REFLECTIONS ON THE FUTURE OF THE LEFT

Building Progressive Alternatives

Series Editors: David Coates and Matthew Watson

Bringing together economists, political economists and other social scientists, this series offers pathways to a coherent, credible and progressive economic growth strategy which, when accompanied by an associated set of wider public policies, can inspire and underpin the revival of a successful centre-left politics in advanced capitalist societies.

David Coates
Flawed Capitalism: The Anglo-American Condition and its Resolution

David Coates (editor)
Reflections on the Future of the Left

Robbie Shilliam
The Deserving Poor: Colonial Genealogies from Abolition to Brexit

REFLECTIONS ON THE FUTURE OF THE LEFT

Edited by
DAVID COATES

agenda
publishing

First published in 2017 by Agenda Publishing

Agenda Publishing Limited
The Core
Science Central
Bath Lane
Newcastle upon Tyne
NE4 5TF
www.agendapub.com

ISBN 978-1-911116-51-6 (hardcover)
ISBN 978-1-911116-52-3 (paperback)

British Library Cataloguing-in-Publication Data
A catalogue record for this book is available from the British Library

Typeset by JS Typesetting Ltd, Porthcawl, Mid Glamorgan
Printed and bound in the UK by CPI Group (UK) Ltd, Croydon, CRO 4YY

CONTENTS

Contributors   vii

1. Introduction   1
    David Coates

2. The political economy of an anti-rent-seeking equality
    agenda   23
    Dean Baker

3. Towards a new paradigm for the Left in the United States   45
    Fred Block

4. Trawling the past as a guide to the future   67
    David Coates

5. A new politics from the Left: the distinctive experience
    of Jeremy Corbyn as leader of the British Labour Party   95
    Hilary Wainwright

6. Social democracy in a dangerous world   113
    Colin Crouch

7. Whose side are we on? Liberalism and socialism are not
    the same   137
    Wolfgang Streeck

8. Class, party and the challenge of state transformation   159
    Leo Panitch and Sam Gindin

9. Closing thoughts   187
    Matthew Watson

    Index   205

CONTRIBUTORS

Dean Baker co-founded the Center for Economic Policy Research in 1999. His areas of research include housing and macroeconomics, intellectual property, social security, medicare and European labour markets. He is the author of several books, including *Rigged: How Globalization and the Rules of the Modern Economy Were Structured to Make the Rich Richer* (2016); *Getting Back to Full Employment: A Better Bargain for Working People* (with Jared Bernstein) (2013); *The End of Loser Liberalism: Making Markets Progressive* (2011); *The United States Since 1980* (2007), and *Social Security: The Phony Crisis* (with Mark Weisbrot) (2001).

Fred Block is Research Professor of Sociology at the University of California, Davis. His most recent books are *The Power of Market Fundamentalism: Karl Polanyi's Critique* (with Margaret R. Somers) (2016), and a coedited book (with Matthew R. Keller), *State of Innovation: The US Government's Role in Technology Development* (2011). He has served on the editorial board of *Politics & Society* since 1980.

David Coates holds the Worrell Chair in Anglo-American Studies at Wake Forest University, North Carolina. He has published extensively on UK and US political economy, labour politics and public policy. His latest publications include *America in the Shadow of Empires* (2014), *Capitalism: The Basics* (2016), *Observing Obama* *in Real Time* (2017) and *Flawed Capitalism: The Anglo-American Condition and Its Resolution* (2018).

Colin Crouch is Professor Emeritus at the University of Warwick and an external scientific member of the Max Planck Institute for the Study of Societies at Cologne. He is vice-president for social sciences of the British Academy. He has published within the fields of comparative European sociology and industrial relations, economic sociology, and contemporary issues in British and European politics. His most recent books include *Post-Democracy* (2004); *Capitalist Diversity and Change: Recombinant Governance and Institutional Entrepreneurs* (2005); *The Strange Non-death of Neoliberalism* (2011); *Making Capitalism Fit for Society* (2013); *Governing Social Risks in Post-Crisis Europe* (2015); *The Knowledge Corrupters: Hidden Consequences of the Financial Takeover of Public Life* (2015) and *Society and Social Change in 21st Century Europe* (2016).

Sam Gindin, now retired, spent most of his working life on the staff of the Canadian Auto Workers union (now UNIFOR) where he was Research Director and later Assistant to the President. He subsequently (2000–10) held the Visiting Packer Chair in Social Justice in the Political Science Department at York University, Toronto. He has written extensively on labour issues and co-authored, with Leo Panitch, *The Making of Global Capitalism: The Political Economy of American Empire* (2012).

Leo Panitch is Emeritus Distinguished Research Professor of Political Science at York University, Toronto. He has been editor of the annual international volume *Socialist Register* for over three decades. Among his many books are: *Renewing Socialism: Transforming Democracy, Strategy and Imagination* (2009); *The End of Parliamentary Socialism: From New Left to New Labour* (2001) and *In and Out of Crisis: The Global Financial Meltdown and Left Alternatives* (2010). His most recent book, *The Making of Global Capitalism: The Political Economy of American Empire* (with Sam Gindin), was awarded the Deutscher book prize in the UK and the Davidson book prize in Canada.

Wolfgang Streeck is Director Emeritus and Professor at the Max Planck Institute for the Study of Societies in Cologne. From 1988 to 1995 he was Professor of Sociology and Industrial Relations at the University of Wisconsin-Madison. His latest publications include: *How will Capitalism End? Essays on a Failing System* (2016); *Buying Time: The Delayed Crisis of Democratic Capitalism* (2014); *Politics in the Age of Austerity* (coeditor with Armin Schäfer) (2013) and *Re-Forming Capitalism: Institutional Change in the German Political Economy* (2009). His current research interests are crises and institutional change in the political economy of contemporary capitalism.

Hilary Wainwright is a researcher and writer on forms of popular democracy, a Fellow of the Transnational Institute (New politics project) and founder editor of *Red Pepper* magazine www.redpepper.co.uk. A long-time activist on the UK Left, she is the author of, among other books, *Reclaim the State: Experiments in Popular Democracy* (2009); *Arguments for a New Left* (1994) and *Labour: A Tale of Two Parties* (1987). She is co-author, with Sheila Rowbotham and Lynne Segal, of *Beyond the Fragments: Feminism and the Making of Socialism* (1979 & 2012) and with Dave Elliot *The Lucas Plan: A New Trade Unionism in the Making* (1981). Her latest (forthcoming) book is *A New Politics from the Left*.

Matthew Watson is Professor of Political Economy in the Department of Politics and International Studies at the University of Warwick. He is also currently a UK Economic and Social Research Council Professorial Fellow. He writes explicitly political studies of the history of economic thought, and sets the concepts that today continue to dominate discussions of the economy back in the historical context in which they were first developed. His single-authored books are *Foundations of International Political Economy* (2005); *The Political Economy of International Capital Mobility* (2007); *Uneconomic Economics and the Crisis of the Model World* (2014) and *The Market* (2017).

CHAPTER 1

INTRODUCTION

David Coates

"Social democracy is at a dead end, but is by no means dead"
Ingo Schmidt[1]

"Europe's centre-left progressive politics is in crisis, maybe in its most existentialist crisis since the foundation of the social democratic movement in the late nineteenth century"
Christian Schweiger[2]

"The unique place of the social democrat to be the champion of the people is over and is never coming back"
Neal Lawson[3]

"Labour is becoming a toxic brand. It is perceived by voters as a party that supports an 'open door' approach to immigration, lacks credibility on the economy, and is a 'soft touch' on welfare spending"
Jon Cruddas[4]

"People are fed up"
Jeremy Corbyn[5]

If further proof were still needed of the fact that one swallow does not make a summer, try comparing the performance of the Labour Party in the UK's June 2017 general election with that of the French Socialist Party in the elections for the National Assembly, the first round of which occurred just three days after the UK election. In both cases, centre-left parties went down to expected defeat: but whereas in the British election, the Labour Party's unexpectedly strong performance cost the Conservative Government its majority, in the French one the Socialist Party and its allies, in government as recently as the previous month, lost all but 44 of their 284 seats. Given that the French performance was by far the more typical of the two, given recent results in both American and European elections, it remains the case, therefore, that – the results of the 2017 UK general election notwithstanding – these are not great days for centre-left parties in developed capitalisms. And a hundred years out from the Russian Revolution, they are even worse days for the revolutionary Left. Indeed, it is quite difficult to think of a recent time in which left-wing prospects of either a moderate or a more radical kind have looked so problematic. Which means, among other things, that reflecting on the future of the Left against such a background is likely to be neither an easy nor a pleasing affair; but then, precisely because it is not, the need for such a reflection has arguably never been greater.

As I have long understood it, the first rule of politics is always this: that if you are in a hole, the initial thing that you must do is to stop digging. Across the western world, the contemporary Left is in a serious hole: which is why the precise nature of the hole, the manner of its creation, the immediate consequence of its existence, and the best way to find the ladder out – understanding all these dimensions of the Left's present predicament are now key requirements for the successful achievement of any political project designed to return progressives to power. The only way to ensure that the present underperformance of progressive forces becomes the lowest point of their political trajectory over time, rather than part of their permanent condition, is to have all of us who care about progressive values concentrate on trajectory improvement. We need, as a matter of urgency, to find a combination of institutions, strategies and programmes that is capable of recreating a broad basis of support for left-wing causes. And because that is so, quite what those institutions need to be, what strategies they should follow, and what policy commitments should go with them – these basic design questions are collectively the subject matter of the essays gathered here. The purpose of this introduction is to set those essays in their shared context, and to explain how and why they have been pulled together.

I

Labour Party supporters in the United Kingdom woke on 9 June 2017 to discover an overnight improvement in the Labour vote, and in its representation in Parliament, that few had anticipated just 24 hours before: and for very good reason. Because until that point, and over the last half-decade, support for left-wing political parties across Europe and North America had steadily sunk to a new low: so low indeed that Árni Árnason recently asked "is 6% the new norm for the progressive left"[6] and Sheri Berman recently wrote that "the European centre-left risks irrelevance".[7] The 2017 UK election stands now as an oasis of hope amid the more general desert of centre-left fortunes across western Europe to which Sheri Berman referred, as in its own way did the size and character of the vote accruing to Hillary Clinton as she fought Donald J. Trump for the US presidency just seven months earlier. But on either side of the Atlantic, it is still a desert out there, when examined calmly from even a moderate (and certainly from a more radical) progressive point of view. Hillary Clinton fought, but she also lost – and lost to Donald J. Trump of all people. Jeremy Corbyn's Labour Party did better than expected, but still lost – and lost in a general election in which *both* main parties increased their share of the vote. How different is all this from the heady days of 1997, when an untested set of New Labour parliamentarians could sweep to power by inflicting on a Conservative Party once led by Margaret Thatcher its heaviest electoral defeat since 1846; or from 2008, when a young and charismatic Barack Obama could reach the White House merely by asserting that "yes, we can!"? Just two decades later in the UK case, and less than a decade in the American one, power in each political system has shifted into highly reactionary hands: leaving progressive forces in the United States facing a deliberate deconstruction of the regulatory state by ultra-libertarian Republicans and a charlatan president; and leaving the Left in the UK watching a minority Tory government (one now suddenly entirely dependent on the support of right-wing Ulster MPs) preparing to pull the United Kingdom out of the European Union – out of the one supra-national institution, that is, within which centre-left values and practices had until recently found their firmest embodiment.

Quite why this change of political fortune had occurred remains a matter of both central importance and huge controversy in left-wing circles on both sides of the Atlantic, as a later reading of the essays gathered here will only underscore. But four things are at least clear, and worth noting as a shared framework for everything that follows.

The *first* is that, on both sides of the Atlantic, significant numbers of voters in traditionally left-wing voting constituencies have, in a series of recent elections, stopped voting for centre-left parties. They have turned instead either to conservative parties offering a more centrist message;[8] or, turning away from both mainstream political currents altogether, have become enthusiastic supporters of right-wing populist parties and figures. Asbjørn Wahl recently put it this way, and he is right.

> Large parts of the western working class now seem to have gathered around right populists, demagogues and racists. They vote for reactionary and fascistoid political parties. They helped to vote the UK out of the EU and to make Trump president of the world's superpower number one, and they vote so massively for the far right political parties that the latter have government power in sight throughout several of Europe's most populous countries. Since working people traditionally are expected to vote for the left, this creates unrest, insecurity, and confusion among experts, as well as commentators and mainstream politicians – particularly in the labour movement.[9]

This working-class realignment is not simply an American and a British phenomenon, though it is certainly the most significant feature of contemporary American politics, and of UK politics both in the 2015 general election and in the referendum on EU membership that followed a year later. For the rise of authoritarian populism is also marked across much of western and southern Europe – from France and Holland in the north to Spain and Greece in the south. At least along the Mediterranean rim, however, the defection from centre-left parties has been as much a move to the left as to the right – politics there have polarized, beaching the moderate centre – but not in either the US or the UK. In the US in 2016, Donald Trump gathered crucial working-class votes in key swing states like Wisconsin, Pennsylvania and Ohio; and in the UK in 2016, right-wing Conservatives and the crude nationalism of UKIP combined to produce a successful referendum bid to take the UK out of the European Union. In the UK case at least, much of that UKIP vote quickly returned to the two main parties; but even there, the gap persisted between the Labour Party and sections of its traditional base. To quote Robert Ford:

> Labour, founded as the party of the working class, and focused on redistributing resources from the rich to the poor, gained the most ground in 2017 in seats with the largest concentrations of middle-class professionals and the rich. The Conservatives, long the party of capital and the middle class, made their largest gains in the poorest seats in England and Wales. Even more remarkably, after years of austerity, the Conservatives' advance on 2015 was largest in the seats where average income fell most over the past five years, while the party gained no ground at all in the seats where average income rose most.[10]

The *second* general point worthy of note as we begin to reflect upon the future of the Left is one related to why this limited but real degree of working class political realignment is now occurring. Many traditionally left-leaning voters seem to have turned away from their normal political loyalties in part because of the severity of the economic and social conditions to which they are increasingly exposed. The collapse of the Soviet Union and the end of the Cold War brought members of well-organized labour movements in western Europe, and of less well-organized ones in North America, into increased competition with lower-paid and even less well-organized workers in former communist states; and facilitated the increasing movement of manufacturing employment out of core capitalisms to developing ones. The years of neoliberal ascendancy that coincided with this Cold War collapse were accompanied by sharp increases in inequalities of wealth and income, before culminating in the most severe financial crisis since the 1930s, and in an associated recession of unprecedented depth and (in many weaker economies) longevity. Both the inequality and the recession hit traditional left-wing supporters hard – particularly those supporters locked away in communities that were heavily dependent for their own prosperity on the production of traditional forms of energy, or of manufactured commodities that could be produced more cheaply elsewhere. It is scarcely surprising, therefore, that as more and more people found their own economic circumstances depleted and the prospects for their children diminished, they should have shifted their political allegiance to parties with no authorial responsibility for any of those adverse developments, and to parties that – because they lacked any role in the creation of these worsened conditions – could address them openly, and offer ostensibly effective and simple solutions for their resolution. And that the solutions on offer, particularly in 2016, were and are invariably backward-looking – Donald J. Trump promising to make America great *again*, and Nigel Farage's UKIP exploiting electoral desires to "take *back* control" – tells us something else of importance too. It underscores the extent to which the underlying premise of centre-left politics – a faith in progress over time – has been eroded in sections of electorates who "no longer believe that the future will bring them material improvement and that their children will have a better life than their own". Or, as Jean Pisani-Ferry recently put it: "They look backward because they are afraid to look ahead".[11]

One might well have thought – certainly at the height of the financial crisis, many of us did – that the main beneficiaries of this growing awareness of the limits of deregulated capitalism would be parties of at least the centre-left, and possibly of more radical leftism too. But the *third* shared feature of our current condition is that this "great moving left show" has not occurred, and has not done so in large measure because of the authorial responsibility for our current malaise that parties of the centre-left in both North America and the European Union share with their more conservative opponents. Centre-left parties are currently hemorrhaging support because of their failure, when last in power, to break fundamentally with the neoliberalism of the Right. It is striking that a financial crisis as severe as that of 2008, and an initially discrediting of neoliberal financial deregulation as sharp as it is possible to find, should have so quickly slipped back into being a political asset for conservative parties and a loadstone around the neck of their centre-left opponents. Yet that is exactly what has happened as, in one northern European country after another, the great economic crisis of 2008–9 generated in centre-left circles only what David Bailey and his colleagues, after surveying them, described as "ideological confusion and/or electoral decline".[12] Being caught by the depth of their previous "Faustian pact" with neoliberalism, and having spent a generation convinced that the Thatcher/Reagan settlement was a permanent one, centre-left parties across both Europe and North America were not well placed, when the financial crisis broke, to quickly disassociate themselves from the "third way politics" into which many of them had by then enthusiastically settled. The result was that, when neoliberalism met its Waterloo in 2008, parties of the centre-left found themselves in solid possession of remarkably few troops. Asbjørn Wahl again:

> The reality is that workers' exploitation and their increasing powerlessness and subordination now hardly have a voice in public debate. Labour parties have mainly cut their connection with their old constituencies. Rather than picking up the discontent generated in a more brutal labour market and politicizing and channeling it into an organized interest-based struggle, middle-class left parties offer little else than moralizing and contempt. Thus, they do little else than to push large groups of workers into the arms of the far-right parties, who support all the discontent and do their best to channel people's rage against other social groups (immigrants, Muslims, gays, people of colour, etc.,) rather than against the real causes of their problems.[13]

The *fourth* significant element of our shared contemporary condition is this; that the general credibility of the European Union – as a more progressive form of capitalism with stronger notions of social partnership – has increasingly lost its electoral elan among both traditional working-class and new middle-class voters, the more it too has succumbed to neoliberal orthodoxies. This was not, and is not, a problem for North American progressives, of course, unless (and to the degree that) the EU was and is used in US progressive circles as a model of how the rules around American capitalism should be reset (most famously of late by Bernie Sanders, eulogizing Denmark).[14] But the embedding of neoliberal principles and practices within the governing institutions of the European Union was, and remains, a particularly acute problem for UK Labour. Heavily engaged as recent UK governments have been with US imperialism in the Middle East – Blair with Bush, no less than Cameron with Obama – the British Labour Party is not now well placed to lead a principled stance on one major, if indirect, consequence of that imperialism – namely the flow of refugees (from Libya and Syria in particular) that has recently made immigration such a toxic issue across the entire European Union. And having been so enthusiastic about flexible EU labour markets when in power as New Labour, and being out of power from 2010, British Labour is equally badly positioned right now to lead opposition within the EU to the severe austerity packages imposed on PIIGS economies by a troika of northern European powers and institutions led by a German government in which the SPD remains a powerful junior partner. The European Union is in internal crisis, and British Labour's indifference to that crisis played its own role in the outcome of the 2016 referendum. What the current condition of both Europe and British Labour therefore demonstrates is that, if there is to ever be a new progressive dawn in the UK and beyond, it will be one that of necessity will have to be created out of the ashes of previous failed centre-left political projects – a demonstration that leaves front and centre the question of whether that progressive phoenix can rise again without first requiring social democracy to have been fully consumed in its own funeral pyre.

II

There is already no shortage of answers to that question. They range from quiet optimism to bleak despair, and they come in a variety of forms: edited collections,[15] programmatic statements,[16] newspaper articles,[17] journal symposia,[18] blog postings,[19] and general overviews. Among the latter, two recent important contributions from the on-going UK debate can usefully be taken as, in some basic sense, speaking for the best of the rest: one by Patrick Diamond, the other by Neal Lawson. Both, it should be noted, were written before the unexpectedly strong performance of the Corbyn-led Labour Party in the general election of 8 June 2017.

Patrick Diamond, in his widely-read survey of the European centre-left, *Endgame for the Center-Left: The Retreat of Social Democracy Across Europe*, turned out to be quite bullish in spite of the retreat he documented, arguing that "for all the difficulties facing social democracy, pessimism can be overstated" and that "despite the apparent demise of centre-left politics, a new progressive era is within reach, underpinned by renewed government activism and a new collectivism that goes beyond the traditional state".[20] His core argument, shared by many similar commentators within the mainstream parties of the centre-left, was that "social democracy stands at a moment of great promise, but also peril". "To write off centre-left politics now would," in his view, "be a great mistake: right and centre-right competitor parties have their own problems," he argued, "and in any case, societies have not rejected social democratic values". The task rather, as he had it, is one of building "bridges between open and closed communities by updating public institutions and policies, just as socialist parties did in the immediate aftermath of the second world war".[21]

Neal Lawson, by contrast, surveying broadly the same scene from his position as chair of *Compass*, saw "social democracy in crisis the world over" with social democrats "nowhere ... ideologically, programmatically or organizationally on the front foot". For Lawson at least, "the crisis isn't cyclical but existential, rooted in profound cultural and technical shifts that scorch the earth for all social democratic parties". As he put it: "social democracy, the belief that one party, in one nation, largely through the state can create a settlement that favours the interests of labour over capital, is dying as a political practice. It is set to join the ranks of 'communism' as a political term of only historic relevance".[22] His is a pessimism about old politics, and a confidence in new coalitions, that is a regular feature of political conversations around the US Democratic Party, as well as around the UK's Liberal Democrats and Greens: a conversation about how to go beyond old class-based forms of politics, and to put away worn-out ways of doing things, and move towards a new politics of identity that is sensitive to the complex modes of exploitation that currently scar contemporary capitalism. For Neal Lawson at least, with the world of work changing so fast, and patterns of consumption proliferating in both scale and variety, it is "the UK franchise of social democracy" that "is first in the firing line," if "for no other reason than it calls itself the party of Labour".[23]

Both answers can't be right, of course; but both can be wrong; and right or wrong, both suggest a distinct and different focus for progressive politics.

For Patrick Diamond, strengthening the Left means getting back inside – in his case – the British Labour Party, and "forging an effective alliance between the middle class, the blue-collar working class, and those in greatest need: the jobless, the economically excluded, the most disadvantaged" around sets of policies that address their constituents' immediate economic and social anxieties, regain the Party's "reputation for economic competence" and reclaim "the politics of national identity" in order to make the case for liberal internationalism and a strong Europe.[24] Forging that effective alliance, if Jon Cruddas's internal review of why Labour lost the 2015 election was correct, requires a firm turn back towards the centre of UK politics – taking what elsewhere Diamond termed "the hard road to power"[25] by reversing its current loss of "connection with large parts of the voter population who are either pragmatists in their voting habits or social conservatives who value family, work, fairness and their country".[26]

For Neal Lawson, again by contrast, reconstructing that Labour Party-electoral class link will no longer suffice. The world has moved on: capital has gone global "and nasty" he said, and irredeemably "infected with the virus of neoliberalism", and is now poised to destroy both the environment that surrounds us and any vestigial collectivism in the consumer culture it is inculcating in all of us. Faced with this new and horrendous reality, since one single progressive party is no longer the answer, there is no alternative for those wishing to blunt the impact of "turbo capitalism" but to focus exclusively on the building of progressive alliances around a new understanding of what now constitutes the good society in a post-material age. And in building that alliance, with Labour so weak after the general election of 2015, it made sense – to quote Lawson's colleague Jeremy Gilbert – "to try to work towards local agreements which would see Labour and other parties of the left and centre stand down in each other's favour".[27]

At one end of the spectrum, that is, successful progressive politics is still about getting "all hands-on-board, making one more push for the New Jerusalem" – finding the programmes inside existing social democratic parties that will make the old politics work again; while at the other, it's all about stepping away from attitudes and institutions inherited from the past, and starting over anew and afresh, building coalitions around consumption and private space as well as around work and public institutions. It's a shared spectrum, but not a shared vision of how best to go forward. And between the two now, in the UK at least – after the unexpectedly effective performance of the Corbyn-led Labour Party in the 2017 election – stands a party that was supposed to be too radical for long-term electoral success if Patrick Diamond is right, and too electorally viable when standing alone to easily fit into Neal Lawson's vision of how best to take the Left forward. So, three UK strategies are now on the table – *go right, go left, or go alliance* – leaving the issue of how best to guarantee a successful future, for the British Left at least, entirely unclear and uncertain!

III

Which is why it seems to us to be potentially useful to add another set of voices to the mix. After all, these general reflective dialogues have happened before, and benefitted then from a multiplicity of views. So why not again now? The previous one much mentioned even in the current debates was that around Eric Hobsbawm's *The Forward March of Labour Halted?*[28] – the publication of which just predated the arrival of Margaret Thatcher in power in 1979. Then, as now, prospects for the Left looked particularly problematic. Stuart Hall and his colleagues at *Marxism Today* were busy documenting "the great moving right show" that Thatcher was implementing (a move that involved not only new sets of policies but also a fundamental shift in dominant modes of thought); and Eric Hobsbawm, as a good and faithful old communist, was pondering the political consequences for the Left of the disintegration and departure of the traditional working class. Then, as now, the temptation to throw in the towel was enormous. A whole way of doing politics that had favoured the centre-left – in this case, Keynesian demand management – had just been rendered mute by the stagflation of the 1970s; and a Labour Party that had been in and out of government for more than a decade and a half had just been roundly rejected by its own electorate after a disastrous "winter of discontent". So, the search was on for how best to respond both to the failure of Old Labour and to the rise of what we would now term "neoliberalism." Re-reading that debate with the wisdom of hindsight, it is striking just how much of what was in debate in 1978 and 1979 was Labour's past rather than the Left's future, and yet how central to that conversation was the political potential of a trade-union movement whose imminent emasculation by Thatcherite policies was nowhere foreshadowed. In retrospect, it is clear that the depth and character of analysis required accurately to anticipate the future was largely missing from the Hobsbawm debate. It is a depth and character of analysis that we cannot afford to leave out again.

Hence the four questions posed to each of the contributors in this collection of reflections. Each contributor was asked to reflect upon (a) what has changed in modern capitalism that has brought us to our contemporary impasse; (b) what role, if any, have errors by (or limits of) particular forms of progressive politics played in the emergence of our contemporary crises; (c) what lessons can we learn from all of this for the form and content of progressive politics going forward; and (d) what are the immediate options opening up before us, and how are they to be seized? The contributors were chosen partly because their previous writings occupied clear and differing positions on the basic spectrum between optimism and pessimism, old politics and new. Each was chosen too so that the focus of the conversation could incrementally shift from the US to the UK, then on to the EU and the wider global stage. Additionally, each was chosen because – to a very large degree – their writings and political activism covered the entirety of the politically-active time span of the baby boomers, so that in a sense each contributor was being asked to reflect on the future of the Left at the very moment when prime responsibility for building that future was passing – baton-like – from one generation to the next. The insights which these eight contributors have gleaned from four or more decades of public engagement on the Left are hopefully condensed here in the pages that follow, on the wager that such insights can only help the next generation of the Left to avoid some of the pitfalls that weakened the political impact of the generation before them.

Eight essays, therefore, each written on the basis of long past experience and political struggle, in the hope that they will be of use to those now carrying, or just picking up, the same progressive baton. The fight for a better tomorrow is always a marathon rather than a sprint, and it is best won if organized as a relay race rather than a steeplechase. Let us hope that, in some small way, the running will get easier because of the essays gathered here.

IV

The first essay is by Dean Baker. Dean makes a powerful case, addressed primarily to the American Left, for not crossing the river to fill the pail, but rather for putting down that pail where we are now: by exploiting to the full the capacity of progressive intervention (particularly at the state level in the United States) to roll back the rigged markets that create such inequality around us. The Left, we are told, should never buy the argument that markets necessarily create those inequalities. Markets are more malleable than that. Contemporary markets create such appalling levels of inequality only because they are set up in ways that favour the rich and the privileged. Their advocates defend them as "free" markets but, in reality, they are anything but free. Instead, they are skewed by federal policies that hold down inflation by increasing unemployment. They are skewed by the excessive privileging of the financial sector, by patent and copyright protections that facilitate rent taking, by lack of effective shareholder control over CEO pay, and by labour market rules that expose workers to global competition while protecting certain professions from any similar pressure on their rates of compensation. As Dean Baker has written elsewhere: "as long as progressives ignore the rules that are designed to redistribute income, they will be left fighting over the crumbs. There is no way that government interventions will reverse a rigged market".[29] The rules rigging the market need to be addressed first. The Baker argument here is that, while for the moment at least progressive intervention to effect meaningful rule-change at the federal level in the United States is unlikely to be effective, that is not the case for equivalent interventions at the level of individual states and cities. His chapter illustrates the potential of grass-roots and labour-movement action at the sub-federal level to deliver real and concrete improvements in the lives of ordinary Americans, and points for inspiration to the recent (and at the time, hard to anticipate) success of such action on issues like gay rights and tobacco-use: arguing that "if progressives hope to turn the tide, we need policies that can produce real benefits in the near term, while at the same time pointing in the direction of larger changes in the future". The argument developed by Dean Baker here is that "there is no shortage of such policies; we just need to think about them clearly".

The second essay is by Fred Block. Fred is less sanguine than Dean about immediate possibilities, but is clear on the longer-term potential for success of a revitalized and reshaped centre-left. Arguing that "parties of the Centre-Left must reinvent themselves if they are to regain their relevance and their electoral support", it is the Block view that such a reinvention requires two broad things; a resetting of party programmes and organization to allow membership influence to grow and relevant policies to emerge; and an explicit recognition of how the context of left-wing politics is changing and must be addressed. That change, in Fred Block's view, is best captured by the notion of a transition to a "habitation society", a transition that both allows and requires the Left to forge "new political strategies that cut across traditional class and locational divides". Conscious of the way in which parties of the centre-left have recently shifted authority and influence internally, away from trade unions and towards professional politicians – and seeing that as a double-edged sword – the Block thesis is that the US Democratic Party in particular should learn from its Republican opponents that a regeneration of activism and power at the base of each party is vital to stop electoral hemorrhaging at the top. Because in a habitation society, "social reproduction becomes primary and production of both goods and foodstuff is secondary, the central challenge becomes finding new and better ways to create sustainable and resilient communities while economizing on inputs of capital, labour and non-renewable materials". This then becomes the task of the Left: to show "various constituencies that are the base of contemporary centre-left politics – women, racial and sexual minorities, labour unions, community activists, and campaigners against inequality and the political power of the wealthy – that they are engaged in a common struggle to create human societies that are inclusive, egalitarian and governed through revitalized democratic practices". It is the Block view that, if done properly, such an understanding of its task could change and strengthen the Left in important and necessary ways.

The third essay is mine. It is written in part to act as a bridge between the American experience of progressive politics and the British – crafted by someone who is British by birth and American by choice – and draws heavily for its content on material and arguments developed more fully in Agenda Publishing's parallel volume to this: *Flawed Capitalism: The Anglo-American Condition and its*

Resolution. The Coates argument there, and here, is that we are in a period of transition between broad social settlements, and the job of the Left is both to recognize that (and to educate its potential electorate in that crucial recognition), and simultaneously to design policies that over time can take that electorate towards a new social settlement (of a more egalitarian and family-friendly form than that created by neoliberalism). This task of creating a new and pro-gressive social settlement is made easier – so the argument runs – because, and to the degree that, neoliberalism is increasingly dis-crediting itself by the economic and social outcomes it is generating. But the task is made more difficult to the degree (very large, actually) to which centre-left parties were junior but acquiescing partners in the design and sustenance of the neoliberal settlement that came so seriously unstuck in 2008. The task is possible, however, and well within our grasp, because of the wealth of appropriate policies of a progressive kind that conservatives in power eschew, and which centre-left parties seeking power should and can adopt. There is, in the Coates view, no programmatic barriers to the creation of a more dynamic because progressively-restructured capitalism, one in which centre-left parties manage capital in the interests of labour, broadly defined. The barrier is, rather, one of agency. "The problem of the Left is overwhelmingly itself" and being itself, it is a problem that the Left can solve, and should address, with all due urgency.

The fourth essay is by Hilary Wainwright, the only one of the eight here who also contributed to the original debate with Eric Hobsbawm on *The Forward March of Labour Halted?* Drawing on her long experience of social movement politics, and writing in a tradition of scholarship heavily influenced by the work of Ralph Miliband, Hilary makes a strong case for understanding the exist-ence of two kinds of power in and around progressive politics. The first – power-as-domination – has been how power is understood in traditional social democratic parties, an understanding they share with more conservative political formations, and which leaves social democrats trying to use particularly state power to meet the needs of supporters whom they do not themselves empower. They demon-strate what she calls "a paternalistic political philosophy". The sec-ond – power-as-transformative-capacity – is, in Hilary's view, the understanding that prevailed in the key social movements of the 1960s and 1970s, and which is now being rediscovered by a new generation of activists disappointed in (and alienated by) third-way social democracy. The Wainwright thesis is that those two forms of power need to coalesce in a new progressive future, with old-style social democratic parties learning that – as she puts it – they must avoid "any separation from the radical social movements from whence the parties came, and on whose transformative power they depend to achieve the changes they promised and for which they won support". That is why, among other things and as its title implies, Wainwright's chapter gives a more sympathetic report on the radical potential of the Corbyn-led Labour Party than is commonplace in mainstream media, even in media of a progressive kind.

The fifth essay, by Colin Crouch, invites us to examine the problems and choices faced by the contemporary centre-left in a longer time frame and against a wider set of issues, returning to themes more fully explored in his remarkable study, *The Strange Non-Death of Neoliberalism*.[30]

The argument developed here begins by noting that the dominant contradictions of contemporary politics are those pulling apart parties of the centre-right, not parties of the centre-left: with the dominant "fault line" being "between the economic globalization fostered by neoliberalism, representing the extraordinary power of business wealth, and the xenophobic form of conservatism, representing the power of mass fear and hatred". It is that fault line that now frames the options facing progressives in both Europe and the United States, with centre-parties struggling to respond to the crisis of neoliberalism in a non-xenophobic fashion partly because of their involvement in the earlier dissemination of the neoliberal settlement, and partly because of neoliberalism's erosion of the old forms of class identity that once sustained successful social democracy. With both religion and class losing much of their capacity to mobilize people politically, the one remaining framework of identity left able to do so would appear to be that of the "nation"; and currently the Left's most pressing problem is that, using that framework to understand the consequences of globalization, "large sections of society [have] finally turned against neoliberal domination, but under the banner of the extreme right". That banner is already visibly tattered, however, and no doubt will tatter more. In Donald Trump's hands, promises to help the forgotten people are already taking second-place to business deregulation favouring the rich; and

Theresa May's hard Brexit strategy will inevitably increase the exposure of "leave" voters to foreign competition, rather than protect those voters from it. Yet none of those likely developments will bring support back to the centre-left, until progressives too develop an adequate response to the janus-face of a globalization process that cannot now be reversed.

It is the Crouch argument here that neither protectionism nor new free-trade agreements are an adequate answer to the economic and social dislocations brought about by neoliberal globalization; and that, moreover, there are sections of the electorate of many leading European and North American economies and societies with whose xenophobia, racism and sexism no progressive should dream of compromising, and from which no progressive support can be expected. In such a polarized and troubled politics, therefore, the centre-left has no choice but to make the case for a more regulated global trading order, to reach out to moderate people worried by immigration and job loss by "standing firmly for redistribution and the rights of low-income workers" (including advocating for high minimum wages and strong labour standards), and to "become part of a broader anti-xenophobic social compromise with internationalist neoliberals and moderate conservatives". The forging of a more assertive form of social democracy is, in Colin Crouch's view, both a necessary and a demanding route forward for the European and North American centre-left. As he has written elsewhere: "European social democracy needs to be shaken out of the defensive posture into which it has shrunk for many years now"; and it can be, "given the widespread revulsion at the behaviour of global finance, which has been the purest expression of neoliberalism to date. 'Let markets work for us, yes; let them tyrannize us, no!' provides a powerful rhetorical base, and a rich and promising political agenda. In parading it, social democrats need have no fear that they are voicing unpopular minority concerns. They stand foursquare in the centre of public opinion and political reality".[31]

In the sixth essay, by Wolfgang Streeck, even the possibility of effecting the kind of alliance that Colin Crouch favours comes under serious and critical review. Deploying arguments which surfaced in fuller form in his recent (and widely discussed) study, *How Will Capitalism End? Essays on a Failing System*, Wolfgang raises one of the biggest questions facing the Left: namely "who are our constituents, our popular base waiting to be organized and mobilized", the ones whose interests we "hope to define so as to coincide with the general interests of mankind?". Not, in his view, the usual suspects. As he says: "whether the future of the left can be an alliance between the old working class and the new human capital owners must be doubted", not least because "interests, worldviews and identities differ widely". They differ particularly on so central a modern issue as immigration, for example, with the old working class threatened by it, the new middle class benefiting from it, and the immigrants themselves likely to want to settle in and remain invisible. Nor does Wolfgang Streeck put much store by any alliance between the new losers in his failing capitalism and a New Left needing, as he puts it, to "somehow steer its potential constituents away from the late capitalist lifestyle of *coping* as test of personal worth, *hoping* as a civic duty, *doping* as a shot in the arm to either help or substitute for individual achievement, and *shopping* as the ultimate reward in an honorable capitalist life".

Adamant that socialism is what the Left must be about – because anything less, liberalism can deliver without it – the Streeck argument on the future of the Left is bleak indeed: that "the task of inventing 'a future for the Left', and indeed for a socialist Left, appears nothing short of awesome". The Streeck thesis is that the Left requires a profound cultural revolution if the excesses of capitalism are to be contained, and yet such a fundamental shift in attitudes to consumption and resources is such a hard sell to a generation obliged to survive by "turning their creative power into human capital". "Our most formidable task", he writes, "may well be to talk people out of the myth that they will be happier in proportion to how much more they consume ... a myth spread and pressed into people's minds and souls every day by the most gigantic, most sophisticated, most expensive propaganda machinery mankind has ever seen". Little wonder that, with such a view, the Streeck conclusion is so bleak. It is this. "While it may be true", the chapter concludes, "that there can be no new socialist left without a culture of politicized de-commodification of consumption, it is also true that no such culture is anywhere in sight. Maybe the historical moment for it has passed?"

In the penultimate essay in the collection, Leo Panitch and Sam Gindin make it clear that they at least think that the historical moment has *not* passed. If any moment has passed, in their view, it is the social democratic one. Writing together, they bring to the conversation perspectives honed around the *Socialist Register,* the non-aligned yearly collection of socialist essays first organized by Ralph Miliband and John Saville in 1964 and now edited by Leo Panitch and colleagues connected to York University in Toronto. Leo is often fond of questioning the sanity of my politics – my commitment to a regenerated social democracy – asking privately lately whether, "insofar as the Left keeps being drawn back into trying to do this [regeneration], does it not display at least some of the traces of the definition of insanity often attributed to Einstein: doing the same thing over and over again, but expecting different results?" But he and Sam are gracious enough to apply that definition of insanity to themselves too; and to defend their refusal (as well as mine) to become sane, if sane means surrendering to the unbridled logics of contemporary capitalism. In their view – one anchored in their unique mixture of long-term reflection and immediate case studies (here, the Sanders campaign in the US, and the Syriza government in Greece) – the increasing de-legitimation of neoliberalism is creating an opportunity for more revolutionary politics again; but it is an opportunity that remains extremely difficult to seize. They take comfort in the movement from protests to politics they see in both North America and Greece, and from the growing sensibility of protesters to the class-based nature of the inequalities that so offend them; but being more Gramscian than Leninist in their analysis of the sources of capitalist stability, Leo Panitch and Sam Gindin are well aware of dangers of social democratic incorporation if the Left does not create, as it moves from protest to power, new political parties that "more than ever, keep their feet in the movements, and far from trying to direct them, remain the central site for democratic strategic debate in view of their diverse activities". As non-social democratic socialists, they remain committed to the importance of what they term a "democratic socialist strategy for entering the state through elections, to the end of transforming the state" itself, while recognizing the enormous difficulty associated with that kind of politics. The future of the Left will not be smooth, they insist, "ruptures, or extended series of ruptures, are inescapable".

V

The final essay in the collection is by Matthew Watson, co-editor of the series *Building Progressive Alternatives* that this volume is helping to launch. His essay is a reflection upon the reflections – an initial response to the essays gathered here, by a leading intellectual of the rising generation to whom academic and political leadership is now beginning to shift. The great hope that I had, in calling this collection together, was that it might act as a bridge between progressive generations – one that might facilitate the transmission of valuable reflections on the Left's past into the collective memory of those who must now shape its emerging future. The best response to the collection gathered here will therefore be one of critique – a calm and careful mapping and measuring of what can usefully be extracted from the past, and an equally careful mapping and measuring of what cannot. Mat's final essay has been designed as a first and tentative example of that critical process of review.

NOTES

1. Ingo Schmidt (ed.), *The Three Worlds of Social Democracy: A Global View* (London: Pluto, 2016).
2. Christian Schweiger, *Progressive politics: permanent austerity stranglehold?* Posted 29 May 2015. https://www.socialeurope.eu/2015/05/progressive-politics-permanent-austerity-stranglehold/ (accessed 7 July 2017).
3. Neal Lawson, *Social democracy without social democrats? How can the left recover?* Posted 13 May 2016. https://www.socialeurope.eu/2016/05/social-democracy-without-social-democrats-how-can-the-left-recover/ (accessed 7 July 2017).
4. Jon Cruddas, *Labour's future: why Labour lost in 2015 and how it can win again* (London: Labour Party, 2016), 8.
5. Jeremy Corbyn, 29 April 2017: quoted on the BBC's "General Election 2017" website.
6. Árni Árnason, *Is 6% the new norm for the progressive left?* Posted on 27 March 2017. https://www.socialeurope.eu/2017/03/6-new-norm-progressive-left/ (accessed 7 July 2017). Perhaps not: social democracy in Iceland has recently made its own unique contribution to that low score. On this, see Thorvaldur Gylfason, *Spineless social democracy.*

Posted on 5 April 2017; https://www.socialeurope.eu/2017/04/spine less-social-democracy/ (accessed 7 July 2017).

7. Sheri Berman, *Europe's centre-left risks irrelevance?* Posted 6 February 2017; https://www.socialeurope.eu/2017/02/europes-centre-left-risks-irrelevance/ (accessed 7 July 2017)

8. Patrick Diamond, *The new "progressive"' conservatism in Europe.* Posted April 2011; http://www.policy-network.net/pno_detail.aspx?ID=3985 &title=The+new+%22progressive%22+conservatism+in+Europe+ (accessed 7 July 2017).

9. Asbjørn Wahl, *Reactionary working class?* Posted on *The Bullet* as e-bulletin No. 1383, 16 March 2017; https://socialistproject.ca/bullet/ 1383.php (accessed 7 July 2017).

10. Robert Ford, "The new electoral map of Britain: from the revenge of Remainers to the upending of class politics", *The Observer*, 11 June 2017.

11. Jean Pisani-Ferry, *Progress Abandoned.* Posted on 18 January 2017; https://www.socialeurope.eu/2017/01/progress-abandoned/ (accessed 7 July 2017).

12. David Bailey, Jean-Michel De Waele, Fabien Escalona & Mathieu Viera (eds), *European Social Democracy during the Global Economic Crisis: Renovation or Resignation?* (Manchester: Manchester University Press, 2014), 12.

13. Wahl, *Reactionary working class.*

14. On the complexities of Danish social democracy, in which Bernie Sanders was clearly not well briefed, see Christoph Arndt & Kees van Kersbergen, "Social Democracy after the Third Way: restoration or renewal?", *Policy and Politics* 43:2 (2015), 203–20.

15. See, for example, James Cronin, George Ross & James Shock (eds), *What's Left of the Left: Democrats and Social Democrats in Challenging Times* (Durham, NC: Duke University Press, 2011); Olaf Cramme & Patrick Diamond (eds), *After the Third Way: The Future of Social Democracy in Europe* (London: Policy Network, 2012) and Ingo Schmidt (ed.), *The Three Worlds of Social Democracy.*

16. Not least the Labour Party election manifesto, 2017.

17. Including one recently by Tony Blair, arguing for a revival of "the progressive centre" and floating the idea of his returning to UK public life to help generate it! On this, see Jason Cowley, "Tony Blair's Unfinished Business", *New Statesman*, 24 November 2016.

18. For the UK, see, for example, *Renewal*; for the US, *The American Prospect*; more globally, *The Socialist Register.*

19. For the UK, see for example *Policy Network* and *Soundings*; for Europe, *social.europe.eu*; for the US, *Alternet.org* and *The Nation*; and more globally, the Socialist Project's e-bulletin, *The Bullet.*

20. Patrick Diamond, *Endgame for the Centre Left?* (London: Policy Network, 2016), ix.
21. *Ibid.*, ix.
22. Lawson, *Social democracy without social democrats?*
23. *Ibid.*
24. Diamond, *Endgame for the Centre Left?* 99.
25. Patrick Diamond, *Can Labour Win? The Hard Road to Power* (London: Rowman & Littlefield, 2015).
26. Cruddas, *Labour's future*, 9–10.
27. Jeremy Gilbert, *A Progressive Alliance: The Progressive Case* (London: Compass, 2017): accompanying notes to his Compass publication, *The Progressive Alliance: Why Labour Needs It.*
28. Eric Hobsbawm, *The Forward March of Labour Halted?* (London: Verso, in association with *Marxism Today*, 1978, 1979 & 1981).
29. Dean Baker, *If Progressives Wanted To Win.* The Huffington Post, 8 February 2011; http://www.huffingtonpost.com/dean-baker/if-pro gressives-wanted-to_b_819871.html (accessed 7 July 2017).
30. Colin Crouch, *The Strange Non-Death of Neoliberalism* (Cambridge: Polity, 2011).
31. Colin Crouch, *From Defensive to Assertive Social Democracy*, UCL SE Journal number 1, December 2013.

CHAPTER 2

THE POLITICAL ECONOMY OF AN ANTI-RENT-SEEKING EQUALITY AGENDA

Dean Baker

Strategizing among progressives is often infected by a sort of millennialism, in which there is an idea that a golden age awaits in the future. This view holds that something will happen that will open a space for progressive ideas that does not exist at present. This something could be an unforeseen upsurge of labour radicalism, or spontaneous organizing like Occupy, but an order of magnitude larger, or perhaps another economic collapse like we saw in 2008–9.

This is not a productive path forward for progressive politics. There will always be unforeseen events, but the idea that these events will open the door for the backlog of progressive reforms we have kept on the shelf is little more than wishful thinking. In fact, the failure of the economic crisis following the collapse of the housing bubble to lead to anything more than minor political changes should be instructive. Even a catastrophic economic event, which is unlikely to be repeated any time soon, does not necessarily open any doors for progressive politics. If we want to see progressive policies advance, then we will have to build from where we are today, not hope for a gift from the heavens to clear the path.

In this respect, we need to learn from the Right. They have made enormous headway by going step by step. They have worked to undermine every institutional basis for progressive support, most importantly the labour movement, but also programs like Legal Aid and the Corporation for Public Broadcasting and other sources of public funds, that could be used to support progressive causes. At least as importantly, they went behind the scenes to restructure the economy in ways that redistributed income upward.

While the right-wing is not shy about demanding a lower tax burden on the wealthy, making the tax system more regressive, their efforts to reshape the before-tax distribution of income have had far more impact on the living standards of the bulk of the population. They have pushed policies, many of them obscure and seemingly unimportant, which have led to the largest upward redistribution of income in the history of the world. If progressives do not address this behind the scenes rigging of the market, there will be little hope for the future of progressive policy.

The basic reason is simple; there is a lot of validity to the complaints of conservatives about the distortions and waste associated with tax and transfer policy. While they hugely exaggerate these costs, they are nonetheless real. If we allow the Right to impose a set of market rules that leads to ever larger before-tax inequality, it will be extremely difficult, if not impossible, to reverse these outcomes with tax and transfer policy. And, this only refers to the economic obstacles. The politics of tax and transfer policy have always been difficult, especially in the United States. It is far better to pursue policies that structure the market in ways that don't lead to enormous inequality in the first place.

Progressives have too often fallen into the trap of seeing the inequality and poverty resulting from a particular structuring of the market as being a natural outcome of a market economy. This leads to a view where the market is seen as the enemy. This makes as much sense as seeing the wheel as the enemy. The market is a tool, it is incredibly malleable. It can be structured in an almost infinite number of different ways. It can be structured so as to generate outcomes that are far more equal than what we see in the US economy today. This restructuring of markets should be the main agenda of progressives for the foreseeable future.

THE SOURCES OF UPWARD REDISTRIBUTION

It would take a longer discussion to fully describe the set of policies that have results in the upward redistribution of the last four decades, but I will briefly outline the five most important here.[1] However before describing these policies it is important to make an additional point about the nature of this upward redistribution. For the most part, it has not been from wages to profits, but rather from workers at the middle and the bottom of the income distribution to workers at the top. While the share of the richest one per cent of taxpayers has risen from roughly 10 per cent in the late-1970s to more than 20 per cent in recent years, there was little change through most of this period in the split in corporate income between labour and capital.

There has been a shift from labour to capital in the years since 2005. This is attributable first to the housing bubble and then to the weakness of the labour market following the Great Recession.[2] Since 2013, as the labour market has tightened, there has been a shift of income back to wages, which has reversed roughly half of the shift to capital. On this topic, it is also worth noting that almost all of the upward redistribution to the one per cent had already taken place by 2005, before there was any notable shift from labour to capital. This means we are primarily looking at an upward shift within the wage distribution, from those at the middle and bottom to those at the top. The big winners have been hedge-fund and private-equity partners, CEOs and other top executives, well-positioned scientists in the tech sector, and doctors and other highly paid professionals. Reducing inequality means undermining the structures that support the extraordinary pay going to these groups.

The first and most important policy fostering the upward redistribution of income is the decision to sustain higher rates of unemployment in order to reduce the risk of inflation. The Federal Reserve Board has placed a far higher priority on fighting inflation in the years since 1980 than in the years prior to 1980. As a result, the average rate of unemployment has been considerably higher in this later period relative to estimates of full employment than in the period from 1945 to 1980.[3]

Low rates of unemployment disproportionately benefit workers at the middle and bottom of the wage distribution. They also disproportionately benefit minorities since African-American unemployment is typically twice as high as unemployment for whites and the unemployment rate for African-American teens is typically close to six times the unemployment rate for whites. The only time since the early 1970s when there was sustained wage growth at the middle and bottom of the wage distribution was the low unemployment years of the late-1990s.

A second source of upward redistribution is the financial sector. This sector has grown enormously relative to the rest of the economy over the last four decades, with the core securities and commodities trading sector growing by a factor of five as a share of the economy. This sector is essentially a drain on the productive economy. While the financial system plays an essential role in allocating capital from savers to investors, there is little reason to believe that it is doing a better job today than it did four decades ago. This means that the additional resources devoted to the sector are pure waste: a tax on the rest of us.

This sector also includes many of the highest earners in the economy such as hedge-fund and private-equity partners. The growth of this sector has been fed by the plunge in trading costs resulting from computerization, which has also allowed for a proliferation of complex financial instruments. The financial sector has also prospered as a result of being largely exempted from taxes applied to other sectors as well as the implicit "too big to fail" insurance from the government that saved the financial sector from collapse in 2008 and 2009.

A third source of upward redistribution is patent and copyright protections. These protections have been made longer and stronger over the last four decades, leading to an ever-larger amount of rents which overwhelmingly go to the top end of the income distribution. The extension of these protections has been a major goal of trade deals in the last quarter century, which are ironically sold as "free-trade" agreements. There is little appreciation of the amount of money at stake in these rents. In the case of prescription drugs alone, the gap between the patent protected price and the free market price in 2016 would have been close to $380 billion or two per cent of GDP. The total gap adding in other protected items could easily be twice this size.

The broken corporate governance structure is the basis for the fourth major cause of upward redistribution. Under the current system, corporate boards tend to hold more allegiance to top management than the shareholders who they are supposed to represent. It is virtually impossible for shareholders to remove directors, with well over 99 per cent of directors who are nominated for re-election getting approved. This corrupt system is what allows even mediocre

CEOs of major companies to draw pay in excess of $10 million a year. This pattern of pay has a corrupting impact on pay structures in the economy more generally. Not only does it lead to bloated pay packages for other top executives, but it spills over into the pay structure in the non-profit sector. It is not uncommon for the presidents of major universities or private charities to be paid more than $1 million a year.

The last source of upward redistribution is the protection that the most highly-paid professionals, most notably doctors, enjoy from foreign and domestic competition. While trade agreements have been designed to put manufacturing workers and other less-educated workers in direct competition with low-paid workers in the developing world, barriers that protect the most highly-paid professionals have been largely left in place. As a result, the average pay for doctors in the United States is more than $250,000 a year, roughly twice as much as the pay of doctors in other wealthy countries.

The structure of the market in these five areas can explain much, if not all, of the upward redistribution over the last four decades. In each case there is nothing natural or intrinsic to the market that led to the current structure. It is possible to design alternative mechanisms that would be at least as efficient and would lead to considerably less inequality.

THE PROGRESSIVE AGENDA: SHOWING THAT INEQUALITY WAS BY DESIGN AND PUTTING FACTS ON THE GROUND

The first part of a progressive agenda is to attack the notion that inequality was simply the result of the natural workings of the market. This is an incredibly powerful view and unfortunately many who consider themselves left of centre share it. The economics profession has been a major culprit in spreading this story. There has been enormous effort devoted to promoting the idea that technology and globalization, acting as natural forces, were responsible for reducing the demand for less-educated workers and led to an enormous pay premium for the most skilled. In this view, it might be unfortunate that the bottom half of the population has seen little benefit from the economy's growth over the last four decades, but the alternative would be to try to block technology or reverse globalization.

In the liberal version of this view, we should look to have somewhat more in the way of tax and transfer policy. As a practical matter this largely boils down to crumbs for the poor, since few are talking about the sort of massive increase in taxation that would be needed to come anywhere close to reversing the upward redistribution of the last four decades.[4] The more conservative version is that we should just accept market outcomes, since the government should not be deciding who gets what.

As I outlined in the previous section, the process of upward redistribution was anything but natural. There was nothing natural about deciding that free trade should focus on manufactured goods and not doctors, putting our manufacturing workers in direct competition with low-paid workers in the developing world while protecting doctors even from their much lower-paid counterparts in other wealthy countries. There also is nothing natural about making patent and copyright monopolies ever longer and stronger. These are very explicit policy decisions that played an enormous role in the upward redistribution of income and making people like Bill Gates incredibly rich.

The economics profession should be quite vulnerable to attack in this area, given its incredible failure to foresee the collapse of the housing bubble and wreckage it would cause. Since the collapse there has been a major effort to rewrite history and treat the Great Recession as the result of a financial crisis which was very hard to see coming since financial matters are so complicated. This relieves the profession of responsibility for a disaster that would have been a career-ending failure for workers in less prestigious occupations, like custodians and dishwashers.

While the sight of major banks collapsing, and many more teetering, captured the headlines, the real story of the downturn was the bursting of an $8 trillion housing bubble in the United States and comparably sized bubbles elsewhere. The demand created by these bubbles was driving the world economy. When they collapsed, there was nothing to replace the demand. The stimulus put in place in 2009 helped for a period of time, but it was too limited in both size and duration to restore the economy to its pre-recession growth path. The economy would have been weak in the years after the collapse of the housing bubble whether or not there had been a financial crisis.

In short, the failure of the economics profession was not its inability to get into the details of complex financial instruments. The failure of the profession was its inability to notice an unprecedented and unexplained run-up in house prices, which was very clearly driving the economy. Recognizing the bubble did not require any deep dives into obscure statistics, only a competent reading of widely available data. For this reason, the economics profession should still be considered to be very much on probation. It should be less able than usual to dismiss serious criticisms of stories that are told because they advance the status quo even though they lack any real evidential basis.

Economists have no serious evidence that longer and stronger patent and copyright monopolies advance growth.[5] We do know that they redistribute income upward. Since when do supporters of free markets push for government imposed monopolies? And why is the financial sector exempted from the same sorts of taxes that we impose on other sectors? Even the International Monetary Fund views the sector as under-taxed.[6] Who could be opposed to transparency in the fees charged by hedge funds and private equity funds to state and local pensions? And what supporter of the free market would be against giving the owners of firms, the shareholders, more say over the pay of CEOs and other top executives?

In these and other areas it is easy to design proposals that show that the supporters of the status quo – the upward redistribution of the last four decades – are very much opposed to the free market. It is important to never treat the battle over economic policy as one between those who want the government to intervene versus those who favour a free market. We must insist on the correct framing: the major economic battle is between those who want to structure markets so that the wealthy are the primary beneficiaries and those who want to structure markets so that growth benefits the vast majority of the population. This is the core issue in economic policy debates both in the United States and the rest of the world. We must make sure that the public understands it.

CREATING FACTS ON THE GROUND

For the immediate future, there is little prospect for progressive economic change at the national level with Donald Trump in the White House and right-wing Republicans in control of both houses of Congress. However, there are many states in which progressives do have considerable influence, including major states like California and New York. These states can provide opportunities for implementing many policies that do not depend on the federal government. The success of these policies will encourage other states to emulate them and also help to generate pressure to adopt them at the national level.

Labour market policy

Of course, there is already much progressive activism at the state level, which has led to victories in many cities and states, such as higher minimum wages and mandates for paid sick days and family leave. It is necessary to build on these victories with the understanding that these policies are not only directly providing benefits for the workers affected, but are also helping to restructure the labour market. If we reduce the average number of hours worked in a year, we are reducing the supply of labour. This makes the labour market tighter, other things equal and gives workers more bargaining power.[7]

The reduction of average work hours or work years can be pressed further with policies like mandating paid vacations and promoting work sharing as an alternative to unemployment benefits. These policies can bring the United States more in line with other wealthy countries. The United States is an outlier in the average number of hours worked in a year. In many western European countries, like Germany and the Netherlands, the average number of hours in a work year is more than a fifth less than in the United States. Reducing work hours is both a way to improve the quality of life for workers – people should have time to take vacations and be with their families or pursue other interests – and to increase the bargaining power of workers. While the trade-off between reduced work hours and increased employment will never be exactly one to one (i.e. a 10 per cent reduction in average hours will not lead to a 10 per cent increase in employment), shorter work years will in general lead to more jobs. Mandating various forms of paid leave, including paid vacation, is entirely within the power of state governments.

Similarly, states have the authority to promote work-sharing as an alternative to layoffs when companies see reduced demand for labour. As it stands more than half the states, including large states like California and New York, already have work-sharing programs as part of their unemployment insurance systems. Work-sharing policies can be an effective way to combat unemployment. In the recession, Germany's downturn was steeper than in the United States, yet its unemployment rate actually fell. The take up on existing state work-sharing programmes is extremely low because many employers don't know they exist. Also, many of the programmes are overly bureaucratic with rules badly in need of modernization.

It is worth noting that efforts to reduce the length of the average work year can be seen as an effort to counteract longstanding government policies that had the effect of increasing average hours. Government policy has long encouraged employers to offer benefits like healthcare insurance and pensions. These benefits typically involve large overhead costs, especially when pensions took the form of defined benefit pensions. As a result, employers had a strong preference for requiring workers to put in longer hours as an alternative to hiring more workers. While the overhead costs are less today than in prior decades, with defined benefit pensions becoming rare in the private sector and healthcare benefits often being pro-rated, there is a substantial amount of inertia in the labour market. This can certainly justify government policies pushing in the opposite direction towards shorter work weeks and work years.

Another way that states can improve the labour market for its workers is by ending dismissal at will, at least for longer-term employees. Montana already prohibits dismissal without cause for workers who have been on the job for more than six months. This sort of protection makes workers more secure in their employment and can also facilitate union organizing since it would be more difficult to dismiss workers involved in an organizing drive.

States could also require severance pay in order to discourage companies from simply laying off longer-term workers and moving operations overseas. For example, if companies had to pay two weeks of severance pay for each year of employment, a worker who had been on the job for twenty years would be entitled to forty weeks of severance pay. This would provide a substantial financial cushion to a longer-term worker facing the loss of their job. More importantly it would change the equation for employers. If they knew they would have to pay a substantial price for dismissing workers they would have more incentive to keep them employed. This would encourage them to modernize facilities and upgrade workers' skills, since this would be preferable to large severance payments for simply getting rid of them.

Severance pay can be set at levels that are too high and discourage hiring and investment, but there is a long way between zero and this point. Germany, which has substantial severance pay requirements, has an unemployment rate of just 4.1 per cent. States where progressives have a voice can make steps towards providing more secure unemployment without worrying about massive capital flight.

Finance

States are more limited in the actions they can take with respect to finance since the most important policy for reining in the sector, a financial transactions tax, can only be effectively implemented in any substantial way at the federal level. However, states and even local governments can take many actions that will limit the waste and abuses in the sector.

Most immediately, state and local governments control their public employee pension funds. These have often been a source of bloated fees for private equity and hedge fund managers, as well as investment advisers. States should insist on complete disclosure of fees with all the information posted on the Web so that anyone who cared could readily make comparisons of fees and returns across pension funds. This should put substantial downward pressure on these fees, which help to enrich many of the richest people in the country.

States can also seek to reduce the fees that workers in the private sector pay on their retirement savings by offering state-operated retirement accounts. Illinois and California are taking the lead in this area, with many other states likely to follow suit in the near future.[8] There is an enormous amount of money potentially at stake for the financial industry. Fees on existing private 401(k) plans average close to 1 per cent a year.[9] Fees on state-operated plans are likely to be in the range of 0.2–0.3 per cent. With almost $6 trillion currently invested in these plans, the difference amounts to more than $40 billion a year in income for the financial industry.[10] The expansion of these state-sponsored accounts would both facilitate retirement savings for the vast majority of workers who no longer have a traditional defined benefit pension and drastically reduce a major source of income for the financial industry.

Financial transactions taxes are a valuable policy because they effectively take a sledgehammer to the waste in the financial sector and in the process can take away tens of billions of dollars of annual income from some of the richest people in the country. The revenue from the tax would come almost completely from the financial sector, since for most investors the reduction in trading volume and the associated costs would fully offset the tax. This means that pensions and 401(k) holders would likely end up spending roughly the same amount on trading costs and the industry pays the price in less revenue. If a tax raises $100 billion a year (0.6 per cent of GDP), as some projections show,[11] this is money directly out of the pockets of the Wall Street traders.

It might be possible for the major financial centres to impose very small financial transactions taxes (e.g., 0.001%), but any substantial tax would quickly shift most trading to platforms in other states. A national tax can be structured in ways that make avoidance difficult, a state or local tax cannot be. The one exception is a tax on mortgage transfers. States do have jurisdiction over the transfer of a mortgage regardless of where it takes place. A modest tax on mortgage transfers (e.g., 0.1%) can be a strong disincentive to the sort of game playing with mortgages that we saw in the bubble years, as well as providing a substantial source of revenue. This can also help to show the potential of broader financial taxes at the national level.

Patents and copyrights

Intellectual property rules are set at the national and international levels, but there is still room for substantial action at the state level in this area. The most obvious course of attack is the place where patents do the greatest harm: prescription drugs. As noted earlier, patent monopolies can cause drugs to sell for several hundred times their free market price. The best way to address this problem is to make it easier for people to buy drugs at their free market price or at least a price that is closer to their free market price.

States can do this in two ways. First, while the law is not entirely clear, the federal government has allowed people to purchase drugs by mail order from foreign pharmacies for their own use. Many people now purchase drugs at far lower prices from pharmacies in Canada, Europe, and elsewhere, frequently saving more than 50 per cent off the price they would pay in the United States. States can encourage this practice by keeping an up-to-date list of credible pharmacies in other countries. This can give people more assurance that they are getting high quality drugs when they choose to go this route.

The other route that states could take would be offering Medicaid patients needing especially expensive drugs the opportunity to travel to a country where the drug is much cheaper and to split the savings with the state. The Hepatitis C drug Sovaldi provides an example of a situation where this could be feasible. The gap between an $84,000 list price, or even the discounted price of around $50,000, and the free market price of $200 can easily cover a trip to India for a patient and family member, with plenty of money to spare. There may not be many cases like this, but even a small number will help to dramatize the enormous price that we pay as a result of granting patent monopolies.

Another path that states could take in challenging patent monopolies in drugs is by demanding open licensing within the state for drugs that were developed in part with the state's funding. This would mean, for example, that patents that stemmed in part from research that was done in part by professors employed by the University of California, would be freely licensed for drugs sold in the state of California. These professors, or the companies with whom they contract, would have full patent rights to their drugs everywhere else in the world, but in the state of California they would be obligated to give free licence to anyone who wanted to use the patent to produce the drug for in state use. This means that drugs developed in California would be cheap in California, even if they were very expensive everywhere else. The same would apply to research at universities in other states. This is a route that would both offer very real benefits for the people of a state supporting research and also call attention to the enormous waste resulting from the patent system.

On the copyright side, a state or even local government could initiate an alternative path for funding creative work. They could go the route of giving their citizens vouchers of modest size ($50–100) that could be used to support the creative worker(s) of their choice. The condition for a writer, musician, singer, etc., to be eligible to receive the money would be that they physically reside in the city or state for most of the year and that all the work they produce for the period in which they are supported is in the public domain.[12]

If even a relatively small city or state went this route it could likely get back much or all of its spending through tourists coming to take advantage of the artistic environment. With most creative workers seeing very little opportunity to support themselves in the copyright system, many would likely view this as an attractive alternative. The residency requirement means they would have to be physically present in the city or state, which means that they would be performing music and plays, offering writers' workshops, and doing other activities that would likely pull in tourists. Also, from the vantage point of creative workers, having a larger public presence would be important for increasing their share of the voucher money.

In addition to possibly providing an effective economic development strategy for the places that take this route, this system would also show that alternatives to copyright financing are feasible. If several cities and/or states went this route it would lead to the creation of a substantial body of work that was outside of the copyright system. If high quality creative work was available at no cost on the Web, it would make it more difficult for the copyright system to survive.

Limiting the pay of CEOs and other top executives

The key issue on CEO pay is giving shareholders more control over the pay received by the company's top management. Since corporations are chartered at the state level, states can rewrite their rules of incorporation so that shareholders are better positioned to vote down CEO pay packages. One possibility would be to set rules that only count directly voted shares in electing directors and on proxy issues.

As it stands now, the asset managers who vote the bulk of shares tend to be friends with top management and see little reason to put downward pressure on their pay. If the asset managers lost their vote, then the people who directly vote their shares, and may actually monitor the behaviour and pay of the CEOs, would be positioned to push back against excessive CEO pay. It is also possible to take advantage of the federal "say on pay" law which requires CEO pay packages to be subject to a non-binding vote of shareholders every three years. States could impose a serious penalty for directors if a pay package was voted down. For example, they could lose half of their pay. This would provide directors with a large incentive to ensure that CEO pay was not excessive.

It is easy for corporations to reincorporate in another state if they don't like a state's rules on incorporation, but this would be of little consequence. With the exception of Delaware, fees for incorporation are not a major part of state revenue and their tax status does not depend on where they are incorporated. Also, the sight of CEOs changing their state of incorporation to avoid giving shareholders more control over their firms should be a great lesson in the structure of capitalism in the United States.

In addition to attacking excessive CEO pay in the private sector, states can also take steps to place limits on excessive pay packages in the non-profit sector. States generally follow the federal government in allowing exemptions from state income taxes for contributions to non-profit organizations. They also usually exempt these institutions from state and local property taxes, as well as a range of other taxes. States could make these exemptions contingent on the pay of employees at these institutions. For example, it could put a strict cap on the pay received by any employee of an institution getting tax exempt status (the president of the United States earns $400,000 a year; that might be a reasonable target for a cap). It is important to note that this is not limiting what a university or hospital pays their CEOs or other high-earning employees, it is just limiting what they could pay if they wanted to receive a subsidy from the taxpayers of the state.[13]

While non-profits would undoubtedly object to imposing pay caps, the consequences are likely to be limited for states that impose them. It is unlikely that Harvard would set up operations outside of Massachusetts if it could only pay its president $400,000 a year. Similarly, it is difficult to imagine organizations devoted to other charitable or public purposes saying they have to relocate because they can't find competent people to work for this pay. Putting pressure to lower pay for those at the top will also have the benefit of freeing up money for lower-paid employees.

Reducing the pay of high-end professionals

The most direct way of lowering the pay of high-end professionals would be to reduce the barriers that prevent qualified professionals from other countries from practising their profession in the United States. As noted before, this is most clearly an issue for physicians where the average pay is more than $250,000 a year, roughly twice the average in other wealthy countries. While the licensing requirements for physicians and dentists are set nationally, states have more discretion in areas like law and other professions. In these cases, they can work to eliminate unnecessary barriers. For example, in the case of law, they can try to ensure that the state bar exams are structured to ensure competence, not to limit the number of people practising law in the state.

The standard that a physician must complete a US residency program to practice in the United States is set nationally as is the requirement that dentists graduate from a US (or Canadian) dental school. While states can't override these requirements, they can try to limit their importance. In the case of doctors, they can authorize doctors to practice under the supervision of other doctors, even if they have not completed a US residency program. Several states have recently passed legislation to this effect.[14] They can also liberalize scope of practice rules allowing nurse practitioners, physicians' assistants, and other health professionals the ability to provide services for which they are qualified.

There would be a similar story in the case of dentists and dental hygienists, where the latter are entirely competent to perform many tasks without the supervision of dentists. States can also try to minimize the need for lawyers by crafting laws to simplify standard legal procedures such as mortgage issuance, house sales, divorces and wills as much as possible.

Another way to reduce the pay of doctors and free up income for state residents is to promote medical travel for expensive medical procedures. In almost all cases, medical procedures cost far less in other countries than in the United States. In some cases, the cost of procedures in high quality facilities in other countries may be less than one-tenth as much as in the United States. With procedures like open heart surgery, which can cost more than $200,000 in the United States, the savings can easily exceed $100,000. This would easily cover the cost of travel and a period of recovery for the patient and family members.

State Medicaid programs could offer beneficiaries the option of having procedures done in other countries while splitting the savings with patients. As is the case with getting low-cost drugs from other countries, this would both directly save money and call attention to the excessive pay of doctors in the United States. In addition, by reducing demand for doctors it would help to put downward pressure on their pay. To further this process states can draft insurance regulations and medical malpractice laws that would provide a clear legal path with appropriate safeguards for offering similar terms.

The net effect of these sorts of measures should be to reduce the pay of high-end professionals in the states that take this route. This will lower the cost of healthcare as well as the other services they provide. This has the same effect of increasing the real wage of other workers as getting access to low-cost imports of clothes and shoes, however in this case the gains occur in a way that increases equality rather than inequality.

THE POLITICS OF RESTRUCTURING MARKETS

In outlining this agenda there is still a big problem as to agency. Who exactly would push the sort of progressive agenda described in the previous sections? It is easy to say labour unions, and for much of this agenda many labour unions would be key allies. However, we have seen enormous shrinkage in the power of unions over the last four decades. It would be great if there were a plausible path to reversing this decline. Some of the measures discussed in the previous sections, notably an end to dismissal at will, would facilitate organizing, but it would be a heroic and unwarranted assumption to envision that this agenda would lead to a massive increase in union membership. While we can look to unions as an important force in promoting any progressive agenda, to succeed any programme will require a much broader range of support.

While it is difficult to say what this broader coalition for progressive reform might look like, there are a few points that can be made. First, there has been a growing effectiveness in the use of the Internet and social media in progressive politics. The Sanders campaign was able to seriously contest the Democratic nomination with a minimal amount of institutional support. His outreach efforts were able to enlist enough activists to work on the campaign and to raise enough money from small contributors that he came close to winning the nomination.

More recently, the spontaneous growth of anti-Trump organizations across the country demonstrates the potential for quickly organizing a large constituency for progressive change. It is far too early to determine the success of these efforts either electorally or in actually affecting policy, but few would have guessed that Donald Trump's election would spark such a large and energetic opposition in just a few months. If this sort of energy can be sustained in pushing progressive policies, it would have considerable potential.

It is also important to note areas of recent success. The successes of the movement for LGBT rights have truly been astounding. It was difficult to imagine that same-sex marriage would be recognized as a constitutional right twenty years ago or even ten years ago. Even in areas that are closer to what is traditionally considered economic policy there have been noteworthy successes. In particular, the anti-smoking movement has managed to ban smoking from almost all public buildings. It was recent memory that ashtrays were standard equipment in cars and even on airplane seat armrests. The tobacco industry was a very powerful and profitable sector, yet anti-smoking activists were able to radically transform the place of tobacco in society and views of smoking.

An important point about the agenda outlined above is that in almost all cases it suggests potential allies within the business community. For example, insurance companies should be allies in the efforts to get lower cost healthcare. The industry has a clear and obvious stake in reducing the income of the prescription drug industry, the medical equipment industry, and doctors. If CEOs really are getting bloated salaries at the expense of shareholders, as opposed to being rewarded for their contribution to the company's stock performance, then investors should be allies in measures to reduce their pay. If state-managed retirement accounts can make it simple and largely costless for small businesses to offer low-cost retirement plans to their employees, then small businesses should be willing to support a measure that removes a competitive disadvantage in trying to retain good workers.

For most of the policies listed in the previous section, there will be substantial segments of business that could benefit if these policies are implemented. Progressives need to take advantage of business allies where they can be found. If we give up on the idea that we will be seizing the means of production, and recognize that markets are here to stay, then we can have a more clear-eyed view of corporations. They are not inherently good or bad: they exist to make profit. It is our job to design policies that allow them to make profit in productive ways and as much as possible prevent large profits from anti-social actions.

Finally, it is worth noting that this is quite explicitly designed as a "slice and dice" incrementalist agenda. We can't expect strong political coalitions to continually fight for big change with nothing to show for their efforts in the interim. We need a set of achievable policies that can both produce results and create a platform for further success. If we can succeed in getting two weeks of mandated paid vacation in Illinois or California, then we will have won an enormous benefit for the large numbers of workers in these states who don't currently get any paid time off from their job. This will be clear evidence of the success of political action and give an incentive for further actions. Perhaps at some point they will push for the six weeks of paid vacation that is now the standard in Northern Europe.

And, if the successes in an Illinois or California don't lead to any increase in unemployment (by reducing labour supply they could actually reduce unemployment), then workers in other states will be tempted to push for similar legislation. And many of these successes will directly weaken the power of the Right. If the drug companies can't get rich from patent monopolies and private equity fund partners can't rip-off pension funds, they will have much less money, and therefore less power, to buy politicians in the future. Just as reducing the number of union members lessens the power of progressives, taking away the rents earned by the wealthy reduces the power of the Right.

If progressives hope to turn the tide, we need policies that can produce real benefits in the near term, while at the same time pointing in the direction of larger changes in the future. There is no shortage of such policies; we just need to think about them clearly.

ADDENDUM

Having the benefit of being three months further into the Trump presidency, and seeing the resistance, as well as having read my co-authors' pieces, I would like to reemphasize my main point. There is enormous potential for reworking the economic system in ways that reverse the upward redistribution of the last four decades and begin to shift power along with income to the bulk of the population. The main obstacle is the need for a better understanding of the economy.

The growth of the anti-Trump movement has been impressive. To a large extent it has been spontaneous, with very little centralized organization. People are angry and scared at the prospect of a Trump presidency and a right-wing Republican Congress. This has already made ordinarily safe Republican congressional seats suddenly contestable. This is inspiring, but the negative side is that there is no real economic agenda attached to this movement, other than being opposed to Trump and the Republicans. If, for example, the Democrats were to retake control of the House in 2018 based on the strength of this grassroots movement, there is no reason to believe that they would be any more progressive than the Democrats who controlled Congress from 2009 to 2011. On the plus side, these will be people who will defend the gains from the Affordable Care Act and who will (mostly) want to protect Medicare, Medicaid and Social Security. However, it is not clear that they are interested in an economic agenda that goes much beyond this, for example taking measures that will seriously downsize Wall Street and the financial industry, commit the country to a full employment economy, and end the corruption that has become the defining feature of the modern patent and copyright system.

It is not clear that this lack of interest can be blamed on the power of the affected interest groups. While there is no doubt that the financial industry will be prepared to go to war to protect their riches, as would the pharmaceutical industry, to date they really haven't had to play hardball. Their foes have been so fragmented and disorganized that they haven't really had to break a sweat in their efforts to preserve the status quo. For the most part, the policy changes that would really hurt them are not even on the political agenda.

To take one very visible example, Jon Ossoff, the great Democratic hope to take the Georgia congressional seat formerly held by Health and Human Services Secretary Tom Price, is a deficit hawk. The commitment to balanced budgets or at least small deficits is a commitment that seriously limits social welfare spending. Even more importantly, in an economy facing chronic demand shortfalls, it is likely condemning large numbers of people (disproportionately African American and Hispanic) to being unemployed. My guess is that Ossoff has no deeply held views on budget deficits. It is likely that a political consultant told him that yelling about eliminating waste and reducing the budget deficit would be the best way to get elected. Odds are that the consultant giving this advice knows next to nothing about the implications of a balanced budget policy. If there was some real push in the opposite direction, toward a full employment policy that might well require larger deficits, it certainly seems plausible that Ossoff would take a different view on budget deficits. While there may be some big money types who will cut off their contributions to Ossoff if he abandoned balanced budget orthodoxy, he can surely raise enough money to be competitive without their help. The issue here is simply that there is no understanding among the people who would most benefit from a full employment budget policy, how they are harmed by the balanced budget orthodoxy.

This can be a source of optimism or of frustration. Those who have benefitted from the upward redistribution of the last four decades have enormous power, which they are prepared to use to protect their gains. But the immediate obstacle to progressive economic policy is not their power; it is lack of economic knowledge among the people who most stand to gain from pursuing different policies. That can change, but it won't be easy.

NOTES

1. This is the topic of my book, *Rigged: How Globalization and the Rules of the Market Economy Were Structured to Make the Rich Richer* (Washington, DC: Center for Economic and Policy Research, 2016). Much of this discussion is derived from this book.
2. The shift to profits in the housing bubble years was partly illusory. The profits made on issuing bad loans were booked in the years the loans

were made. Recorded profits were later depressed when the loans went bad in the years 2008–10.

3. In the years from 1947 to 1980 the unemployment rate averaged 0.5 percentage points below the Congressional Budget Office's (CBO) estimate of the non-accelerating inflation rate of unemployment (NAIRU). The years from 1980 to 2016 has averaged 0.8 percentage points more than the estimates of NAIRU. Even if we pull out the years since the 2008 crisis, the average unemployment rate in the post-1980 period was more than 0.6 percentage points above the estimates of NAIRU. While the CBO estimates of the NAIRU can themselves be questioned as measures of the full employment level of unemployment, they do at least provide an independent benchmark against which to measure the tightness of the labour market in these two periods. See Dean Baker & Jared Bernstein, *Getting Back to Full Employment: A Better Bargain for Working People* (Washington, DC: Center for Economic and Policy Research, 2013).

4. On this point, it is worth noting one of the inaccurate claims often made by economists. The story goes that since the winners from trade gain more than the losers lose, it should be possible to redistribute from winners to losers and make everyone better off. This assumes a costless redistributive process. In other words, it means taxes that don't create distortions and compensation or retraining programs that don't involve waste or corruption. Neither exists in the real world. In other words, this is one of those claims made by economists, without any real foundation, in order to promote policies they like.

5. M. Boldrin & D. Levine, "The case against patents", *Journal of Economic Perspectives* 27:1 (2013), 3–22.

6. International Monetary Fund, "A Fair and Substantial Contribution by the Financial Sector" (Washington, DC: IMF, 2010), https://www.imf. org/external/np/g20/pdf/062710b.pdf (accessed 3 August 2017).

7. The minimum wage does go in the other direction of creating a deliberate obstacle to a market outcome. Minimum wages have led to substantial wage gains for millions of workers at the bottom of the wage distribution, but clearly there are limits as to how high a minimum wage can be raised before the employment losses more than offset gains to wages to those who have jobs.

8. This possibility could depend on the survival of a Labour Department ruling on the application of Employment Retirement Security Act (ERISA) to these accounts. The Republican Congress was seeking to overturn this ruling at the time of writing.

9. A 401(k) is a retirement savings plan sponsored by an employer. It lets workers save and invest a piece of their paycheck before taxes are

taken out. Taxes aren't paid until the money is withdrawn from the account.

10. Data on the assets of defined contribution pension plans are available from the Federal Reserve Board's Financial Accounts of the United States, Table L.118, https://www.federalreserve.gov/releases/z1/current/html/l118c.htm (accessed 3 August 2017).

11. Baker, *Rigged*.

12. This sort of system is described more fully in Baker, *Rigged*. It is worth noting that Seattle adopted a similar sort of approach to funding political campaigns. Residents are given vouchers that they can spend on the candidate(s) of their choosing. The condition for candidates to be eligible for the money is that they must accept strict limits on donations from other sources.

13. At many universities, the highest paid employees are the football or basketball coach. This raises the question of why the public should be providing a tax subsidy to what for practical purposes are professional sports. There is no reason that the football or basketball team of a major university with a large fan base could not operate as an independent entity, subject to the same tax rules as any other for profit business.

14. C. Morgan, "Doctors who fail to match with a residency program head back to school to become nurses", *Daily Nurse*, 23 December 2016, http://dailynurse.com/doctors-fail-match-residency-program-head-back-school-become-nurses/ (accessed 3 August 2017).

CHAPTER 3

TOWARDS A NEW PARADIGM FOR THE LEFT IN THE UNITED STATES

Fred Block

Recent political earthquakes including Trump's election, the Brexit vote, and the electoral threat from the far right in the French and German elections make it obvious that parties of the centre-left must reinvent themselves if they are to regain their relevance and their electoral support. I agree with much of David Coates' diagnosis in his chapter in this volume, but I would formulate the issue somewhat differently. For these parties to become once again serious governing parties, they must meet both an organizational and a programmatic challenge. The organizational challenge is to rebuild the parties on a democratic and inclusive basis so that rank and file party members exercise real influence on party leadership. The programmatic challenge is to develop strategies that would actually improve the lives of much of the electorate.

My focus here is on the US case, but I think some of the analysis is relevant for other advanced societies in Europe and Asia. Most of my attention is on the programmatic challenge since solutions to the organizational challenge are outside of my areas of competence. After a brief description of the organizational challenge, I argue that the United States and other developed societies are experiencing a transition to a "habitation society" and this diagnosis opens up the possibilities of new political strategies that cut across traditional class and locational divides. In the conclusion, I suggest that this diagnosis can also be helpful in thinking about how to meet the organizational challenge.

THE ORGANIZATIONAL CHALLENGE

It was socialist organizers who invented the modern mass political party.[1] Before the emergence of these parties based in the industrial working class, political parties had been loose alliances of notables who gathered together under a party umbrella to compete for elected offices. This conformed to Schumpeter's definition of democracy as a political system in which voters have the opportunity to choose which elite groups will rule over them. To be sure, the programmatic differences between such parties could be extremely serious, but the process of articulating connections between candidates and voters was limited to the period of hotly contested electoral campaigns.

This arrangement was upset by the emergence of socialist parties in Europe at the end of the nineteenth century and beginning of the twentieth century. While the precise organizational linkages between unions and socialist parties varied from country to country, participation in unions provided millions of voters with an ongoing, albeit imperfect, channel of connection with their party's leaders. This meant that these parties formulated their political programmes through an ongoing dialogue with the party's political base creating something that, at times, was a qualitative advance over Schumpeterian democracy.

In response to this challenge, non-socialist parties were forced to transform themselves, to some degree, into mass parties that established durable links between the party leadership and the party membership. In the US, there was no direct threat from a Socialist Party after 1920, but the New Deal linkage between the Democratic Party and the labour movement created something comparable to the European model. In the years that followed, both major parties moved to empower party members through the primary process. The consequence was that the control of the parties by notables and elected officials began to decline as evidenced by successful insurgencies by "outsider" candidates such as Goldwater in 1964 and McGovern in 1972.

In the meantime, however, the industrial working class has experienced a precipitous decline in all of the developed societies as a consequence of technological changes and the movement of production to low-wage countries. In the US, this transformation is exemplified by the fate of Detroit, once the centre of auto production. Between

1947 and 2007, the number of manufacturing workers in the city fell by 97 per cent.[2] The declining political clout of the United Auto Workers was demonstrated by its inability to block a Republican governor from turning Michigan into a right-to-work state in 2014. And, of course, Michigan was one of the critical states that handed Donald Trump the presidency in 2016.

Because of the decline in union membership, the mechanism that historically made these centre-left parties somewhat democratic has atrophied. These parties have instead followed the trajectory of non-socialist mass parties that have used primaries and other feedback mechanisms to create some weaker connection between party membership and the party leadership. Over the last three or four decades, all mass parties have come to rely on new cadres of experts including pollsters, campaign strategists and messaging professionals. These professionals manage the relationship between party leadership and both party members and the broader electorate. They figure out what promises candidates should make and how they should formulate their political appeals.

This new form of expertise is itself a double-edged sword. Obama's successful candidacy relied heavily on young cadres who mastered the art of targeting certain demographic groups and getting them to show up at the polls. Similarly, Jeremy Corbyn's surprising campaigns for party leadership similarly relied on these new experts who were able to mobilize rank and file Labour Party members. But the dark side is that these new forms of expertise tend to displace more durable forms of party organization at the local level. This helps to explain the familiar paradox that Barack Obama handily won two national presidential elections, but over those eight years, the Democratic Party lost a huge amount of ground in filling seats in state legislatures, state houses and the Congress.

Obama's people created a national campaign structure that parachuted campaign workers into battleground states to organize local volunteers to use sophisticated computer targeting to reach out to rank and file voters. At the time, this looked like an ideal blending of grassroots politics with advanced technologies. But in retrospect, it appears that all of this worked not because of the technology but because of Obama's extraordinary appeal as a candidate. When Hillary Clinton's campaign closely followed the same model, it failed miserably. The campaign officials who parachuted in were unfamiliar with the localities where they were working and simply ignored the growing anxiety of party officials in places like Michigan and Wisconsin who were warning of significant defections of traditional Democratic voters.

It is hardly rocket science to recognize that political parties need to have vital local organizations that create strong linkages with voters and the high-tech Obama model does not do that. The point is clearly made by the state that represents an exception to this general pattern. Nevada is a traditionally Republican state, but successful organizing campaigns by the Hotel and Restaurant Employee union in Las Vegas has created the kind of union–party linkage that was characteristic of the industrial era. The union's ability to turn out tens of thousands of voters, predominantly Latino, made it possible for Hillary Clinton to carry the state and for a Latina Democrat to win the US Senate seat.

The weakening of the Democratic Party at the state and local level is also a result of the party's focus on exerting power in Washington as the key to delivering results for its supporters. This developed organically out of the party's commitment to equality for African Americans, women, and gays since these causes could only be assured through federal action to overcome fierce resistance at the state and local levels.[3] But instead of developing a nuanced mixture of strategies that focused at the local, the state and the national level, the Democratic coalition's thinking on most issues was concentrated on the federal level whether the issue was union rights or healthcare reform or local economic development. So, for example, in the case of healthcare, the Democrats focused during both the Clinton and Obama administrations on national legislation. Ironically, it was a Republican, Mitt Romney, who implemented a near-universal health insurance reform in Massachusetts.[4] It was the relative success of that state-level reform that became the model for Obama's Affordable Care Act.

To be sure, any effective reform strategy in the United States depends on a complex combination of decentralized initiatives. Given the power and resources of the central government, most significant reforms require some shifts in national policy. But there is no question that over the last five decades, the Democratic coalition has focused almost exclusively on Washington to the detriment of using state governments as "laboratories of democracy". This has a number of highly negative consequences. It drives the decline of local political organization because there is much less sustained focus on what the state government can do to solve problems. Why should citizens remain engaged on a day-to-day basis when all that matters is who wins the White House every four years? It also means that future party leaders focus on building careers in Washington rather than at the state level.

The Republican Party has followed the opposite course since it recognized the possibility of using state government as "laboratories of reaction". They legislate at the state level to reward grassroots religious right advocates and to implement measures that weaken the political capacity of their opponents. Republican controlled states have passed multiple state bills to limit abortion access, defund Planned Parenthood, discriminate against gays and transgender people, and provide direct funding to various religious right initiatives. But equally important has been the rollback of union rights, creating barriers to voting for traditionally Democratic constituencies, and the gerrymandering of legislative districts to make Republican control permanent.[5]

It seems clear that centre-left parties must find a way to revitalize themselves at the local level by developing strong and durable links to their supporters. But doing this requires a political strategy in which day-to-day actions at the local level holds out the promise of leading to something important beyond electing better people to political office. There is the need to recreate the kind of organic connection that existed when membership in a local union fighting for better wages and working conditions was closely linked to being an active supporter of the local branch of the socialist party.

Finding ways to create those kinds of organic linkages is not enough. Rebuilt political parties must find new ways to structure themselves at the local level to become both democratic and inclusive of the multiple identities that the centre-left needs to represent. This means bringing together people across formidable divisions of race, ethnicity, class, gender, immigration status and life styles. Obviously, the Internet and social media can play an important role in creating a two-way flow of information and influence, but there also needs to be ongoing face-to-face interactions where people have the opportunity to hear different views and deliberate together. Solutions to this organizational challenge will have to be worked out through trial and error by different groups trying different approaches until a few institutional innovations emerge that prove effective both in maintaining high levels of participation and creating more democratic and inclusive political party structures.

THE PROGRAMMATIC CHALLENGE

In some fundamental sense, centre-left parties have been adrift since the political economic changes of the early-1970s constructed major barriers to the Keynesian and welfare-oriented policies that had prevailed in the quarter century after the end of the Second World War. Ever since, there have been a succession of efforts to seek new programmatic directions. On the Left in the 1980s, there was Mitterrand's left turn and the Swedish initiative for wage-earner funds. In the 1990s, there was also the centrist Third Way of Clinton, Blair and Schroeder that achieved some electoral successes but proved unable to reverse the market-oriented trajectory initiated by the Right. More recently, New Leftist parties such as Syriza and Podemos have raised hopes for a new kind of breakthrough. But so far, none of these initiatives has generated anything vaguely resembling the synergy between left politics and economic policies that existed in the Keynesian era.

This record of failure is hardly surprising given the dramatic transformations of the economy that have occurred over the last five decades. Think, for example, of the shift in what are the most profitable and powerful giant corporations. Fifty years ago, that would be General Motors with its vast investment in giant factories and 400,000 workers who belonged to the United Auto Workers. Today, it could be Google (now renamed as Alphabet) that has no factories, offers most of its products for free, and employs only about 61,000 people worldwide. Close on Google's heels is Facebook whose business model is based not on appropriating the surplus labour time of its 16,000 employees, but rather, appropriating the surplus leisure time of literally billions of people so they can better connect with each other.

Another key signpost is the shift in consumption patterns that have occurred over that time period. In 1970, the purchase of all goods, including food, clothing, appliances and cars represented

56 per cent of consumer outlays in the US. By 2015, goods had fallen to less than 33 per cent of consumer expenditures. To be sure, this overstates the case somewhat because housing is treated as a service that consumers purchase, but even in housing construction, the cost of the materials used has been falling for decades as a percentage of total costs. But the basic reality is that when most people think about economic production, they think about products on the shelves of stores and yet these represent only about a third of what the economy now produces.[6]

Since the 1960s, academics have sought to name and describe this transformation as a transition from an industrial to a postindustrial society.[7] But while postindustrial arguments have had considerable resonance in academia, they have not been successfully translated into political programmes. To be sure, Bill Clinton and Tony Blair used the related rhetoric of a "new economy" fuelled by computer technology and finance to justify some of their initiatives that supported the growth of financial activity. More recently, advocates of "green economy" strategies that focus on replacing fossil fuels with renewables have gained some greater political leverage, but they also have had difficulty making the case that the energy transition could be the key to a new era of sustainable growth.

The obvious explanation for the lack of political success is that the terminology of postindustrialism is abstract. When one thinks of agricultural society, one envisions a farm. When one thinks of industrial society, it brings to mind factories with smokestacks. But the term postindustrial has little by way of concrete associations; it is simply a place-holder saying that all we know is that the central economic activity is no longer raising crops or factory production.

But now, fifty years into this transformation, it is possible to give this new historical stage a less abstract name. We are experiencing a difficult and uneven transition to a habitation society.[8] The central economic activity, both in terms of employing the most people and in creating the most value, is now the production and improvement of the communities in which people live. Of course, human beings have always attended to their habitation, but in past times, the physical and social construction of communities was a secondary activity that people engaged in when not doing the primary activity of raising crops or working in factories. Now, however, creating and improving the physical and social infrastructure in which we live is what most people do whether we are construction workers, teachers, health-care workers, software engineers or government workers.

In a habitation society, social reproduction becomes primary and production of both goods and foodstuff is secondary. The central challenge becomes finding new and better ways to create sustainable and resilient communities while economizing on inputs of capital, labour and nonrenewable materials. In the industrial era, there was a powerful logic of centralizing complex production processes, a trend that culminated in the movement of a substantial share of global manufacturing to Chinese factories. But the logic of a habitation society is the opposite; it is towards increasing the self-sufficiency of sub-national economic regions. Communities prosper by getting better at providing housing, infrastructure, healthcare, education, energy and other services. To be sure, regions cannot be entirely self-sufficient; they will still need to import some goods and services. Hence, there will continue to be pressure to specialize in some types of production to trade for those imports.

For both self-sufficiency and export success, innovation is central to habitation.[9] Using new technologies and new organizational techniques is essential to improve the production of quality services. We see this process in embryo as cities use new technologies to make more effective urban transit systems that improve mobility while reducing problems of traffic and pollution. Moreover, cities and regions also need innovation to develop goods and services to export to other parts of the world.

But our political arrangements and institutional structures are relics of the industrial era; they systematically constrict and distort the process of making a habitation society function in an effective way. The result is an economy that doesn't work and that, in turn, generates deep dissatisfaction with the political system. This, of course, presents centre-left parties with an opportunity. If they could become the proponents of a transition to a habitation society, they would be able to reinvent themselves and give new meaning to the Left's historic commitments to equality and democracy.

THE CONTRADICTORY NATURE OF THE TRANSITION

The best example of the contradiction between a habitation society and industrial era structures comes not from the advanced economies but from China that is still predominantly an industrial society. The Chinese have invested massively in the project of building entirely new cities to prepare for future migration from the countryside. On one level, the regime's logic in doing this is impeccable. The need for labour on farms will continue to fall, so many in the countryside will ultimately need to move to urban areas. But since existing megacities have already reached 20 or 30 million people, it makes sense to spread this increased urban population across a number of newer cities that are organized on a more manageable scale.

But on another level, the logic is deeply flawed with the consequence that some of these urban developments have become uninhabited "ghost cities".[10] For one thing, the Chinese planners do not have an answer to how these migrants will earn a living in these pre-built cities. Ordinarily, construction puts a lot of people to work, but if the apartment towers are already completed, that cannot be a significant source of employment. And China's coastal cities have already exhausted the possibilities of export-oriented factories to produce clothing or smart phones to sell to the rest of the world. Presumably, in these new cities, many will work in restaurants and big box retail stores, but this is hardly sufficient to make these new cities economically viable.

But the deeper problem is that people do not want to move into pre-built cities and forcing them to do so does not make sense. In the industrial era, people moved to where the factories were out of economic necessity and they made do with the housing that was available or they gradually constructed their own homes in their limited spare time. This was the reality; habitation had to take a back seat to earning a living. But as the creation of habitation becomes the central economic activity, people want to choose the physical environment and social communities in which they live. In other words, the Chinese model is exactly the opposite of what is developmentally necessary in a habitation society which is the expansion of democratic mechanisms so that people are able collectively to shape the kind of human communities that they want.

These democratic mechanisms are necessary because the market is deeply flawed as an instrument for deciding on many habitation issues. Whether we are talking about the infrastructure for transportation, energy, communication, health, education, community amenities, or the distribution of activities across space, the choices cannot be made by individual actors on the market. These are inherently collective decisions even if the providers of particular services are private entities. But during the industrial era, many of these decisions were put outside the realm of politics to be handled instead by technocratic decision makers. This no longer makes any sense since habitation is at the core of what people consume, and they need to be part of choosing if there is going to be a decent match between what is produced and what is consumed.

There is, of course, a line of argument that people choose the kind of community in which they want to live by their decisions as to what real estate to purchase or rent. But the reality is that desirable communities or neighbourhoods are rationed through market prices. Attractive neighbourhoods are scarce and most people cannot even think of matching the high prices needed to own or rent in those districts. But the key issue is that even when there is extremely strong demand, this is not sufficient to create more good neighbourhoods. Private developers do not have the resources to provide the infrastructure needed for good neighbourhoods, and city officials in the US have neither the incentive nor the funds to invest in significant upgrading of existing neighbourhoods. So what one gets instead is the process of gentrification in which better neighbourhoods are created by kicking out most of the historic residents. The basic reality is that the market mechanism fails in providing most people with the kind of habitation they want. This can be seen clearly in data showing that large portions of the labour force in metropolitan areas now face long and difficult commutes to get to their workplaces.

To be sure, the mismatch between what people want and what they get is not as extreme in the US and Europe as it is in China's newly built ghost cities. But the point still holds; the existing political and budgetary arrangements prevent progress towards a well-functioning habitation society. As in Marx's classical formation, existing power relations are blocking society from realizing the possibilities inherent in current patterns of social and economic development. The result is a period of crisis, when the new cannot be born and existing arrangements decay at an accelerating rate. Our deepest social and economic problems can be understood as resulting from this crisis of a blocked transition to a habitation society. While these problems intersect in complicated ways, four central issues can be identified.

1. Lost economic dynamism

Since the global financial crisis in 2008, the world economy has grown only slowly and has constantly been on the edge of a new economic downturn. While the US economy has fared somewhat better, the Obama-era expansion left many people behind and the decline of unemployment has occurred with many prime-age people not returning to the labour force. Moreover, growth as a goal of economic policy is increasingly being questioned because the top one per cent receive a disproportionate share of any gains and the environmental costs of continued growth along industrial era lines are increasingly obvious, particularly with the danger of catastrophic climate change.

At the same time, the system of national income accounting that was developed in the 1930s and 1940s no longer measures what we need to measure. In a habitation society, the inflation adjusted dollar value of the things that people consume is no longer the key indicator of economic welfare. Moreover, the statistics we gather for the output of key parts of the economy such as the health sector or the education sector are indifferent to the quality of the services that consumers receive, and many of the things that are increasingly important to people such as economic security, protecting the environment, meaningful work, and the quality of their neighbourhoods are simply not measured.

This disjuncture puts political leaders in a bind. Significant new investments in infrastructure spending and on health and education are needed to fund the kind of growth that would improve people's quality of life. But political leaders cannot justify that spending or generate the needed revenues because the prevailing economic measures are unlikely to vindicate such outlays. In fact, in the US, continuing fiscal pressures at all levels of government have crippled infrastructure spending, so that the dynamic possibilities of a habitation economy are not being realized.

A similar problem can be seen with national innovation systems. Recent decades have seen the decline of corporate laboratories as the key locus of innovations that translate scientific and technological advances into new products, new processes and new ways of delivering services. Such innovations now emerge out of public–private collaborations where publicly-funded scientists work with private sector technologists to overcome technological barriers.[11] But while these new collaborations have been highly effective in pushing forward such key products as smart phones, solar photovoltaics, advanced batteries and electric cars, continued innovation is threatened on several fronts.

First, budget constraints endanger continued national investments in research and development. In the US, such spending has been declining as a percentage of GDP since 2009 with negative consequences for scientific research at universities and federal laboratories. But public scientific spending is the cornerstone of this new system. Second, the aggressive and increasingly predatory behaviour of established firms also puts these collaborations at risk. In their eagerness to command the profit stream associated with a breakthrough innovation, these firms can easily sabotage the sharing of information that is critical to effective collaboration. Moreover, we are also increasingly seeing firms use their patent portfolios as a weapon to cripple potential challenges from start-up firms. The absence of adequate funding means that start-ups are often forced to sell their innovative technologies to large firms that are less likely to stick with the product long enough to bring it to the market.

A third problem is that the corporate model often stands in the way of successful deployment of significant innovations. One recent example is Twitter which has become hugely successful as a communications tool, but the company has not been able to find a way to create a sufficient stream of profits. It is possible that the tool will disappear if the firm were to fail. We have already seen with some key pieces of computer software that they are much more effectively provided through non-profit or cooperative mechanisms. Finally, there are many cases where deployment of an innovation requires significant infrastructure spending, but ongoing fiscal crises and conflicts over who gets the profits have interfered with those needed infrastructure investments.

In short, innovation is central to a habitation society as more and more people work at using technology to improve the quality of life and protect the environment. But effective collaborations for innovation have now outgrown the corporate form and require new institutions and new governance mechanisms. Until progress is made in reorganizing governance arrangements and funding, the potential for renewed economic dynamism will not be realized.

2. Growing inequality and social exclusion

Periods of socio-economic transition often see huge surges in economic inequality. The gilded age at the end of the nineteenth century was characterized by the creation of vast fortunes as a small number of aggressive entrepreneurs were able to take advantage of the shift from locally-based economic activity to the creation of a unified national market. In some cases, there were real technological breakthroughs that underpinned the rise of giant firms. In other cases, the abrupt shift in scale provided people in certain strategic locations with the opportunity to command monopoly profits. It took decades before legislative initiatives to change regulatory structures and taxation finally contained this trend towards greater income and wealth inequality.

Something similar has happened over the last forty years with a similar shift in scale that has allowed entrepreneurs in the US to operate on a global scale in both consumer and financial markets. The result has been the extraordinary increase in income and wealth inequality that has been so effectively documented by Thomas Piketty and his colleagues.[12] Moreover, the success of the top one per cent in gaining a substantially larger share of income flows has intensified all of the racial, ethnic and gender inequalities and resentments, including the division between native-born and immigrants, since groups outside of the elite have been forced to struggle over a shrinking portion of total national income. Moreover, the right-wing's success in preventing effective changes in regulation and taxation has meant that this transitional intensification of income and wealth inequality has continued unabated.

The rollback in public spending and dramatic increases in incarceration of minority populations has also intensified problems of poverty and social exclusion. The number of households living in extreme poverty, defined as living below 50 per cent of the federal poverty line, has increased dramatically. And paths out of poverty have been blocked as the poor are increasingly marginalized in urban housing markets with little prospect of establishing stable housing situations. Even the minority of poor children who are able to overcome unstable housing and finish high school are often unable to pursue a college education because of mounting financial barriers.

There is also another dimension of intensified inequality that has received less attention; it is the growing divide between metropolitan areas and rural areas. This division erupted into politics in 2016 when rural areas and small towns voted overwhelmingly for Brexit and for Donald Trump, while metropolitan areas did the opposite. The irony is that despite the multiple problems of metropolitan areas including social exclusion, gentrification and rising real estate prices, and issues of traffic and inadequate infrastructure, cities and surrounding suburbs have generally fared far better than small towns and rural areas.

Part of the issue is that most areas with low population density do not receive the public or private infrastructure spending that are now necessary for modern business activity. Access to broadband is almost always slower and cell phones coverage is spottier. So with agricultural and industrial employment continuing to fall, these areas have much greater difficulty attracting new service industries than urban areas. And, of course, low population density also limits the possibilities for small retail businesses. The consequence has been ongoing unemployment and continued out-migration of young people. Moreover, in the context of continuing fiscal pressures at all levels of government, there have been few policies to respond to rural distress. The result has been intensified populist resentment of the political establishment.

But it is also important to recognize the paradoxical way in which this rural–urban divide is mapped on to the US political system. Rural voters have become overwhelmingly Republican and their weight is augmented by institutional arrangements such as each state having two senators regardless of its population size and partisan gerrymandering of legislative and Congressional districts. However, rural, largely Republican states get back more in federal outlays than they pay in taxes. Similarly, within states, rural counties usually get back substantially more than they pay in. Logically, rural voters should favour higher taxation to finance more services and more infrastructure spending since much of the tax burden would fall on city dwellers. Yet they give their votes to a Republican Party that pushes for lower tax rates at both the federal and the state level. In other words, the current intense polarization between rural and urban voters makes it impossible to address the problems experienced by both groups.

3. The crisis of care

Care work has always been necessary for human communities, but substantial parts of it have usually been defined as women's work and rewarded inadequately in both status and compensation. In a habitation society, care work moves to the centre of economic activity because sustaining the ability of people to thrive and to innovate, even into old age, makes communities more productive. However, the effective organization of care giving is blocked either by continued reliance on the unpaid work of family members or by trying to mass produce care using industrial technologies. In both healthcare and education, we can see that standardized procedures organized around cost containment end up producing substandard care.

Here again, ongoing fiscal pressures have often blocked experiments to expand access to high quality care. The US, in particular, lags far behind other developed countries in providing family members with income support to deal with the addition of family members through birth or adoption or to make it easier to combine paid employment with care of elderly relatives. Similarly, the US suffers from a particularly acute shortage of quality childcare slots, and there is virtually no public support provided to offset the high cost of such care.

Acute problems around the financing of higher education are also part of this same crisis of care. On the one side, financial barriers are increasingly cutting low-income students off from access to higher education. On the other side, even middle-class students are required to take on huge debt burdens to finance their educations. Meanwhile, in this sector as well, the logic of cost cutting is systematically undermining quality as mass production techniques undermine students' ability to learn the critical thinking skills that are supposed to be at the core of higher education.

4. The environmental crisis

Sustainability and reducing the human burden on the environment is central to the promise of a habitation society. Once people are self-consciously creating their own communities, it follows that they need to work at protecting both the local and global environment.

But here, as well, the inherited institutions and practices of the industrial era constitute a barrier to effective environmental practices. Corporations built on the exploitation of fossil fuels have waged ferocious campaigns to interfere with the needed transition to renewable energy sources. And here again, ongoing budget constraints have slowed the massive public and private investments that are needed to finance a shift to clean energy.

But the environmental agenda also involves restructuring the relationship between cities and the countryside. On the one side, this involves pursuing "smart growth" and higher density urban living in order to counter urban sprawl. On the other, it means rewilding portions of the countryside and encouraging the planned use of designated areas of rural space for recreational and touristic purposes. Such efforts need to be oriented both to the protection of nature and the creation of stable livelihoods for people living in rural areas and small towns. Initiatives to address these issues face enormous obstacles, and the result is that growing political divide between metropolitan areas and the countryside.

TOWARDS A POLITICS OF HABITATION

This analysis is meant to show that the various constituencies that are the base of contemporary centre-left politics – women, racial and sexual minorities, environmentalists, labour unions, community activists and campaigners against inequality and the political power of the wealthy – should understand that they are engaged in a common struggle to create human communities that are inclusive, egalitarian and governed through revitalized democratic practices. Such an understanding could change left politics in several important ways.

First, there is a need to move beyond the Left's historic definition of socialism that defines the project of emancipation as the transformation of property relations. From historical experience, we have learned that this is too narrow a foundation on which to build a left politics that struggles against racial and gender hierarchies and environmental degradation. We need instead to employ a Polanyian definition of socialism as the "the tendency inherent in an industrial civilization to transcend the self-regulating market by consciously subordinating it to a democratic society" to signal that the primary task is the creation of a more deeply democratic society.[13] There is still a need to confront the power of the wealthy and large corporations, but this must happen by strengthening both regulatory institutions and the control that citizens exert over their government.

Second, this emphasis on democratization leads directly to a politics of transforming governance arrangements both locally and at whatever territorial units exist below the national level.[14] At times, this will require creating new governance structures, such as decision-making bodies for entire metropolitan areas that cross both county and state lines. The idea is not just to involve more citizens in periodic elections to choose office holders, but to experiment with a broad range of participatory structures that are designed to give citizens more voice in decisions about budgets, infrastructure and the organization of services such as policing and education.[15] The basic organizing principle is that we are creating our own habitation and this requires a collective, inclusive and ongoing conversation about what kind of community we want and how we are going to get closer to it.[16] And such a conversation requires that we empower historically marginalized communities to participate fully in that conversation.

This bottom-up orientation to democratization does not mean neglecting national politics. On the contrary, as citizens increase their political clout at the subnational level, their ability to influence national politics will increase as they develop the skills needed to hold elected representatives accountable. But it is also the case that the bottom-up initiatives will quickly hit roadblocks without changes in national policy, especially on issues of government spending, financing arrangements and the regulation of private entities. What is required is a paradigm shift from thinking about solving problems through national legislation to using national legislation to facilitate decentralized initiatives that solve problems while increasing the political agency of citizens.

Third, this agenda makes the democratization of the financial system one of the core priorities of centre-left politics. One of the deepest contradictions of the last half century is that while production processes and innovation have been significantly decentralized, finance has become highly centralized. As a result of banking consolidation, most consumer deposits are held by small numbers of giant banks. Similarly, pension funds and retirement savings are channelled through a handful of enormous financial intermediaries. As we saw in the global financial crisis, this process of centralization is highly dangerous since these giant institutions are both too big to fail and too big to jail. But equally important, this centralization leaves all kinds of economic activity at subnational levels starved for financing at reasonable interest rates.

This creates an enormous opening for a left initiative to rechannel people's saving into public and non-profit financial entities that will make credit available for a wide range of decentralized economic initiatives including local economic development, rebuilding of urban areas and the development of small and medium sized businesses.[17] This democratization of financial decision making is a critical tool for realizing the goal of giving citizens the capacity to shape the communities in which they live since control over flows of capital would make it possible to establish the infrastructure, the services and the amenities that they want.

Here again, we see a politics in which there needs to be a synergy between initiatives at the local and subnational levels and federal action. Bottom-up initiatives can be halted if the federal government is effectively captured by Wall Street interests. But federal action alone will not create the new network of public and non-profit financial institutions; they have to be built from the bottom-up by activists who understand the importance of gaining greater control over financial flows.

Fourth, this agenda finally makes it possible to build a durable bridge that connects those engaged in the "politics of everyday life" with electoral politics. For at least fifty years, there has been a growing constituency of people seeking to live in a different way by creating alternative communities, engaging in grassroots initiatives from food cooperatives to urban gardens, pursuing alternative practices of consumerism, and periodically mobilizing through actions such as Occupy Wall Street. Such activities are frequently seen as a better and more authentic form of political action since mainstream parties are seen as either corrupt or ineffective.

But once a centre-left party turns its focus to the project of creating a habitation society, it should be able to mobilize the considerable energies and talents of people who have remained mostly marginal to mainstream politics. Artists of all types, for example, would gain a new social role. As people begin collectively to design their own communities, they would draw on the insights, ideas and work of both visual artists and performing artists.

CONCLUSION

What I have suggested here as a new direction for centre-left parties built around the idea of creating a habitation society is obviously just a preliminary sketch. There are many important issues that I have left unaddressed. The goal is simply to start a discussion and stimulate people to question some deeply ingrained ideas about politics that emerged out of a very different political economic conjuncture.

But in concluding, it is important to return to the organizational challenge that I talked about earlier. The resurgence of populist politics on both the Left and the Right is a response to the broad perception that there is a deep divide that separates ordinary citizens from most members of the political class. This divide has been growing for the last forty or fifty years; it reflects the reality that these political elites have a diminishing ability to "deliver the goods" for citizens. As a consequence of globalization, declining industrial jobs and ongoing fiscal crises, it is rare that members of the political class are able to take actions that actually make life better for some significant group of citizens.[18] This is, of course, the context in which electoral support for centre-left parties has eroded.

To escape this bind requires that centre-left parties have a strategy for rebuilding the economy so that it meets the needs of people. By necessity, this project of rebuilding has to unfold in a decentralized fashion; it will not work to focus on creating wealth in Silicon Valley, Hollywood and New York City and simply redistribute resources to the rest of the nation. This requires increasing the capacity of people to meet their own needs in communities, both rural and urban, across the country. The project involves creating high quality services to meet people's need for healthcare, education from pre-school to lifelong learning, housing, transportation, nutrition and connections with each other. It also involves continuous innovation to develop new products and new services, some of which will be exported to other communities.

Since this is necessarily a decentralized, bottom-up process of rebuilding, it requires the leadership of political organizations that are able to mobilize and represent large numbers of people from diverse constituencies at the local level. Such entities would lead the fight to expand the scope of democratic participation in governments at the subnational level. As new institutions to democratize key decisions at the level of municipalities and metropolitan areas are created, there is a vital role for political parties in informing the public, aggregating interests, brokering compromises and mobilizing citizens against technocratic or oligarchic power grabs.

This is the challenge that centre-left parties face. It will require experimenting with new organizational forms that facilitate more democratic and inclusive party decision making. The process will bring to the surface the deep divisions within the party's base in terms of race, class, gender, religion, life style and so on. But the hope is that as citizens obtain a real voice, they will rise to the occasion and move beyond an exclusive focus on their specific group's immediate concerns. And there will be inevitably setbacks, failures, power grabs by trusted allies, and enduring divisions between groups that should be able to find common cause. Nevertheless, the goal is important enough to keep organizers and activists inspired. It is, after all, the same vision that empowered the New Left of the 1960s. The project of building a habitation society requires that we create a truly participatory form of democracy.[19]

NOTES

1. See S. L. Mudge, *Leftism Reinvented: Western Parties from Socialism to Neoliberalism* (Cambridge, MA: Harvard University Press, 2018).
2. R. Farley, "Detroit in bankruptcy" in M. P. Smith & L. O. Kirkpatrick (eds), *Reinventing Detroit: The Politics of Possibility*, 93–112 (New Brunwick, NJ: Transaction, 2015).
3. This focus had deeper historical roots that are explained in G. Gerstle, *Liberty and Coercion* (Princeton, NJ: Princeton University Press, 2015).
4. There were campaigns in states such as Vermont and California to implement a single payer healthcare system, but they were ultimately unsuccessful.
5. For a powerful account of corporate-led economic initiatives at the state level, see G. Lafer, *The One Percent Solution* (Ithaca, NY: Cornell University Press, 2017).

6. This remains true even if you were to adjust the figures for housing because this data omits all of the services that citizens receive from government that do not involve user fees. The failure to measure the flow of services from government is a major flaw in the national income accounts. See L. Daly, "What is our public GDP?", Demos, 7 July 2014, http://www.demos.org/publication/what-our-public-gdp-valuing-government-twenty-first-century-economy (accessed 8 August 2017).

7. Daniel Bell's book, *The Coming of Post-Industrial Society* (New York: Basic Books) was published first in 1973 but he had prefigured the argument in papers published in the late 1960s. Alain Touraine published his book, *La société post-industrielle. Naissance d'une société* (Paris: Denoël) in 1969.

8. The term "habitation" has Polanyian roots. In Chapter 3 of *The Great Transformation* (Boston, MA: Beacon Press, 2001 [1944]) in his discussion of enclosures, Karl Polanyi describes a conflict between habitation and improvement. Improvement or raising agricultural productivity destroyed the foundations of traditional rural communities. The same conflict persisted through the industrial era, but there is now the possibility of overcoming this conflict as technological advances can be mobilized to improve human habitation.

9. The innovation process itself is becoming increasingly decentralized with much of the action occurring in regional clusters that bring together publicly-funded researchers with small and large firms. See F. Block & M. R. Keller (eds), *State of Innovation* (Boulder, CO: Paradigm, 2011); F. Block & M. R. Keller, "Explaining the transformation in the US innovation system: the impact of a small government program", *Socio-Economic Review* 11:4 (2013), 629–56.

10. C. Sorace & W. Hurst, "China's phantom urbanisation and the pathology of ghost cities", *Journal of Contemporary Asia* 46:2 (2015), 304–22, http://dx.doi.org/10.1080/00472336.2015.1115532.

11. Block & Keller, *State of Innovation*.

12. T. Piketty, *Capital in the Twenty-First Century* (Cambridge, MA: Harvard University Press, 2014).

13. Polanyi, *Great Transformation*, 242.

14. In this respect, I agree with much of what Dean Baker lays out in his chapter as possibilities for reform at the subnational level. See also G. Winant, "Who works for the workers?", *N+1* 26 (Fall 2016), https://nplusonemag.com/issue-26/essays/who-works-for-the-workers/ (accessed 8 August 2017).

15. A. Fong & E. O. Wright, *Deepening Democracy: Institutional Innovations in Empowered Participatory Governance* (New York: Verso, 2003); G. Baiocchi & E. Ganuza, *Popular Democracy: The Paradox of Participation* (Stanford, CA: Stanford University Press, 2017).

16. Such efforts should be informed with an ethic that could be termed cosmopolitan localism – that affirms the importance of locally-based identities without excluding those who have only recently arrived. Such an ethic is a way to address the issues raised by Colin Crouch in his chapter.

17. F. Block, "Democratizing finance", *Politics & Society* 42:1 (2014), 3–28.

18. Expanding the rights of gays is a possible exception, but most of these victories came through the courts. The passage of the Affordable Care Act under Obama is another, but the new legislation has been an imperfect fix; many people still face high premiums and the continuing threat of bankruptcy in the event of a serious medical crisis.

19. I am grateful to David Coates, Larry Hirschhorn and Margaret Somers for comments on an earlier draft of this chapter.

CHAPTER 4

TRAWLING THE PAST AS A GUIDE TO THE FUTURE

David Coates

"Onions can be eaten leaf by leaf, but you cannot skin a live tiger paw by paw: vivisection is its trade, and it does the skinning first. If the Labour party is to tackle its job with some hope of success it must mobilize behind it a body of conviction as resolute and informed as the opposition in front of it. The way to create it, and the way when created for it to set about its task, is not to prophesy smooth things. Support won by such methods is a reed shaken by every wind."
                                                    R. H. Tawney[1]

"So why is the centre-left by and large not benefiting from the failures of [its] political opponents? The answer lies in its absorption of the politics of the centre-right, going back almost three decades."   Wolfgang Münchau,
                                                    20 September 2016

"If Jeremy Corbyn is the answer, then Labour is asking the wrong question."   *The Observer*, 19 July 2015

It is a feature of very dark nights that they tend to be followed by particularly bright mornings – or at least that the contrast between the two states of being always seems to be remarkably sharp. The morning of 9 June 2017 in the United Kingdom was one such moment of sharpness: a morning of unexpected brightness after an otherwise long night of political darkness for centre-left parties on both sides of the Atlantic – a night that stretched back to at least the May 2010 general election in the UK case, and in the US one to the Republican Party's recapture of the House of Representatives later in that same year (with that capture softened only slightly by Obama's retention of the presidency in 2012). There was brightness for the UK centre-left in June 2017 in the fact that the election result was far better for the Labour Party than most commentators, including sympathetic ones, had thought likely; and there was brightness too in the simple partisan pleasure of watching more conservative political figures no longer sweep all before them. But elections always tell wider stories, and the one in June 2017 certainly did. The unexpectedly strong performance of the Corbyn-led Labour Party in that snap general election undoubtedly offered a glimpse into the possibilities that more orthodoxly-timed UK general elections could open-up for a revitalized centre-left. But at the same time, the fact that the Labour Party still lost the 2017 contest, and by some margin, told us much about the continuing weakness of progressive forces even in the UK; and the elation (and indeed, relief) in most Labour ranks that the party only "just" lost the election told us equally much about how low the expectations-bar had recently been set, and how lacking in self-confidence centre-left forces currently remain.

This lack of confidence is, however, hardly to be wondered at, given the overall pattern of voting to which centre-left parties and individuals have recently been exposed. The election of Donald Trump to the presidency of the United States, for example, was both unexpected by (and traumatic for) many American progressives, and put back onto their agenda a whole swathe of defensive fights. They now find themselves obliged to protect again modest gains in civil rights and social justice that had been squeezed out of a conservative political establishment over a fifty-year period, and which many progressives had come to treat as permanent features of the American social landscape. And the June 2016 vote in the UK to leave the European Union had been equally traumatic for many left-leaning people in Britain. It was rightly seen at the time as a harbinger of things like Trump to come, and as a vote that also spoke to the diminution of support in traditional working-class areas for the Labour Party in either its New Labour or post-New Labour form.

Not surprisingly, therefore, the contemporary centre-left in both the United States and the United Kingdom is currently awash with critics. There are plenty of commentators out there ready to throw in the towel entirely, and to declare the search for a more civilized and managed capitalism to be well and truly lost. There are also plenty of voices, less pessimistic than that, who see the need for more conservative policies on the Left.[2] They see in the Brexit vote (in the UK) a yawning gap between a supposedly conservative electorate and a tentatively radicalizing Labour Party leadership that can be bridged only by Labour moderating its stance, and in the Trump vote (in the US) a parallel need for the Democratic Party platform to accommodate white working-class antipathy to immigration and civil rights. There are even those in the UK right now who are willing to treat the June 2017 election result as yet more evidence that the Labour Party's move to the left is entirely to be abandoned. "Labour missed an 'open goal' to beat Theresa May", the former Labour shadow chancellor Chris Leslie insisted immediately the results were known: "I've never known a more beatable prime minister", he said: "We shouldn't pretend that this is a famous victory. It's good, as far as it's gone, but it's not going to be good enough". Labour's key problem remains – in his mind – unaddressed: namely that of convincing "voters it can move from protesting about a government into being the government".[3]

If you listen to voices of that kind, then you are bound to come to the view either that the Left has no future, or that it has one which will be only a pale reflection of its earlier radical self. But the trick is not to listen to those voices, because history needs to be read within a longer timeframe than the immediate. The centre-left has survived dark days before, flourishing after adversity, and as the June 2017 UK election result suggests, it can survive and flourish again. Indeed, it may do so this time around even more easily than in the past, because the Cassandras on the contemporary Left are far outnumbered by the legions of decent progressive people on both sides of the Atlantic who are hungry for a new social settlement: one that can combine rising prosperity for themselves with greater social justice for others. Over 63 million of them in the United States voted for Hillary Clinton in November 2016 – far more people, indeed, than voted for Donald Trump; and 40 per cent of the UK's voting population just supported the Corbyn-led Labour Party – 10 per cent more than in 2015, and probably as many as two in every three of young first-time voters. The job of progressive intellectuals, therefore, is not to abandon the task of designing and advocating programmes of substantial economic and social reform. The job of progressive intellectuals is to explain why currently that task is so difficult, and to point ways forward to its eventual realization.

That task involves at least four distinct stages. The *first* is to explain the nature of our contemporary condition, and the agenda it releases upon us – the better to know what we face. The *second* is to map out what will not work in contemporary conditions, no matter how often conservative commentators tell us otherwise: and, therefore, what in consequence the centre-left should avoid. The *third* is to survey the plethora of centre-left proposals designed to put our contemporary condition behind us – proposals that will indeed work if effectively applied; and the *fourth* is to examine the state of leading centre-left parties, the better to clarify how they need to change if they are ever to deliver fully on these programmatic commitments.

As we do all four of those vital things, we need to hold the line for a politics of managed capitalist transformation that is neither as pessimistic as those who would despair of our ambitions, nor as optimistic as more radical socialists are prone to be about the possibilities of total capitalist transformation. Centre-left politics have always to be built on the recognition that the task of the Left is to manage capitalism rather than to replace it, because no credible politics has yet emerged on how best to replace capitalism entirely; and because it has not, the centre-left's task is always the same. It is to build a progressive social settlement wrapped around a still predominantly privately-owned economy. *It is to manage capital in the interests of labour.* It is, in a real sense, to ride the tiger.

THE NATURE OF OUR CONTEMPORARY CONDITION

To understand our present condition requires a certain reading of the past, and a developed sensitivity to the importance of history in the understanding of our contemporary condition. Studying the past enables us to place the present in relation to the future, by making the present a moment in a distinctive economic and social trajectory, rather than having it be simply a set of events that turned up yesterday for which no easy label or explanation is available. Studying the recent past of both the US and the UK, with the concerns of the centre-left in mind, enables us to see at least three important things: namely that our contemporary condition is one of transition between the broad social settlements necessary to sustain contemporary capitalism; that the latest settlement, the one first put in place under Reagan and Thatcher, is now well past its sell-by date; and that the task of progressives therefore is to speed the creation of a new settlement that is more progressive in design and effect than the one which fell to pieces so dramatically in 2008.

Given the limitations of space here, the character and contradictions of the social settlements that have stabilized post-Second World War Anglo-American capitalism can be only briefly documented (though a fuller specification is available elsewhere[4]). Quickly put, twice in the years since the Second World War social settlements have emerged to frame sustained periods of capitalist economic growth; and in that sense the period of neoliberal-inspired growth that ended so abruptly in 2008 was not the first growth period in the postwar British or American story. It was the second. The Thatcher settlement of the 1980s replaced in the UK the development of a welfare-Keynesian state and society that from the late 1940s had maintained full employment and rising living standards for a generation. The parallel Reagan settlement followed on the heels of a period of economic growth in the United States that between 1948 and 1973 had created the affluent living standards of what we now term the American "middle class". Each of those earlier growth periods had rested on a distinctive (domestic and international) economic, social and political order – on what regulation theorists call a particular "social structure of accumulation"[5] – each of which took at least a decade to call into existence, and each of which disintegrated over time as its component elements began to change.

Anglo-American economic growth between 1948 and 1973 was built on the generalized application across the manufacturing sectors of both economies of the semi-automated production systems first pioneered by Henry Ford – a generalized application that simultaneously raised the productivity of labour and strengthened the bargaining position of organized workers. With the US economy dominant globally from 1945 (and with the UK as the US's main ally in policing the capitalist borders of a world divided east–west by the Cold War and north–south by colonialism) productivity, profits and wages in core manufacturing industries rose together for a generation, in the process steadily transforming both the US and UK social landscape and removing the memory of the Great Depression from the agenda of Anglo-American politics. Politically, the superintendence of this first growth period switched in Washington back and forth in the 1960s between Republicans and Democrats, and in the UK between Conservatives and what Tony Blair later called "Old Labour". But in both capitals, the initial level of policy consensus was high, and the commitment to Keynesianism at home and neocolonialism abroad was near total.

Social settlements of the kind constructed in both the US and UK after 1945 do not remove the basic contradiction between capital and labour that sits at the heart of modern capitalism. That is why there is an unavoidable rhythm to all social structures of accumula-tion, including to this first postwar one – a rise and then a fall – a pattern ultimately driven by the inability of any capitalist-based social settlement permanently to hold at bay the contradictory class forces precariously balanced within it. The first postwar growth period ended in the stagflation of the 1970s as the productivity potential of Fordist-type production systems levelled off, as protest movements within the United States challenged the exclusion of minorities from the emerging prosperity, as trade union resistance to the intensification of work processes grew in the UK, and as rebellions against western dominance abroad drew the United States into the cauldron of Vietnam. Like the decade that later would follow the financial crisis of 2008, the 1970s in both countries was in consequence a decade of *transition* between settlements, as the one already in place disintegrated and as its replacement only slowly crystalized out from the resulting ashes.

Eventually, however, a new social settlement did emerge: one initially orchestrated internally by the Thatcher Government in the UK and by the Reagan Administration in the US, and one characterized externally by the unexpected end of the Cold War. Under this new settlement, capital was freer to move about globally in ways that had been impossible while the communist world remained a sealed bloc; and capital was freer to accumulate domestically to the extent that trade union power was broken and working-class wages frozen or depleted. Deregulation of business behaviour at home and out-sourcing of production abroad came together, from the 1990s, to generate renewed growth in both the UK and the US economies, growth that this time was anchored in a widening gap between productivity and wages. Profits and wages did not rise together on this occasion as they had in the generation before. Instead, economic growth in both countries was accompanied in the 1980s and 1990s by soaring income and wealth inequality; by a lengthening of the working day and an intensification of prevailing work processes; and by the growth of mass consumption that this time was financed out of wages not yet earned – financed, that is, only by rising levels of personal debt.

At the core of each economy under this second postwar settlement, the wage-effort bargain shifted in favour of capital. Both economies ended up as predominantly low-wage, long-hour economies with huge service sectors, an over-developed financial system and a diminished manufacturing base; and both made this transformation first under political leadership from the centre-right and then from the centre-left. But this debt-driven growth model, over which Reagan/ Thatcher conservatives and New Democrats/New Labourites presided with equal ease, did not disintegrate slowly as had the first one in the 1970s. Instead it crashed overnight in the financial crisis of 2008, generating as it did so mass involuntary unemployment on a scale not seen since the 1930s. Then, just as the collapse of the first postwar settlement had left the second half of the 1970s and much of the 1980s as years in which centre-left parties struggled for programme and for votes, so the collapse of 2008 left behind it a decade or more of electoral trouble for the centre-left – trouble evident early (as we noted at the outset) in the general election defeat of the Labour Party in 2010 and in the mid-term "shellacking" of the Obama Administration by a resurgent Republican Party later that same year.

THE POLITICS OF TRANSITION

This electoral trouble should not totally surprise us, for centre-left politics is more difficult in periods of transition between SSAs ("social structures of accumulation"[6]) than it is when an SSA is up and running. When a particular social settlement is up and running, the task before both the political Left and the political Right is simply to manage it and make it work. Politics in those periods becomes largely an issue of marginal differences amid high levels of basic consensus, a jockeying for positions of leadership within a broad political class that is largely at peace with itself. But in the period of transition between social settlements, the job of the political class becomes harder. Political leadership then requires some understanding of why the previous settlement fell and how it can best be replaced. Political leadership also requires sufficient agility to design and advocate long-term changes while simultaneously dealing with the fall-out from the collapse of the old ways of organizing the society and running the economy – dealing, that is, with an electorate whose expectations cannot now be met in the old way and who in consequence often feel cheated and let down, even scared and desperate for a return to some imaginary preferable past. Periods of transition can be periods of crazy politics, as Antonio Gramsci recognized in the early 1930s. "The crisis consists", he wrote then, "precisely in the fact that the old order is dying, and the new cannot be born; in this interregnum, a great variety of morbid symptoms appear".[7] Nigel Farage's UKIP moment in 2016, and that of Donald Trump later that same year, stand in their different ways as evidence of this underlying truth about morbid symptoms.

When trying to respond in an electorally-credible way to the problems generated by the collapse of a once-dominant social settlement, what complicates the task still further for the centre-left is the degree of complicity of past generations of centre-left politicians in the design and implementation of each of the dominant settlements of the immediate past. The second of the two great postwar social settlements and growth trajectories – the Thatcher/Reagan one – was entirely a conservative construction. The first, of course, was not. On the contrary, it was New Deal legislation on trade union rights and basic welfare provisions that empowered organized labour in the US in the years immediately after the Second World War, just as it was the Attlee Government's welfare programme, commitment to full employment and embrace of Keynesian economics that underpinned the postwar consensus in the UK. Indeed, it was precisely because of the organic link between that first postwar settlement and the Anglo-American centre-left that its demise in the 1970s was so traumatic an experience for both American Democrats and the British Labour Party.

The rise of the Thatcherite/Reagan neoliberal alternative during the decade of stagflation that followed the oil crisis of 1973 required of centre-left parties on both sides of the Atlantic divide that they make a fundamental set of policy responses. And that response was indeed made. Indeed, it was made twice: first as *challenge* (in the form of the 1983 Alternative Economic Strategy in the UK, and in the Democratic Party's flirtation with industrial policy in 1984) and then as *capitulation* (under first Clinton and then Blair). It was the inadequacy of the Clinton/Blair accommodation to neoliberalism – in the new conditions left behind by the financial crisis of 2008 – that now makes it imperative that centre-left political parties make yet another fundamental rupture with their own immediate past if they are to emerge from the political wilderness one more time. What the centre-left now has to do is *not* to break from the politics of constructing a progressive social and economic settlement around a still privately-owned economy. What the centre-left has to do is to design a *new and better* settlement – one that can address the inadequacies of the previous settlement and create sustained and progressive growth again that is capable of remaining in place for at least as long as its predecessors.

The great dilemma of centre-left governments is that they invariably find themselves elected into office, to do such a job, only when the economic conditions surrounding them are so difficult as to effectively preclude the easy implementation of centre-left programmes. Paradoxically, if economic times are good, parties offering extensive sets of social reform have difficulty persuading electorates that they are even necessary. And yet when times are bad, and electorates turn away from governing parties of the Right in the hope of something better, the economic surpluses needed to allow the easy funding of those reforms are invariably denuded by the scale and severity of the bad times themselves. Invariably, the result is that by trying to make a failing settlement work for at least another electoral cycle, centre-left parties come to be identified by many of their potential voters as either the cause of that failure, or too constrained in their critique of it. Either way, as periods of transition open-up, parties of the centre-left are often seriously tarnished by their involvement in what had immediately gone before – in the 1990s embrace by the Clinton Administration of Reaganite policies on welfare-to-work, for example, or the later flirtation of New Labour with Thatcherite neoliberalism – which is why it is vital that, if sufficient progressive electoral support is ever to be won again, centre-left parties use their years *out* of power to make a fundamental break with the practices of their party when last *in* power. Off with the old, in with the new, mining the past for lessons for the future – this has to be the fundamental pattern of reflection and change that stands at the very core of effective progressive politics.

NEW NEEDS AND OLD SOLUTIONS

Each SSA throws its own unique shadow forward, the content of that shadow being primarily determined by the nature of the central contradictions that brought it down. The first post-1945 SSA fell in wage-push inflation as the inability of Fordist production methods to maintain their rate of productivity growth coincided with working-class militancy engendered by the years of rising wages. The second SSA – the Reagan/Thatcher one – did not fall that way. In fact, just the reverse: it fell as rising productivity ran up against the barrier of stagnant real wages and exploding levels of personal debt. It is at the legacies of that second fall, therefore, that the new thinking and policy of the centre-left has now to be directed. Three major legacies are of central concern here. One is the *deindustrialization* of both the US and UK manufacturing base by the outsourcing propensities of increasingly deregulated business communities. A second is the resulting *wage-race to the bottom* (the so-called Wal-Mart syndrome: of American and British jobs going overseas, leaving only low-wage service employment available in any volume for large sections of each working class, and consolidating a retail sector selling shoddy goods made abroad that are all that low-wage Anglo-American workers can now afford). The third is the *lack of adequate levels of demand* from the mass and generality of Anglo-American consumers that results from three decades of stagnant or falling real wages, and from the associated intensification of wealth and income inequality.

In relation to all three legacies, as is presumably clear from the source of the list itself, the old economic growth models will no longer work – in the UK case, neither the growth model of Old Labour (based on Keynesianism) nor that of New Labour (based on post-neoclassical endogenous growth theory). Nor will right-wing "austerity" packages work either. If their aim is to lower taxes to trigger innovation and growth, we have evidence enough that "trickle-down economics" simply does not work. It certainly did not work for the United States under George W. Bush between 2000 and 2007.[8] Nor did it work in the UK under George Osborne between 2010 and 2016, where any balanced view of recent UK economic performance data makes abundantly clear that the rate of recovery quickened again in 2013 and 2014 only *after* the Coalition Government eased back on the austerity pedal.[9] Nor should that surprise us, since cutting government programmes and public sector employment in periods of low economic growth only compounds local manifestations of secular stagnation. It does not reverse them. Cutting public spending erodes levels of demand, and the quality of life, without any commensurate leap in labour productivity. The Reagan/Thatcher-induced productivity leap of the 1980s was anchored in the fear of job loss and an associated intensification of the work process, and by a defensive lengthening of the working day (people worked longer and harder in the 1980s if they had a job than they had a decade before, in an attempt to ensure that their job stayed secure). But it simply is not possible to cut our way to enhanced productivity in that way again. People cannot work harder and longer this time around than they are already doing – that low hanging fruit went in the 1980s – and it isn't possible to get more productivity out of service employment if (as is likely now the case) that employment has been as computerized as it is likely ever to be.

There is also now growing evidence – not least from international agencies that once stood at the heart of the neoliberal settlement – that at this stage of capitalist development, economic growth and social inequality do *not* go together: that on the contrary any long-term successful growth strategy has to be based on reduced levels of inequality and the full development and mobilization of all levels and forms of human capital. The well-paid boss in the top office is no longer – not that in truth s/he ever was – sufficiently significant as to be able to trigger prolonged economic growth by his/her initiative/genius alone. The reality is beginning to dawn, in key parts of the international governing strata, that because production is inherently a social process, its success over the long term requires the full motivation of all involved economic players. On the demand side of the economic equation, those players require a capacity to buy goods and services from the wages they earn rather than from the credit they borrow; and on the supply side of the equation those same players need to be able to sustain over the long period high-quality inputs into the creation of goods and services that others buy (and so require, among other things, working environments and work-life balances that will enable them – and motivate them – to do so).

What has ultimately to replace the neoliberal politics of austerity is a progressive resetting of public policy and the social order in ways that stimulate the full use of existing productivity capacities. If (as is likely) we now face a sustained period in which there is no systemically-induced new technology to lift productivity across the entire economy, any incoming progressive government will need to lift that productivity by fully utilizing the productivity potential that is already there. As is discussed more fully in *Flawed Capitalism*, it is only possible to stimulate greater labour output/hour across the entire economy in a limited number of ways. Some of those ways, like intensifying the work process by managerial dictat, are neither possible in the present conjuncture nor progressive in any conjuncture. But other ways are both those things – possible and progressive. 1. Productivity/hour can be raised, by *rebalancing the distribution of labour* from low-productivity to high productivity sectors (the traditional Swedish model solution, now requiring both active industrial policy and an active labour market one). 2. Productivity can be raised by *fully employing the entirety of the available labour force and increasing its skill level* (the traditional left-Keynesian solution, now requiring quantitative easing as well as long-term public spending/borrowing); and 3. productivity can be raised by *fully mobilizing the existing set of economic skills, a set now so heavily skewed by gender.*

This last source – the full use of an educated young female labour force – is now key. Under present circumstances, the only way to generate greater output from a fully-mobilized population is to create an economy and a society in which the organization of work articulates seamlessly with the needs of a fulfilling private/family life, and where the rewards to work are visibly fair, equitable and just. There is no Anglo-liberal austerity route to long-term economy recovery and prosperity for all. That route benefits only the rich and the privileged. That is why they like it, and advocate it so. Progressive politics need to go off in an entirely different direction

– one based on the recognition that the restoration of long-term economic growth now requires the implementation of a new and progressive set of social policies, an entirely new social settlement focused on the needs of working families, and particularly on the needs of the women within them. In that third strategy, policies on equal pay, on flexible working hours, on affordable child care, and on the de-gendering of family responsibilities, must move centre stage: no longer to be add-ons to be cut the first time the national budget needs to be balanced, but rather the first thing to be funded to make sure that the budget balances at a higher and more generous level. They must remain core priorities, because the alternative being canvassed against them – the continuation of a low-wage, long-hours, route to productivity growth – is simply no longer a viable option. It no longer works, and even when it did, it was in no sense progressive.

THE TREASURE TROVE OF POLICY

There is no shortage of policy proposals on the current centre-left in either the US or the UK that can meet these new requirements. On the contrary, policy proposals abound across the full spectrum of needed policy response: a spectrum that includes external and environmental economic and military concerns, domestic industrial and financial policy, wages and working conditions and the associated reconfiguration of civil society. The problem with the existing policy agenda is not, therefore, its range. It is the degree of radicalism within that range, and the linked level of explicit rupture made with the neoliberal accommodation of leading centre-left parties in the era of Bill Clinton and Tony Blair.

The range of available policies is at least this deep and this wide:

Active context policy

- Shift resources from the military to the civilian sector;
- Reset trade policy to generate a race to the top, not the bottom;
- Ensure environmental sustainability over time by developing a green economy now;
- Strengthen human rights, and reduce development inequalities, globally;

- Work externally as well as internally for a growth model based on equality and inclusiveness.

Active industrial policy

- Bring failing industries/companies into temporary/permanent public ownership;
- Establish tight regulation/ownership of key sectors/companies, especially finance;
- Fund the state orchestration of research and development;
- Strengthen the small- and medium-size business sector;
- Reconfigure economic options spatially by active industrial location policy;
- Stimulate demand via infrastructure spending;
- Eliminate tax avoidance by large corporations and rich individuals;
- Rebalance the economy by bringing home manufacturing employment.

Active labour maket policy

- Increase real wages, link wage rises to growing productivity, and reverse trends to income and wealth inequality;
- Strengthen trade union and individual worker bargaining rights: extend industrial democracy;
- Increase rights to job security;
- Consolidate and expand rights to paid vacation time, paid maternity/paternity leave, and flexible working hours;
- Extend public funding of extensive training and retraining programs, including the redevelopment of high-quality apprenticeship schemes;
- Establish minimum and maximum salary/wage ranges, supplemented by wage subsidies for the working poor;
- Establish equal pay for equal work, regardless of gender/race.

Active civil society policy

- Put in place affordable child care and pre-kindergarten educational provision;
- Ensure free healthcare at the point of use, and enhanced pensions for the working poor;
- Make college affordable, and reconfigure existing student debt;

- Increase welfare payments to single-parents and to the permanently disabled;
- Increase the provision of social housing, and of rent subsidies for the working poor;
- End mass incarceration;
- Extend progressive taxation to finance improved welfare, housing and education provision;
- Create a basic income for all citizens.

Unfortunately, to date the scale of radicalism associated with each sphere of policy activity varies, from the moderate to the radical: from a list of proposals (which elsewhere we catalogued for the US case as List B[10]) that make hardly any rupture with dominant neoliberal orthodoxies, to a list (which we termed List C[11]) that make the greatest break. At the moderate end, stand policies of the kind found in both the Labour Party's 2015 election manifesto and the Democratic Party platform in 2016. These are policies perhaps most easily accessible in the *Report of the Commission on Inclusive Prosperity*, a commission jointly chaired in early 2015 by Larry Summers and Ed Balls, and published in the US by the Clinton-sympathetic Center for American Progress. Taking as its goal the delivery of "high-employment, high-productivity economies with rising employment and rising wages" that could "help bring budgets down and put national debt on a downward trajectory", many of the commission's detailed proposals later figured prominently in Labour's 2015 manifesto and in Hillary Clinton's pre-election platform. In the hands of Summers and Balls, successful contemporary centre-left politics requires no break with what they termed "globalization and technology". Instead, their commission preferred to generate their inclusive prosperity by raising wages, increasing female labour-market participation, extending educational opportunities, encouraging regional innovation clusters and longer-term forms of investment, and fostering "international co-operation on global demand, trade, financial instability, and corporate tax avoidance".[12] A parallel and similarly motivated report from the middle-of-the-road Brookings Institution in the United States argued for new skills and innovations strategies modelled on German best practice, and so emphasized the need for public-private-civic partnerships, and for the creation of a highly-trained technologically-savvy labour force.[13]

Another common theme in the contemporary US progressive rethink – one that also surfaced in the Summers/Ball report – was what was later dubbed "the infrastructure route to growth"[14]: the call for a regeneration of economic growth and greater international competitiveness through federal spending on the *modernization of the US economy's physical infrastructure* (roads, bridges, rail and Internet). Other, more radical voices, also added a demand for *progressive taxation* to redress the "theft" of wealth by the top US income earners,[15] to slow the rate of growth of/reverse the trend to income and wealth inequality,[16] and to generate demand for goods and services across the entire US economy by concentrating extra purchasing power in the hands of those most likely to spend it – the American middle class and the American poor.[17] Such demands for progressive tax reform also now tend to be accompanied in the US by a call for a higher minimum wage, for more generous earned-income and child-tax credits, for renewed trade union rights, for greater rights for women and minorities at work, for corporate tax changes to encourage profit-sharing with employees, for a bigger federal pension (increasing Social Security for all but high income earners), and for policy designed to reverse the outsourcing of well-paid American jobs.[18] In more radical circles still, that last demand is often linked to one calling for less spending on the US military[19] – a call for a redistribution of resources and efforts into more nation-building at home and less overseas – and for the use of public procurement policies to strengthen home-based manufacturing industry.[20] And although the extension of public ownership has yet to surface as a major progressive demand in the post-2008 United States, the demand to either more tightly control or break-up large financial institutions certainly has; as too has the demand for the placing of a green agenda at the heart of any future US progressive growth strategy.

So that in the United States at least, Larry Summers and Ed Balls may stand in the moderate core of the contemporary debate on the centre-left, but surrounding them, in more radical positions, are groups like the Congressional Progressive Caucus, think-tanks like the Economic Policy Institute and the Center for Economic and Policy Research, and individual public intellectuals and activists: a long list that runs at least from Bernie Sanders and Barney Frank, through Paul Krugman, Joseph Stiglitz and Robert Reich, to Harold Meyerson, Robert Kuttner, Dean Baker, Jacob Hacker and Robert

Pollin.[21] Collectively, these more radical voices provide an effective arsenal of policies which if fully implemented would indeed reset US economy and society onto a new and more progressive path.

There are clear echoes of much of this policy-rethink in the parallel debate in the United Kingdom as well. In the UK, the policy-rethink after 2015 initially went more slowly and covered less policy distance than in the United States. It covered less distance partly because it had less distance to go (much of what Bernie Sanders, for example, advocated in 2016 as "democratic socialism" was standard European social democratic stuff, as he himself openly acknowledged). It went more slowly because unlike Bernie Sanders, Jeremy Corbyn and his new team had a whole parliamentary party to bring on board behind them, significant sections of which remain unenthusiastic at best, openly hostile at worse. Yet from very early on, there were signs of new policy emerging from Jeremy Corbyn's post-New Labour party, including renationalizing the basic railway system, abolishing fees for attending university/college, and resetting the industry department into what the Shadow Chancellor, in his first party conference address in that role, called "a powerful economic development department, in charge of public investment, infrastructure planning and setting new standards in the labour market". Jeremy Corbyn later termed this "a strategic state" in contradistinction to the "absentee state" of the Tory years, a strategic state willing to create and deploy a National Investment Bank to "promote infrastructure upgrades and support for innovation."[22] And although this process of policy innovation was cut short by the calling of an unexpected general election in June 2017, the Labour Party was still able to go to the country that year with its most radical set of proposals since 1983: *renationalizing not just the railways but also the Post Office and energy and water companies; providing free childcare for all two years olds, and 12 months maternity leaves for their mothers; committing to the creation of 100,000 council and housing associations new homes per year; and paying for a stronger NHS and student maintenance grants by raising corporation tax, taxing derivative trading in the City, and taxing high earners (those earning £80,000 a year) at new income tax rates of first 45 and then 50 per cent.*

There is also a growing supply of progressive policy proposals now emerging from a set of UK-based think-tanks that parallel the US ones, and which – as in the US – run the full progressive gambit from moderate to radical. Particularly noteworthy here are the series of policy papers emerging from the Social Market Foundation, the Policy Network, IPPR, Compass, Soundings and the New Economics Foundation – a whole slew of options from Joe Cox's *Plan B* from Compass[23] through Mariana Mazzucato's proposals on reforming finance,[24] and Soundings' policy proposals in the wake of its *Kilburn Manifesto*[25] to the series of reports and policy proposals now emerging regularly from SPERI (Sheffield Political Economy Research Institute) not least their *Civic Capitalism*.[26] Will Hutton's writings remain too an important source of new ideas.[27] Joe Cox's *Plan B*, for example, urged the UK centre-left to learn from Germany the importance of *local banking, employee empowerment, control over working hours, industrial policy* and the *benign constraints* that trade unions can set on private firms to trigger long-term industrial productivity. Hardly rocket science, but visibly a step in the right direction.

The incremental shift by the Corbyn-led Labour Party towards the creation of a Mazzucato-type "entrepreneurial state", and to the parallel restoration and *extension of trade union and worker rights*, built on the incremental movements away from the New Labour paradigm that had begun under Ed Miliband. The Miliband-led Labour Party fought (and lost) the 2015 general election on a policy platform that remained committed to the rapid balancing of the public accounts, so retaining one foot in the old policy camp. But it also went to the country committed to *a modest increase in top rates of tax; a higher minimum wage; new labour rights; more free child care; protected funding for the NHS and for publicly-provided education and skills training; enhanced infrastructure investment; a state-run investment bank; and proactive policy to slow down climate change.* Many of these policy changes were briefly labelled as "predistribution" policies by Ed Miliband,[28] based on the growing realization in leading Labour Party ranks that, as he put it later, "there is good reason to believe that inequality isn't just unfair but that it actually inhibits economic growth",[29] and that therefore one critical task for any incoming progressive government was to develop a "predistribution" agenda – a set of policies designed to level the social playing field surrounding private entrepreneurial economic activity. At the heart of those policies were social ones facilitating individual opportunities (things like funding preschool education and providing paid parental leave), labour market ones strengthening trade unions and individual worker rights, and economic ones focused on the regulation of finance and business.

THE QUESTION OF AGENCY

The problem the centre-left in both the US and the UK faces, therefore, is not one of programme. The kind of economy and society the centre-left could call into existence if empowered to do so is now broadly clear. So too is the fact that such a progressive social structure of accumulation, were it to be implemented, could sustain a successful period of economic growth and social justice for at least a full generation. The current problem of the Left does not lie, therefore, in the quality of its proposals. It lies elsewhere. It lies in the lack of electoral support for that programme, and in the internal weaknesses of the political parties available for the programme's dissemination and delivery. The weakness of the centre-left in both countries are less those of policy, therefore, than they are of agency. The problem of the Left is overwhelmingly itself!

Political success is always a product of the interplay of party and context, and currently that interplay is working differently in America and Britain in ways that suggest ways forward for the centre-left in both. Both the Democratic Party in the US and the Labour Party in the UK are having electoral difficulties with their traditional working-class base, but in 2016 the losing Democratic presidential candidate still out-polled her Republican opponent by a significant margin. The Democratic Party may have lost the Reagan Democrats, but their hold on minority electoral support is still strong – and demographic changes will increasingly play to that strength in presidential elections to come. Where the Democrats are weak is down-ballot, where they face formidable opponents organized at state and local level as Christian conservatives, as anti-statist libertarians, and as Tea Party fanatics. America is a country of edges and middles, with some version of a social democratic (in US terms, New Deal) culture still firmly entrenched on the West coast and in parts of the East, but largely missing in vast swathes of the middle of the country, particularly in the South. Political culture in the UK, by contrast, is far more social democratic than it is libertarian, and is as much shaped by "one nation" Toryism as it is by neoliberalism of the Thatcherite variety. The Labour Party therefore has far less of an uphill battle on its hands to persuade people that the public provision of welfare services, for example, is both necessary and superior to any privately-provided equivalent. And for all that the Party out-performed expectations in 2017, the fact that it has now lost three elections in a row tells us just how weak programmatically Labour had become by 2010, and how tarnished the Party remains by its long New Labour dalliance with Thatcherism.

As Jeremy Corbyn's leadership is quietly demonstrating, the Labour Party needs to rebuild an electoral base for itself as passionate and as committed as the Democratic Party will soon enjoy as the limits of the Republicans' austerity policies reveal themselves, and as opposition to Trump excesses grows. That will require Labour to continue to sharpen its critique of its own immediate past as New Labour, and to fill the ranks of the Parliamentary Party with a new and more radical generation of politicians untainted by that past. It will also require that the party leadership take to heart what Hilary Wainwright explains so clearly later in this volume – that the party must become one of movements and locally-based civic alternatives, and not just of parliamentarians and the London-based UK state. The call is currently on, from every current of opinion within the broad Labour-Party tent, for the Party to reconnect to key groups of voters, to re-establish public confidence in its economic competence, and to make clear its underlying vision. Of course, it must do those things: but it will not achieve any of them if, as some now propose, it prioritizes "the concerns of Conservative marginal voters in the south and the midlands", and redefines its central task as that of reversing "the drift away from voters in southern England".[30] For there are always two ways of reconnecting a party to its voters: you can transform that connection by transforming the party or by transforming the voters. A truly progressive political party has no genuine option – if its progressive goals are ultimately to be achieved – but to prioritize the transformation of its electorate. The new and predominantly young membership that flowed into the Labour Party to support the Corbyn leadership – 360,000 and counting – spoke to a wider recognition of the important political truth that there is no "centrist" route back to power for UK Labour. The Conservative Government is completely in control of that pass out of the mountains.[31] To regain power, and to regain it on terms that will enable power to be used, Labour has no choice other than to turn itself again into a movement of principled social reform and economic regeneration, and then show both the sense and the courage to invite its electorate to join it in that struggle.[32]

Meanwhile in the United States, the Democrats need to find a way to build and disseminate a more social democratic understanding of the vital role of public provision in the maintenance of a civilized capitalism. As an electoral machine, the Democrats have been losing ground steadily since 2010, and doing so despite holding the White House until 2017. The result: currently more than two-thirds of all US states are run by Republican governors, the ranks of state legislators contain at least 9,000 fewer Democrats than they did a decade ago, and the White House is now lost. So even as an electoral machine, the Democratic Party is not performing adequately – just the reverse, in fact – and that is largely because too many local Democratic Parties see themselves as just that, as mere electoral machines. They raise money. Every two or four years, they canvass; and between elections they hunt out candidates. What they do not do is then hold those candidates tightly accountable to a previously agreed set of policies and principles. Only Republicans – from Tea Party activists to socially-conservative evangelicals – do that. It is time for the Democrats to take a leaf from their opponent's playbook, and to learn lessons from the practices of progressive parties in parliamentary systems – parties held together by programme and ideology rather than simply by money and electioneering. More than just an effective electoral ground game, the Democrats need an ideologically coherent and generally-agreed programme, to mirror and replace that now pursued with such resolution by their Republican opponents. The Democratic Party needs to start putting programme first and candidate second, and look to ideas rather than simply to money and organization to eventually win the day, because – as we have argued more fully elsewhere – "progressive politics requires programmes that select candidates, not candidates that select programmes".[33]

It is also time for centrist Democrats to concede what 2016 made abundantly clear: namely that "the new American electorate could offer [them] a durable majority – if Democrats address economic needs with progressive policies, not centrist ones".[34] The future lies with the Sanders' wing of the Party, and no longer with

the Clintonites; and the sooner Democrats unite around that recognition, the sooner the Party's electoral fortunes will begin once
more to turn.[35] At the very least, therefore, in this next phase – one
of defensive battles against Republican excess and Trump bombast
– the Democratic Party must stay together as a federal as well as a
state/local force between elections, and must widen its understanding of what winning elections entails. And most crucially of all, the
key messaging issue with which the Democrats must now deal is
how best to articulate the identity politics they have been playing
so successfully for the last four decades with the class politics they
pursued so successfully through the New Deal period,[36] because by
not articulating those two things successfully in the last 25 years,
they have lost contact with key parts of their white working-class
base. For the future success of the Democratic Party, rekindling that
broad class alliance around issues of poverty and rights, rather than
around race and rights, is the most pressing issue of the day. As was
clear as early as 2015, and is certainly clearer now:

> poverty is the one thing in America that ultimately is both
> color- and gender-blind. Without money, nothing else is
> possible: least of all the realization of the full potential of
> ethnic minorities and of an oppressed gender discrimi-
> nated against by the racism, sexism and homophobia that
> still scars the daily reality of so much American life. Until
> the poverty that threatens at least one-third of the entire
> American labour force is put front-and-center by a more
> progressive Democratic Party, until poverty AND discrim-
> ination are presented to the entire American electorate as
> the two *dominant and linked* political issues of the day, the
> fear of that poverty will continue to fuel deep and damaging
> divisions between groups of Americans – white, black and
> Hispanic, male and female, straight and gay – who, if united,
> could really transform America into a land of opportunity
> for each and every one of us.[37]

The Sanders' 2016 campaign focus on income inequality constituted
an important moment in the building of that broader alliance, but in
truth the Democratic Party now needs more than merely a critique
of millionaires and billionaires. It needs to develop a focus on the

interplay on class and power at every level of contemporary US society, and not just at the top – offsetting the Republican Party's presentation of Americans as simply consumers with that of Americans as also workers – a focus making worker rights and trade union growth as central to American freedom as civil rights and equal protection under the law, and one making the Democratic Party not simply more progressive but also more social democratic.

FINAL THOUGHTS

In the end, Jeremy Corbyn and Bernie Sanders may each be – by virtue of their age alone – transitional figures; but the social forces they have mobilized, the discontent into which they have tapped, and the radicalism they are espousing – all those things are going to last. And on all those things the centre-left now needs rapidly to build – not by going back on them, but by going forward through them. Much of that radicalism derives from growing dissatisfaction with the distributional consequences of full-blown neoliberalism: tensions between generations over access to jobs and pensions, between debtors and creditors over access to housing and consumption, and between whole classes over access to income and wealth. The task of the moment is to link the centre-left's long-term vision to the immediate pressures now operating on the various elements in the potential progressive coalition, by simultaneously demanding immediate action to increase job security and social justice whilst designing and advocating policies directed towards a longer-term resetting of the relationship between capital and labour. The need now, therefore, is for transformational policies – policies bridging that gap between an old social order in decline and a new one in formation. A decade ago, I suggested focusing for that purpose on issues of work-life balance, the green agenda, and the resetting of overseas trade and aid.[38] More recently, Rasmussen and Bullmann have proposed building transformational policies around, among other things, the pursuit of a fair and managed globalization, sustainable development, and fair wealth and income distribution.[39] The adequacy of the detail is less important here than the recognition of the importance of the strategic task – which is to effect a kind of policy-making double-shuffle, developing policy that leaves the old social order behind as centre-left politics incrementally shifts its electorate's focus to the requirements of building a new and better social settlement.

No part of that trilogy – the immediate, the long-term, and the relationship between the two – lends itself to the soundbite politics of the modern media era; but that incompatibility simply under-scores the extent to which a successful centre-left politics needs to break with the contemporary trivialization by the right-wing media of issues whose resolution requires the development of complex pol-icy after careful thought. Taking charge of the content and the speed of the public discourse on contemporary politics is itself, therefore, a key requirement for long-term progressive success. For although elections are formally won or lost on a specific date, as we saw most recently in the UK in June 2017, they are invariably won or lost much earlier in the electoral cycle. Examining the past of centre-left pol-itics makes that very clear – for the Left has lots of experience of losing – and often in doing so has had only itself to blame. Elections are lost by the centre-left whenever the dominant political discourse is one shaped by their political opponents. They are lost whenever centre-left politicians seek votes by trying to outflank their conserv-ative opposition on their right. They are lost whenever progressives fail to capture the political narrative of the age,[40] and they are lost if all that people are told to expect from politics is a modest change in this, or a tiny alteration in that. Margaret Thatcher knew well enough that her electoral success required a prior "great moving right show".[41] The Reaganites knew well enough that they had to debunk the New Deal political narrative before their hold on power could be complete. Indeed, it is a measure of their contemporary success that American public opinion treats Ronald Reagan as a great president but hardly these days mentions Franklin Delano Roosevelt at all; and it is a measure of the lasting legacy of Margaret Thatcher's years in power that the modern Labour Party is obliged to justify any tax-and-spend policy more succinctly than do conservative politicians insisting on an austerity route to growth.

Political power is ultimately about establishing the hegemony of ideas in the minds of voters, and the Right has been extremely effective at hegemonic politics of late. It is time, therefore, for the centre-left to imitate and outmatch them. Austerity politics do not lead to growth, so there is always fertile electoral ground in which to replant social democratic seeds. The planting will take time, but less time if it starts now. As Antonio Gramsci had it, we will need a long war of position before we are ready for a successful war of manoeuvre. But as he said too, he was "a pessimist because of intelligence but an optimist because of will". Progressive politics is always a fusion of "pessimism of the intellect and optimism of the will". It is time for a large dose of that optimism. There is a better world to be created out there, if progressives act now with the total courage of their convictions to call it into existence.

NOTES

1. R. H. Tawney, "The choice before the Labour Party", first published in *Political Quarterly* in 1932, and reproduced in William A. Robson (ed.), *The Political Quarterly in the 1930s* (London: Allen Lane, 1971), 103–4.
2. This, for example, from Richard Reeves of the Brookings Institution, the day after the UK vote: "There is a good chance that this is Corbyn's high-water mark; in which case, Labour faces a long road to government" (R. Reeves, *"Everyone loses in UK election"*, posted on the Brookings website, 9 June 2017) https://www.brookings.edu/blog/fixgov/2017/06/09/everyone-loses-in-uk-election/ (accessed 15 August 2017).
3. Press Association, "Labour should have won against May's 'open goal', says MP", *The Guardian*, 10 June 2017.
4. See D. Coates *Flawed Capitalism: The Anglo-American Condition and Its Resolution* (Newcastle upon Tyne: Agenda, 2018) and D. Coates, *Capitalism: The Basics* (Abingdon: Routledge, 2016).
5. See D. M. Kotz, *The Rise and Fall of Neoliberal Capitalism* (Cambridge, MA: Harvard University Press, 2015).
6. See T. McDonough, "Social structures of accumulation theory: the state of the art", *Review of Radical Political Economics* 40:2 (2008), 153–73; and D. M. Kotz, T. McDonough & M. Reich (eds), *Social Structures of Accumulation: The Political Economy of Growth and Crisis* (Cambridge: Cambridge University Press, 1994).
7. A. Gramsci, *Prison Notebooks* (New York: International Publishers, 1971).
8. See D. Coates, *Answering Back: Liberal Responses to Conservative Arguments* (New York: Continuum, 2011), chapter 3.
9. See D. Coates, "Building a growth strategy on a new social settlement: the UK case", SPERI Paper No. 25 (October 2015), 8.

10. In "Democratic primaries in the shadow of neoliberalism" in D. Coates, *Observing Obama in Real Time*, 428–41 (Winston-Salem: Library Partners Press, 2017); and originally posted at http://www.davidcoates.net/2016/05/18/democratic-primaries-in-the-shadow-of-neoliberalism/ (accessed 1 August 2017). List B included: the maintenance of demand through public spending and the toleration of public debt; the avoidance of further financial crisis by tighter financial oversight; the infrastructure route to growth (public spending to modernize roads, bridges, rail and Internet); progressive taxation to reduce excessive inequality and to spread the cost of welfare provision to those best able to bear it; greater rights for women and minorities at work, more childcare and paid parental leave; and moves towards a carbon-free energy policy.

11. List C included: greater rights for trade unions, and a major hike in both the minimum wage and Social Security; a systemic attack on the sources of poverty, with affirmative action while poverty persists; the deconstruction of the system of mass incarceration and the ending of the war on drugs; new trade policy to reverse the outsourcing of well-paying jobs; the breaking up of banks that are too big to fail; and less spending on the military and on foreign wars: more nation-building at home, less abroad. (List A was the standard neoliberal one).

12. Center for American Progress, *Report of the Commission on Inclusive Prosperity* (Washington, DC: 2015).

13. Brookings Institution, *Skills and Innovation Strategies in Strengthening US Manufacturing: Lessons from Germany*, Washington, DC: Metropolitan Policy Project, 2015.

14. See, for example, K. DeGood *et al.*, *An Infrastructure Plan for America* (Washington, DC: Center for American Progress, 2016); and J. Bivens, "The Short- and Long-Term Impact of Infrastructure Investments on Employment and Economic Activity in the US Economy", Economic Policy Institute Briefing Paper #374, 1 July 2014.

15. A core claim in the 2016 Sanders campaign. Now enshrined in *The People's Budget*, prepared and published in May 2017 by the Congressional Progressive Caucus.

16. See, for example, J. Bernstein, *The Impact of Inequality on Growth* (Washington, DC: Center for American Progress, 2013).

17. Congressional Progressive Caucus, *Restore the American Dream for the 99% Act*, (Washington DC, 2016).

18. Economic Policy Institute, *Agenda to Raise America's Pay* (Washington, DC: Economic Policy Institute, 2015).

19. B. Frank, "The new mandate on defense", *Democracy* 27 (Winter 2013), 50–6; and L. J. Korb & A. Rothman, *Nation Building at Home: How*

Sensible Cuts to Defense Spending Can Offset the Cost of the American Jobs Act (Washington, DC: Center for American Progress, 2011).

20. R. Pollin, J. Heintz & J. Wicks-Lim, *Strengthening US Manufacturing Through Public Procurement Policies*, University of Massachusetts-Amherst: Department of Economics and Political Economy Research Institute, December 2015.

21. See, for example, such works as: J. Stiglitz, *The Great Divide* (New York: Norton, 2015); R. Reich, *Saving Capitalism: For the Many, Not the Few* (New York: Knopf, 2016); P. Krugman, *End This Recession Now* (New York: Norton, 2012); D. Baker, *The End of Loser Liberalism* (Washington, DC: Center for Economic and Policy Research, 2011); and J. Hacker & N. Loewentheil, *Prosperity Economics: Building an Economy for All* (Washington, DC: Creative Commons, 2012).

22. This in Jeremy Corbyn, "The Tories are taking us back to 1979 – we need a strategic state", *The Guardian*, 23 August 2015; and his *The Economy in 2020*, July 2015.

23. Joe Cox, *Plan B* (London: Compass, 2011).

24. M. Mazzucato, *Rebalancing What?* (London: Policy Network, 2012).

25. S. Hall, D. Massey & M. Rustin (eds), *After Neo-Liberalism: The Kilburn Manifesto* (London: Soundings, 2015).

26. http://speri.dept.shef.ac.uk/ (accessed 13 August 2017).

27. See W. Hutton, *How Good We Can Be* (London: Little, Brown, 2015).

28. J. Hacker, "How to reinvigorate the centre-left? Predistribution", *The Guardian,* 12 June 2013.

29. E. Miliband, "The inequality problem", *London Review of Books*, 4 February 2016.

30. P. Diamond & G. Radice, *Can Labour Win? The Hard Road to Power* (London: Policy Network, 2015).

31. See D. Coates, "Labour's historic defeat: learning the right lessons", SPERI Comment, 14 May 2015.

32. For one pro-Corbyn take, see A. Murray, "Corbyn's Labour", *The Bullet*, 15 October 2015. For the counter-argument, that with Corbyn "the party has ended up in policy and culture pre-New Labour, when we need to be post-New Labour", see D. Miliband on "Why the left needs to move forward, not back", *New Statesman* 21 September 2016.

33. "The mid-term election: taking the longer view" in D. Coates, *Observing Obama in Real Time*, 385; and originally posted at http://www.davidcoates.net/2014/11/19/the-mid-term-elections-taking-the-longer-view/ (accessed 3 August 2017).

34. S. Greenberg, "A new formula for a real Democratic majority", *The American Prospect*, Spring 2015.

35. See, for instance, A. Gabbatt, "Bernie Sanders lambasts 'absolute failure' of Democratic Party's strategy", *The Guardian*, 11 June 2017.
36. See M. Lilla, "The end of identity liberalism", *New York Times*, 18 November 2016.
37. "The invisibility of class, and the hegemony of conservative ideas, in contemporary America" in D. Coates, *Observing Obama in Real Time*, 415; and originally posted at http://www.davidcoates.net/2015/04/10/the-invisibility-of-class-and-the-hegemony-of-conservative-ideas-in-contemporary-america/ (accessed 3 August 2017).
38. D. Coates, "A different double shuffle", *Renewal* 15:2/3 (2007), 114–5.
39. P. N. Rasmussen & U. Bullman, "The social democracy to come", *Social Europe*, Occasional Paper, No. 11, October 2016.
40. R. Reich, "The lost art of Democratic narrative", *New Republic*, March 2005.
41. S. Hall, "The great moving right show", in his *Selected Political Writings* (London: Lawrence & Wishart, 2017).

CHAPTER 5

A NEW POLITICS FROM THE LEFT
The distinctive experience of Jeremy Corbyn as leader of the British Labour Party

Hilary Wainwright

Writing as I have been – first in the middle and then at the end of an election campaign in which I feel some engagement – I have had to exert self-discipline and resist the temptation to chase fast moving events. I found the advice of writer Italo Calvino useful. He says: "I reject the role of the person chasing events. I prefer the person who continues his discourse, waiting for it to become topical again, like all things that have a sound basis".[1] It's not for me to judge whether my discourse has a sound basis, but I will argue the case on the assumption that it does. And so, tempting as it is, I will not chase the events leading up to election day, 8 June 2017, or the consequent repercussions for the Labour Party, for Jeremy Corbyn, and for the movement that his campaign to be and then to remain leader of the Labour Party – though I do intend to reflect on the movement's prospects, the new openings since the electoral successes of Corbyn-led Labour, the obstacles it still faces and the pitfalls it needs to avoid, drawing on lessons from the experience of Syriza.

My discourse in this chapter concerns "a new politics from the left", in particular, the importance as a foundation of this politics of an understanding of power learnt from social movements of the past half-century; and related to this, a distinct understanding of knowledge and what kinds and sources of knowledge matter in public decision-making. My argument will focus on the incubation of this new politics, and its underlying understandings of power and knowledge, in the movements of the late-1960s and 1970s; and their re-emergence after decades of neoliberalism in the twenty-first century – with the movements of the squares in Southern Europe followed by Syriza and Podemos (though with scattered, regionally specific, antecedents in the 1980s). I also will explore the under-standings of power and knowledge that underpin the "old politics" historically associated in the UK with the Labour Party. This exploration will give some indication of the likely obstacles that the agencies of the new politics will be (and indeed are already) up against.

I will use the Labour Party as a case study, not only because the struggle both in and against the Labour Party is my daily political reality, living and working as I do in London and co-editing a national magazine and website (*Red Pepper*), but also because such a case study can help throw the key relationships of social democracy into sharp relief. I am thinking here of the Party's long-established uncritical (and indeed, positively deferential) approach to the British state; its "parliamentarism", as Ralph Miliband termed the elevated importance the Labour Party gave to electoral and parliamentary politics throughout the twentieth century: the division on which it was founded between its industrial wing (the trade unions, with their focus on industrial relations) and its political wing (the Parliamentary Labour Party, with its focus on Parliament). If you doubt that, you will find in Ralph Miliband's classic *Parliamentary Socialism* an exemplary study of the dynamics and conditions of sustainability of this social democratic party – and in works directly inspired by Ralph Miliband's work, clear evidence of the limits of this kind of politics.[2]

I will consider the case of Jeremy Corbyn's challenge to the Labour Party as we have known it, and as Miliband analysed it, not because a new politics of the left stands or falls with Corbyn. Rather, I will focus part of what follows on the Corbyn-led Labour Party because the movement for which he has become a voice, an amplifying voice, is an important expression of a new politics from the Left, and in its successful campaign against Theresa May – the epitome of the old politics at its most remote, arrogant and cruel – an answer to a widely felt need and desire to bring down the political class. Not only has Corbyn and the movement that he inspired challenged and shaken the political establishment. They have also challenged, through the Labour Party's 2017 election manifesto, the parliamentarism that tied the Labour Party so closely to this establishment. What is also now effectively under challenge is the Party's "Labourism": the sub-ordinate position of labour that was built into the institutions of the Labour Party and its relations with the unions from its inception (in particular, the separation of politics from economics, reflecting the limitations of liberal democracy and containing/restraining the wider political repercussions of periodic moments of workplace trade union militancy).

The most distinctive – and probably unique – feature of the Corbyn phenomenon is that this radical transformative left politics has emerged *within* a social democratic party, though driven signifi-cantly by long marginalised – one might even say suffocated – move-ment energies *outside* (energies and activists that were attracted to Corbyn, as an emphatically *non-parliamentarist* Member of Parli-ament, and in spite of their hesitations about the Labour Party). The obstacles that this uniquely hybrid movement faces are especially revealing about what this new politics is up against. My conclusions, while not trying to predict the likely scenarios for left politics in Britain, draw from the Corbyn experience and from the experience of Syriza in Greece, to argue for a radicalization of the relations between electoral politics and extra-parliamentary alternatives – a radicalization that is embryonic in the former and partially realized in the latter.

A COOL STRAIGHTFORWARD LEADER REFUSING TO PERFORM A ROLE IN A DYSFUNCTIONAL STATE

Moreover, while insisting that the sustained development of a new politics does not stand or fall with Corbyn, I do not want to dimin-ish the importance of his distinctively modest and supportive style of leadership – quite contrary to the parliamentarist and somewhat superior stance of the bulk of the British political class, including even some of the most left-wing Labour MPs. The presence of Jeremy Corbyn – one of the most radical Labour MPs in Parliament, and one who had persistently disobeyed the leadership of his party and always stood up for struggles against injustice – on the ballot for leader of the Labour Party was not the result of a long-prepared plan. The Parliamentary Left could hardly fill a telephone box. None of the three main figures had leadership ambitions; it was simply Corbyn's turn to be the Left option, slog around the country to keep up the morale of the faithful and to be torn apart by the right-wing press. Once he was on the ballot paper, however, he became, as we have just intimated, a powerful magnet for the kind of discontent expressed by the movements of the squares in Greece and the Indignados in Spain: discontent which, within the specifics of the British context, had at its core an angry reaction to Tony Blair's New Labour government with its continuation of Thatcher's agenda of deregulation, privatization and austerity.

The energies of the movement that lifted Jeremy Corbyn to the party leadership came primarily from outside the Labour Party. They came from environmental campaigners and direct-action groups, those radicalised by growing inequality, austerity and the 2008 financial crash, and by the mounting threat to the survival of the planetary ecological system, as well as from thousands of trade union members angered by government cuts and their consequences for public services, local government and the lives and prospects for young people. Jeremy Corbyn was no Tony Benn, although his political development had taken place through his 30-year collaboration with Benn and the Socialist Campaign Group of MPs. For whereas Tony Benn championed radical change through his charisma and established status as a leading UK politician, Corbyn symbolised a new effort from below to open the party to becoming a movement for radical change through his very modesty and daily support for others in struggle. Alex Nunns, author of the most authoritative description of Jeremy Corbyn's "improbable path to power", comments that this participatory ethos, rather than the specific detail of policies, "was really the essence of Corbyn's entire campaign".[3] For disempowered party members in particular, it was the reason Corbyn was so appealing. He was offering them empowerment, and there was no mistaking the message – every aspect of Corbyn's candidacy, from his own selfless demeanour to the specific form of rail nationalization he was proposing, was about inviting people to take part.

This appeal of his example, especially under pressure in his first year as leader from his fellow MPs behaving, or misbehaving, and treating the party members with contempt, when combined with Corbyn and John McDonnell's unrelenting commitment to resisting austerity (in a society where the lives of the vast majority, young and old, were being devastated by several decades of increasingly brutal austerity imposed by Tory and Labour governments alike) has proved dramatic. It has produced the first example, beyond the extraordinary circumstances of the immediate post-Second World War period, of Labour Party electoral success – though not yet victory – on the basis of an appeal from the Left (and even in 1945, it was not the Party leadership but the activists and the voters who were on the Left). This electoral success from the Left removes one important sustaining principle of centre-right parliamentarism and labourism: the insistence – an article of faith, really – that because of the peculiarities of the British electoral and party system, Labour can only win elections by moving to the centre; and that accordingly, given the importance of unity against the Conservatives in a two party system, the left in the party and the trade unions alike have always to moderate their demands and subordinate themselves to the imperatives of unity and electoral success.

What is most striking and attractive (from a progressive viewpoint, at least) about Jeremy Corbyn, and makes him different from other European leaders of the radical left – often called "left populists" – is that his appeal is not centred on himself as a charismatic leader. It is based rather on an invitation actively to join an urgent crusade for a new politics based on popular participation. His promise is to invite people to participate in developing the policies that the government he seeks to lead would implement. He is not a left-populist in the sense of a leader in whom the people are encouraged to invest their faith against the elite. His appeal has been his encouragement to people to have confidence in themselves. Jeremy Corbyn's approach to knowledge and wisdom reflects this break from traditional, elite notions of expertise. He described his personal attitude to "expertise" in an interview soon after the election: "I never held in awe those who have had higher education", he said, nor had "a sense of superiority over those who don't. Life is life. Some of the wisest people you meet are sweeping our streets".[4]

RETHINKING POWER AND KNOWLEDGE

This approach of Corbyn's accords closely with the new understanding of power which I believe underpins what is new about the new politics. My argument is based on a distinction between two kinds of power and on the possibility of new institutions and relationships between parties and social movements/radical initiatives in civil society. This understanding of power also shapes how the two combine to achieve radical social, economic and political change.

On the one hand, there is "power over", which could also be described as "power-as-domination", involving an asymmetry between those with power and those over whom power is exercised. Historically, social democratic and communist parties have been built around, at best, a benevolent vision of the understanding of power-as-domination. Their strategies have been based on winning the power to govern and then steer the state apparatus to meet what they identify as the needs of the people. It is a paternalistic political methodology. On the other hand, there is "power to" or "power-as-transformative-capacity". This is the power discovered by social movements of students, radical workers, environmentally-conscious technicians and feminists as they moved beyond protest to proposing and directly creating practical, pre-figurative solutions.[5]

The distinction between the two forms of power is central to the experimental search for appropriate forms of transformative democratic political organization in the context of extreme fragmentation, precarity and dispersal of working people. At a time when older forms of organization, notably the traditional mass workplace-based organizations of labour, have either been defeated or are inadequate in today's changed circumstances, this distinction helps us to focus on the exact and distinct purposes that any new organizations have to be fit for. It is a search also stimulated by the failures of the traditional parties of the Left to bring about the changes in which their supporters had believed, and for which they had originally built those organizations.

The notion of power-as-transformative-capacity emerged out of widespread frustration at the workings of power-as-domination exercised by political parties of the traditional left. The distinctive feature of the rebellions of the 1960s and 1970s was that students, workers, insubordinate women and others took power into their own hands, discovering through collective action that they had capacities of their own to bring about change; and that through rebellion, they had leverage because the power of their oppressors depended on their complicity. These were not simply movements of pressure, demanding with extra militancy that the governing party do something on their behalf. Their approach was more directly transformative. For example, women took action directly to change their relations with men, with each other and with public services; workers took militant action in their workplaces not only to improve their working conditions but also to extend control over the purpose of their labour; and community groups squatted in empty buildings, occupied land against speculation, and campaigned for alternative land-use policies for the wellbeing of their communities. They no longer focused primarily on the parliamentary politics of representation.

A common theme of these rebellions involved overturning conventional deference to authority and the forms of knowledge that those in authority deployed as their source of legitimacy. The other side of the movements' rejection of these forms of authority was a pervasive and self-confident assertion of their own practical and sometimes tacit knowledge, as well as their collaborative capacity, against the claims of those in authority to know "what is best" or what "needs to be done". Along with this self-confidence in their transformative abilities went inventiveness about the forms of organization that would build that capacity. While acknowledging the mixed and uneven legacy of the 1960s and 1970s, I would argue that a distinctive feature of the radical movements of these years was their tendency to emphasize and value the sharing of different kinds of knowledge, practical and experiential as well as theoretical and historical. In their refusal to defer to authority, such movements broke the unspoken bond between knowledge and authority that underpinned the postwar settlement – the paternalistic idea that those in power know what is best for the mass of people. The uncertain, experimental process of democratizing knowledge tends, in practice, to involve an emphasis on decentralized and networked organizations sharing and developing knowledge horizontally, and breaking from models that presume an expert leadership and a more-or-less ignorant membership (the model assumed by Robert Michels in his study of social democratic political parties and his hypothesis of "the iron law of oligarchy"). The radically democratic approaches to knowledge pioneered in the 1960s and 1970s (most notably by feminists but also by networks of workplace, community organizations, and critical technologists) laid organizational and cultural foundations that have partially underpinned many civic movements ever since, from the alter-globalization movement of the late 1990s through to Occupy and the Indignados.

The wisdom of the streets and the workplaces are also evident in the many and diverse locations where grassroots trade union and community alliances have since the 1980s been a driving force in the defence and improvement of public services or utilities in the face of privatization. (I'm thinking here of the networks of co-operatives, social enterprises and radical NGOs involved in renewable energy, fair trade, non-industrial food and agricultural production, the growth of alternative media projects, the networks of open software production, peer-to-peer collaboration, communication, and production[6]). These networks have become a means of sharing knowledge and building transformative power, not only to defend public resources but also to advance projects of democratization.[7] They have shown they can strengthen citizens' resilience in the face of policies that threaten their material security, offering a degree of autonomy and control that would not otherwise be available to them. And ultimately, by illustrating in daily practice that there are alternatives, the realization of which lies in significant part with the people themselves, they have often become an important part of strategies for political hegemony. In this way, power-as-transformative-capacity has begun to produce elements of an institutional-, and a communications-, infrastructure, which can be recognized as distinct from the institutions of representation, through an understanding of its basis in a distinct and effective source of power.

Yet what has also become very clear in developing new institutions through social and labour movements is that the autonomy of non-state sources of power tends to be precarious and difficult to sustain, however transformative and creative they can periodically be. This repeatedly has raised the question of how far, and under what conditions, power-as-domination (essentially, in this context, having control over state institutions, national and municipal) can be a resource for power-as-transformative-capacity. It is important to recognize that although there is a sharp distinction between these two types of power, they are not necessarily or invariably counter-posed. We therefore need to probe further into both concepts of power, and then into what new forms of institutions of representation could enable the two to best combine for purposes of transformation, perhaps revitalizing representation in the process. How, for example, could power-as-domination be a resource for power-as-transformative-capacity, as distinct from weakening or overwhelming forms of social power originally autonomous from the state? And what kinds of transformative capacity are strategically relevant to bring about change, with resources from power-as-domination?

Moreover, civic sources of power cannot automatically be assumed to be transformative or strategically significant. Under what conditions, if any, could institutions of representative democracy provide a framework or platform through which these two kinds of power could combine in a process of social transformation?

LESSONS FROM THE GREEK DEFEAT

The recent experience of Greece highlights the challenges involved in exploring the relationship between these two sources of power in the context of what is, formally at least, representative democracy. Following its electoral success in 2015, winning 36 per cent of the vote and leading a government with a small nationalist party, Syriza, as a coalition of movements and political organizations of the radical left, faced the problem of negotiating its rejection of the Troika-imposed austerity Memorandum and gaining both time and financial support to work with civil society to drive and support social and economic transformation in Greece, including radical reform of the corrupt and undemocratic Greek state. This, at any rate, was the stated intention. There was a widespread assumption, not only among the leadership of Syriza but also those sections of the Left across Europe that shared Syriza's predominant political outlook, that the EU bureaucracy and its constituent government would, albeit reluctantly, respect Syriza's electoral mandate for ending the Memorandum – and would negotiate on that basis.

The reality turned out to be rather different. "I was astonished", reported Yanis Varoufakis, Greece's new finance minister and leading negotiator, "to hear the German finance minister [Wolfgang Schäuble] say to me verbatim, that 'elections cannot be allowed to change established economic policy'".[8] Varoufakis and his fellow Syriza negotiators were acting on the basis of a more or less radical variant of the Left's understanding of democracy and its relationship

103

to it, shared across postwar Europe. As Andreas Karitzis, a member of the party's political committee, put it at the time: "the assumption was that the elites were committed to accepting the democratically shaped mandate of an elected government".[9] The response of the EU to the Greek government's refusal, on behalf of the overwhelming majority of Greek people, to accept the continued austerity regime imposed on previous Greek governments, was brutal. Not only did EU negotiators, led by Schäuble, treat Syriza's original electoral mandate with contempt, they also rebuffed the July 2015 referendum in which Greek voters again rejected the renewal of the austerity regime.

The consequences for the lives of ordinary Greeks have been disastrous. The experience has been a terrible reversal of high hopes and expectations, on the part not only of the leaders of Syriza, but more significantly, of the majority of party and movement activists. Many are engaged in deep debate about what went wrong and what can be learnt for the future, including for the Left across Europe and worldwide. Varoufakis resigned from the Syriza government and has founded a movement, DiEM25, for the democratization of Europe. Others left Syriza to set up a new political party arguing for Greek exit from the Eurozone. Some, however, have left, not to found a new party but to experiment with a new strategy based on developing the capacity of organized citizens to take over basic social functions of daily life. In doing so, they have turned to the infrastructure of solidarity which was created after 2010, as a politically conscious strategy of survival against the relentless austerity measures coming from the institutions of the EU and IMF, which are now also effectively controlling the Greek government. These networks involve the self-management of basic social functions: health, the distribution of food, childcare, some aspects of education, and so on. It also increasingly involves links with agricultural production, especially with small and medium-size farmers who share the aims of the solidarity movement and have turned their farms into becoming parts of a solidarity food chain and into centres of education in eco-agriculture.

Some of these solidarity social organizations, especially the volunteer-run health centres, act as laboratories for new relations of social care at the same time as providing essential services. A volunteer psychologist described to me the contrast between his relationship with a patient in a conventional mainstream hospital and in the voluntary clinic where he worked. "In the solidarity clinic", he said, "I was able to treat him as an individual and with respect, talking to him, one to one; whereas in the hospital, the institution prescribed a relationship in which patients were more like a production line. In the clinic, there is an egalitarian ethos. We are all volunteers self-managing the service; patients are fellow citizens with whom we are in solidarity". If in the future there were the resources to re-establish public hospitals to take on such services, then he says, he and his colleagues would introduce improvements they had learnt from the collaborative, egalitarian culture of the self-managed clinics to transform the management and quality of service they provided. Andreas Karitzis has explained very well what impelled him to turn to these networks as the foundation for a new way forward after the experience of Syriza in government:

> A strategy that wishes to be relevant to the new conditions must take on the duty of acquiring the necessary power to run basic social functions. It is the only way to acquire the necessary power to defy the elites' control over our societies ... We must modify the balance between representing people's beliefs and demands and coordinating, facilitating, connecting, supporting and nurturing people's actions. We must contribute heavily to the formation of a strong 'backbone' for resilient and dynamic networks of social economy and co-operative productive activities, democratically functioning digital communities, community control over functions such as infrastructure facilities, energy systems and distribution networks. These are ways of gaining the degree of autonomy necessary to defy the control of elites over the basic functions of our society.[10]

PREREQUISITES OF AN ORGANIZATION RADICALIZING THE RELATIONSHIP BETWEEN SOCIAL STRUGGLES AND ELECTORAL POLITICS

The Greek and British experiences point, above all, to the importance of overcoming the separation of politics from economics. Historically this separation was inherited from the transition from feudalism to the capitalist market and representative democracy, and later reproduced in the separation – in a particularly rigid form in the UK – between the industrial and political wings of the labour movement. This division between economics and politics, and the prohibition (often self-imposed) on unions becoming political, has weakened the potential for workers to exercise their collective transformative capacity. This is something that transformative party-union relations would have to change. Such a change would also involve a break from the still-lingering mentality that sees the capture of/gaining office over centralized state power as the key strategic objective for a party committed to change. On this conception of change, the main role of the party is of representation.

By contrast, the notion of party strategy and organization that flows from an understanding of power as transformative capacity as well as of the varied forms of knowledge and of the collaborative nature of creativity – is one in which the party is a source of experimentation and capacity-building, rather than an organization focused exclusively on political representation. Such a party would act more as a catalyst to building power as transformative capacity in the here and now, than as an army bent on capturing the citadels of government in the future. We need therefore to envisage a party as a means of experimenting and prefiguring in the present the relations we envisage in the future between politics and everyday material and cultural life, rather than letting the party's representative role predominate.

The party's work then becomes rooted in daily production and reproduction, and its task becomes to build and realize citizens' capacities for self-government and social and economic transformation. It would need to work with labour and community organizations for this purpose. If power as transformative capacity is understood to include political economy and to recombine politics and economics in new ways, then a new kind of radical party would need to shift exclusive attention from both macroeconomic flows (the supply of money, levels of taxation and the regulation of trade) and the purely national institutional framework of ownership towards questions of the content and social organization of production: Production for what purpose? With what technology? With what environmental and social consequences? And drawing on whose knowledge, with what relations to its workers and users? The planetary imperative towards a low carbon economy gives added impetus to create or at least illustrate transformed relations of production in the present (from which national policies for state support could be generated and popularized). The ICT revolution and the Web have opened up potential opportunities for a new socially- and ecologically-driven economy (and challenging the monopolies that now dominate the sector). The new party, in its policies and its practice, needs to be attentive and hence immersed in the development of these new possibilities. It could act as a political space for those engaged in the new production, overcoming the rift between politics, economics and society that has held thought and institutions in its vice since the early nineteenth century.

This would imply a party membership that is self-educated and practically involved in the many social innovations that are emerging globally: open source software, co-operative platforms, collaborative consumption, new ways of growing and eating food, of producing and using energy, of light footed transport, of forms of trade and finance, of "soft" care and health enabling systems, of cultural production and all those other aspects of a sufficient life. These would be the contemporary forms of knowledgeable citizen participation that would be the life of a pre-figurative, catalytic party. Power-as-domination always implied that power is exercised most distinctively through government, which can turn aspects of state power into resources for power as transformative capacity. But state institutions, like all institutions, depend on social relations that people can reproduce or refuse and, under some conditions, take action to transform. I would call this *revolutionary gradualism*, distinct from the insurrectionary model implicit in the "reform or revolution" model, but not underestimating the resistance it will face and the likelihood of intense conflict and moments of radical rupture. An opportunity for a transformative party to support pre-figurative change in the present, as a way of preparing for more widespread systematic change when the party eventually won government power, would be at the level of municipal governments, which are increasingly under attack from national governments imposing austerity policies but are already sites of radical and visionary experimentation. It would be important for a transformative, catalytic party to use municipal government as both a site of experimentation and learning and a basis for educating members in the new culture of the party in sharing power between elected government and organized citizens. Cities especially tend to be both where citizens are regularly engaged in forms of formal and informal self-management and where the mechanisms are most easily invented for supporting them and acknowledging their capacity. City government can also be an institutional space where a radical party can consolidate its power and improve its ability to gain national governmental power. It is most important, therefore, for any radical party to campaign for the devolution of power to cities and regions.

All this might seem a long way from the Labour Party as we have known it, focused on elections, deferential towards state power, defensive about its trade union links. But in another sense, this approach continues, in contemporary form, traditions embedded in the party's origins. Traditions which gave us Clause 4, the party's famous commitment not only to common ownership but also to the "popular administration and control of each industry and service" and "to secure for the workers by hand or by brain the full fruits of their industry and the most equitable distribution thereof". Note here the emphasis on "workers by hand and by brain" and that it refers explicitly not to state or public administration and control but to "popular administration and control". Surely an implication of this is that in the preparation for gaining power, the type of party leadership needed is one that not only prepares its shadow cabinet for managing the affairs of state, but also engages in a process of empowering education amongst its members and supporters, the labour movement and its social allies, for the process of "popular administration and control of every industry and service".

Several of Corbyn's promised initiatives indicated how much his leadership is potentially open to this kind of process, as in various commitments already made: for Labour's Manifesto to be drawn up through a process of popular participation; for participatory processes for constitutional reform; for an "Arms Conversion Agency" to involve workers in the defence sector in proposing alternative socially useful projects to which their skills could be put. Whatever the continuing opposition to such initiatives inside the PLP, there is no lack of resources and will outside parliament to make them viable. Corbyn had been so pinned down by hostile pressures that he had been unable before the recent general election to develop these commitments in practice. The election process, however, opened up new possibilities, of which the Party's election manifesto was exemplary. It was the product of the party leadership actually listening to and giving credence to the policies of many different civic organizations, including but not restricted to the unions. The quality of the manifesto was able to benefit from several initiatives autonomous of the Party, initiatives that were not simply resisting austerity but also proposing and involving people in developing alternatives. Good examples include recent positive campaigns by the National Union of Teachers reaching out to parents and the wider community; also the environmental movement around experiments in democratically organized renewable energy sources, and the housing movement promoting ideas and practical initiatives for social and co-operative housing, and for controlled rents. A younger generation of activists concerned with the future of our cities is retrieving and popularizing the history of radical municipal governments, like the Greater London Council in the early 1980s from which John McDonnell, who was Deputy to Ken Livingstone, drew for his economic policies.[11]

As far as political reform is concerned, the rise of the movement for Scottish independence in its grassroots form, autonomous from the Scottish National Party, has had repercussions across the border and lent urgency and possibility to the need for a democratic constitution – an issue yet to be adequately addressed by Corbyn's Labour Party, but under discussion and debate, especially at events of "The World Transformed" a cultural and educational initiative of Momentum, the diverse and very active organization consolidated out of the movement for Corbyn to become leader. However, the separation of MPs from the people, and the crisis over Corbyn's leadership, makes the issue of democratizing the British state an urgent issue for those who joined the Labour Party or became supporters as a result of Corbyn's leadership, as well as for a broader constituency. What is needed is a fully participative process of creating a convincing alternative to Britain's unwritten constitution and the immense but opaque executive powers derived from it – from the extensive powers of patronage to the power to press the nuclear button, and in general the power to preserve the continuity of the British state. It is exactly this that the establishment feared and continue to fear most from the dynamics unleashed by Corbyn's leadership: that is, the democratic potential to realize a transformative politics beyond "parliamentary socialism". For this reason, they and their allies in the Parliamentary Labour Party have worked hard to ensure that Corbyn is never able truly to lead.

Much to the stunned surprise of these hostile forces, in the Parliamentary Party and in the liberal media as well as in the right-wing media – in *The Guardian* as well as in the *Daily Mail* – Corbyn, given the focus and publicity of a general election campaign, unleashed a suppressed radicalisation arising from the experience of over a decade of austerity. This occurred especially but not only amongst young people (who have in turn often galvanised their parents). A section of the PLP and the previously entirely hostile party apparatus are simply impressed by Corbyn's ability to win votes – winning elections was always one aspect of parliamentarism. Another less responsive, more entrenched, dimension of parliamentarism, however, is deference to the British state, the Union, the Queen in Parliament, and with it the power of private capital as organized through the City of London. These ideological Blairites, committed to the British state and to the free market – whose ideal world would be run by Hillary Clinton, Emmanuel Macron and Tony Blair – will continue to organize to ensure that Corbyn will never be prime minister. The problem for them is that in the past they have always been the electorally successful part of the Labour Party and therefore hegemonic within the party which after all is united by a desire to defeat the Tories and form a government, however much left and right differ about what they want a Labour government to do.

The newness of Jeremy Corbyn and his team is that they have broken the ability to win elections from what Miliband called "parliamentarism" with its deference to the British state. They have shown that – after decades of neoliberal economics – it is possible to win from the left. This gives them a window of hegemony in the party and greater legitimacy in wider society. Exactly how this should be followed through is unclear but hopeful: what an electorally successful left party, aiming for a radical transformation of the capitalist state, involves in practice is uncertain; but the negative lessons of Greece warn harshly against any separation from the radical social movements from whence such parties came, and on whose transformative power they depend to achieve the changes they promised and for which they won support.

A NEW POLITICS FROM THE LEFT

NOTES

1. Italo Calvino, *Hermit in Paris: Autobiographical Writings* [1985], Trans. M. McLaughlin (New York: Pantheon, 2003).
2. On this, see R. Miliband, *Parliamentary Socialism* (London: Merlin, 1961/1972); D. Coates, *The Labour Party and the Struggle for Socialism* (Cambridge: Cambridge University Press, 1975/1981) and Leo Panitch, *Social Democracy and Industrial Militancy* (Cambridge: Cambridge University Press, 1976). Many relevant essays by Miliband-inspired academics and activists are gathered in D. Coates (ed.), *Paving the Third Way: The Critique of Parliamentary Socialism* (London: Merlin, 2003).
3. A. Nunns, *The Candidate*, second edition (New York: OR Books, 2018).
4. Leo Panitch & H. Wainwright, "'What we've achieved so far', an interview with Jeremy Corbyn", *Red Pepper*, December 2015, available at www.redpepper.org.uk (accessed 13 August 2017).
5. Here I build on distinctions made, as part of entirely different theoretical frameworks, by John Holloway in *Changing the World Without Taking Power* (London: Pluto, 2002) and Roy Bhaskar in *Dialectic: The Pulse of Freedom* (Abingdon: Routledge, 2008).
6. See R. Murray, "Global civil society and the rise of the civil economy" in M. Kaldor, H. L. Moore & S. Selchow (eds), *Global Civil Society 2012* (London: Palgrave Macmillan, 2012).
7. For descriptions of detailed examples, see H. Wainwright, *The Tragedy of the Private: The Potential of the Public* (Geneva: Public Service International & the Transnational Institute, 2014).
8. Y. Varoufakis, *And the Weak Suffer What They Must? Europe, Austerity and the Threat to Global Stability* (London: Bodley Head, 2016).
9. A. Karitzis, *The European Left in Times of Crisis: Lessons from the Greek Experience* (Amsterdam: Transnational Institute, 2016), available at www.tni.org (accessed 13 August 2017).
10. *Ibid.*
11. see www.glcstory.co.uk.

CHAPTER 6

SOCIAL DEMOCRACY IN A DANGEROUS WORLD

Colin Crouch

The most fundamental fault line in contemporary politics runs through the centre of its dominant right-wing alliance, that between neoliberals and conservatives, and sets two different kinds of political power against each other. It is a conflict that leaves the political left to one side, with the ironic consequence that what should be a moment of major opportunity for social democrats to break that alliance is in fact having the opposite consequence. The fault line is that between the economic globalization fostered by neoliberalism, representing the extraordinary power of business wealth, and the xenophobic form of conservatism, representing the power of mass fear and hatred.

It is in relation to these that the political left is weak. It has become routine for debates about "the state of the Left" to bewail a lack of ideas to challenge neoliberalism, but in his contribution to this book David Coates shows how in fact there is an abundance of ideas and practical policies coming from left of centre; the weakness lies in a mobilizing capacity strong enough to confront its opponents. I would go further and argue that, so important are centre-left policies, these opponents cannot avoid embracing aspects of them. Nowhere in the democratic world, and particularly in Europe, have neoliberal governments been able completely to destroy public health and education services, public pensions, publicly funded infrastructure, regulation of business behaviour and consumer rights, or taxation that has some redistributive effect. On the conservative right, leaders who are building their power base on hostility to immigrants, the European Union (EU) and foreigners in general, such as Marine Le Pen in France, Theresa May in the UK and the Danish People's Party, feel a need to reinforce their position by rejecting the neoliberal approach to social policy. Social democratic policies live on and even revive, despite the growing weakness of the parties to which they belong.

In this essay, I shall concentrate on constellations of power in the electoral and other mass mobilization arenas, but always bearing in mind that this is by no means the only and probably no longer the most important place where political power is wielded. As Wolfgang Streeck has argued, the "market people" (*Marktvolk*) have become far more significant than the "state people" (*Staatsvolk*) in shaping the contemporary world.[1]

THE SHIFTING CONSTELLATION OF LEFT AND RIGHT

The original confrontation between Left and Right, in the assemblies following the French Revolution, pitted a liberal left pursuing the Enlightenment values of modernizing rationalism and universalism (*liberté, fraternité, égalité*) against conservative defenders of monarchy and the church, hierarchy and acceptance of what was sanctified by tradition. As the nineteenth century progressed, liberals everywhere divided into those who stressed *liberté* and saw the market and private property as the core embodiment of reason and universalism, and those who gave weight to *fraternité* and *égalité* and became social liberals or even socialists. Most of the conservative right resisted, often violently, the Enlightenment project and feared its translation into democracy, though some conservatives saw the potential attraction of the security of tradition and belief in the unity of the nation as a potential popular base against both liberalism and socialism. Associated as it was with science and capitalism, liberalism advanced insistently throughout the nineteenth and early twentieth centuries. Even where monarchs and archbishops continued to receive the honour accorded to superior social status, the conservative values with which they were associated were in retreat. In France, Britain and elsewhere their best chance of survival was their growing alliance with their old liberal enemies as major segments of the capitalist bourgeoisie preferred alliances with co-defenders of private property to those with socialism. As the suffrage expanded, liberals found that their rationalistic language was unable to mobilize masses in a way that both conservative traditionalism and the class appeals of the labour movement could do. The conservative alliance was therefore important to them.

One route to understanding this defect in liberal mobilization capacity is to note the odd position of *fraternité* in the revolutionary triad. Forgetting for present purposes its gendered formulation, the idea of *fraternité* belongs more in the field of feelings and loyalties than in the rationalism of the other two components; more obviously with traditionalism than with universalism. It works as a liberal slogan only in the sense originally intended, of a "brotherhood of man" that transcends the particularism of communities, nations, religious faiths and the other locations of conservative "brotherhood". But that has never been a powerful appeal. The kind of loyalty implied by brotherhood is local, restricted to persons who are actually and closely known, especially blood relatives. When Napoleon Bonaparte set out to bring (through military means) the rationalistic values of the revolution to the rest of Europe, the language was universalist, but premised on the idea that the French nation had a special mission as the bearers of those values. As we shall see below, a similar implicit nationalism has applied, though quietly and often only implicitly, to the mass appeals of socialist and social democratic movements.

The quadrilateral of political forces

To make sense of what has been happening to political mobilization, we need to analyse the political space that we have inherited from past decades and the ways in which different interests and ideologies move around it. The core conflicts over *liberté* (authority versus freedom) and *égalité* (more versus less equality) can be represented as the axes of a typical two-by-two matrix (see Figure 6.1). Conservatism originally represented the quarter "authority with inequality", but as conservatives came both to accept democracy and to align their interests with liberal capitalism, they were able to encroach on the space of other political traditions as shown in the figure. The socialist force that emerged during the late nineteenth- and early twentieth centuries originated as the egalitarian wing of liberalism. As many socialist movements came to accept the capitalist economy and became what we now call social democrats, they too were able to encroach on liberal territory, again as shown in the figure. There was also an important element of traditionalism in the labour movement, especially when working-class communities were challenged by economic change and crisis, and looked to their parties and unions to defend them. As a consequence of these aggrandizing movements by conservatives and socialists, liberals increasingly became a minoritarian political force, sharing their liberal inegalitarian quarter with these two larger forces.

This leaves the fourth quarter: traditionalist egalitarianism. This might seem to be an oxymoronic position and therefore necessarily empty, as traditional European societies were strongly hierarchical,

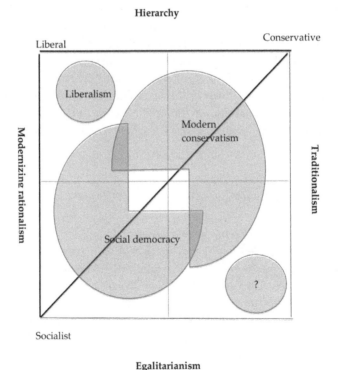

Figure 6.1 The principal dimensions of political space

with lower classes giving considerable deference to higher ones. The fact that we usually recognize three dominant political traditions rather than four suggests that this is the case. On the other hand, tradition does not just mean the defence of established elites. It can also mean the security of the familiar and hostility to the new; people in economically poor and insecure positions may well find in tradition, or social conservatism, a source of stability. This is where the ambiguity of *fraternité* as an Enlightenment slogan becomes important.

Since working-class traditionalism has historically referred to the familiarity of local communities and working environments, trade unions and the institutions of the welfare state, movements of the Left have had access to the oxymoronic final quarter. There is in principle tension with the rational universalism of socialism, but for much of the twentieth century this was concealed by the fact that the "universalism" of the welfare state stopped at national boundaries; more strongly, people accepted the sharing and mutual support necessary to the moral strength of a welfare state because, as David Goodhart and Wolfgang Streeck have separately argued[2], they shared identity as members of the same national family. This can be seen most clearly in the role of the experience of wartime solidarity in the construction of modern welfare states after 1945 – though the idea of the welfare state as a symbol of national belonging was nowhere more strongly developed than in Sweden, which had not participated in the war and had started to construct its powerful social policy in the 1930s. This nationalism was not strident and could co-exist with some serious exercises of internationalism by social democratic governments, such as the exceptionally strong international development efforts of the Nordic countries, or the role of the British and Dutch Labour parties in welcoming immigrants. Provided the tensions implicit in this position were not placed under stress, social democracy was able to gain access to sentiments associated with the fourth quarter.

The situation on the conservative right was a mirror image of this. Given the rejection of democracy by early twentieth-century conservatives in several countries, their only survival strategy in an increasingly mass polity had been to shape working-class traditionalism as solidarity within the nation against foreign challenges of various kinds, prioritizing that struggle over domestic democracy. When this combined with deference to traditional national elites (as for many rural and Christian workers it did) it could be completely absorbed by conservatism itself in the original *ancien régime* quarter. Where there was dissatisfaction with existing elites, there needed to be compromises with movements that attacked these elites while also rejecting the universalism of social democracy. This is one way of interpreting what happened with fascism: movements representing disgust with liberal governing elites and sympathy with the aspirations of working-class people, not as class solidarity, but as a nationalistic rally against foreign nations, ethnic minorities and immigrants. In this way the oxymoronic nature of the fourth quarter could be resolved. The emphasis of the different movements was very diverse. Italian fascism included a version of modernism entirely lacking in Portugal and Spain. German Nazism was highly modernizing economically, but culturally reactionary, religiously ambiguous, and very divided over capitalism. However, it gave itself the name that summed up the fourth quarter: national socialism. In every case however the promise of the intrinsically unstable fourth quarter was betrayed, as fascist leaders befriended aristocratic and capitalist elites, and social inequality grew.

Following the disaster of their flirtation with fascism and Nazism, conservative interests learned to accept democracy, to reduce or even eliminate the stridency of their nationalism, and to accept substantial parts of the social democratic agenda. If social democrats appealed mainly to those working people who, while valuing both tradition and egalitarianism, prioritized the latter, conservatives could appeal to those with the reverse priorities. In such a context, there was no room for autonomous movements representing the fourth quarter alone. Conservatives and social democrats crowded them out, even more than they did liberals. This mid-twentieth-century position is the one represented in Figure 6.1. No name, only a question mark, is given to the fourth quarter. It is so unstable that it has produced no enduring political tradition. Fascism has been its principal expression, but it would be inaccurate to define the space in general as fascist. Fascism was necessarily violent, and this is not necessarily the case with all movements that try to represent this position.

Social compromises

As the postwar years developed, different patterns appeared in different places. Although conservative–liberal alliances predominated, each of the three great political families of democratic Europe could combine with one or both the others, and they could do this across or within parties. Conservatives and social democrats shared a concern for protecting the security of working-class lives from the vagaries of the liberal market; social democrats and liberals could unite on programmes of reform, particularly over issues of family, religion and sexual relations. Further, none of these groups pushed their claims too far. Conservatives remained sensitive to the past fascist associations of parts of their ideology. Liberals knew that extreme forms of the market were unpopular. Social democrats wanted to avoid association with the increasingly bleak image of Soviet state-socialism, and also calculated that they would never have the strength to overwhelm capitalism but would have to make compromises with it. Social democrats' strength lay in their capacity to mobilize manual workers and various other junior-level personnel – a working population, divided by various national regimes, on whom modern mass capitalism depended as both workers and consumers for its success.

Liberals, in the form of neoliberalism (never democratically strong, but central to the aspirations of the *Marktvolk*), were the first to break rank from the various forms of this social compromise of the first three postwar decades. Following the revealed weaknesses of Keynesian demand management during the 1970s, they were able to persuade both conservatives and eventually many social democrats of a need for far more reliance on market forces. This led to an agenda of economic deregulation, in particular the elimination of barriers to global capital movements, producing in turn a major strengthening of the political power of corporations able to make use of highly mobile capital. Capital was increasingly liberated from dependence on the citizens of any one country. *Marktvolk* began their domination of the democratic *Staatsvolk*.

There were many casualties as globalization led to the closure of manufacturing industries in developed economies. The strength of both industrial and political wings of the labour movement declined with the sectors in which their power had been based. Pre- and post-tax income inequalities grew as a result of neoliberal policies and the changed political balance. There were however compensations that enable us to describe the post-1970s period as a new, neoliberal social compromise, albeit one highly skewed towards the interests of capital and the wealthy. Globalization brought cheaper products to consumers in the wealthy countries, at least partly compensating them for declining or static incomes. Employment grew in new services sectors, including public services, which continued to elude neoliberal attacks on them, and a greater proportion of populations benefited from extended education. If people were still finding it hard to manage, from the 1990s constantly expanding deregulated financial markets started extending credit opportunities on soft terms.

Like the postwar consensus before it, the neoliberal one lasted three decades. It was brought down, in the financial crisis of 2007–8, by its last-mentioned component, the increasingly irresponsible lending behaviour of deregulated finance. Since this was a crisis of neoliberalism, why, in general, did social democracy, neoliberalism's main antagonist, not benefit from it? The answer lies partly in the fact that all major social democratic movements had shared in the neoliberal consensus, no longer able to appear as its antagonists. Also, given the numerical decline of the industrial working class, there was no major class capable of mobilizing the enormous forces needed if *Staatsvolk* were to challenge the growing power of *Marktvolk*. Although the behaviour of the world's leading banks had caused the crisis, their resources and capabilities were needed to resolve it, so they emerged from the crisis more powerful than before.

THE MOTIVATIONS OF POLITICAL PARTICIPATION

I have argued elsewhere[3] that most people can become seriously engaged in politics only if social identities that they strongly feel have political meaning thrust upon them, usually in conflicts over exclusion and inclusion. Class and religion provided such mobilizing identities during the struggles for political and social rights of the late nineteenth- and early twentieth centuries. Once universal adult citizenship was gained, and the classes associated with those struggles replaced by the less distinct ones of post-industrial society, class lost that capacity. In Europe, though not the US, religious identification also gradually collapsed. By the time of the 2008 crisis it seemed that no social identity would be strong enough to produce the mass popular mobilizations necessary to shake the confidence of neoliberal domination. Initial waves of activity like the Occupy and anti-global movements had little effective mass appeal beyond their activist core, and subsided.

However, one social identity remained that could quickly acquire political meaning, one that was particularly relevant when globalization in its various forms could be identified as the enemy: nation. This had the added advantage for mobilization that, while there had to be a critique of remote, powerful and obscurely understood global financial elites, there was another feature of globalization that was close at hand, easily perceived, weak and easily kicked (sometimes literally): immigrants and ethnic minorities. The coincidence that in the years following the financial crisis the various wars in the Middle East and North Africa were generating both large numbers of refugees and tiny but effective numbers of Islamic terrorists helped strengthen a general xenophobia, and a major growth of political movements and parties associated with it. Large sections of society had finally turned against neoliberal domination, but under the banner of the extreme right. The fourth quarter was finding new occupants. Like their fascist predecessors (though only a few of these movements are fascist), these have solved the oxymoronic nature of egalitarian traditionalism by concentrating their attacks on ethnic minorities and international organizations. They have also been helped by the fact that almost no major political forces had been defending true social conservatism for some time. In economic policy, most conservatives had almost fully accepted the change-hungry implications of neoliberalism. Neoliberals, social democrats and many conservatives had all embraced anti-traditional policies on the increasingly salient issues of family, gender and sexuality.

The new movements make no real attacks on *Marktvolk*. In the United States President Trump makes rhetorical attacks on globalization, but almost immediately on taking office repealed the measures taken by the Obama administration to regulate financial transactions, the form of globalization that has had the most damaging consequences. In the UK the Brexit referendum was won on the basis of discontent with economic disruption, but the Conservative government is interpreting the outcome as meaning that the country should be subject to more, not less, global competitive pressure, and should model its social policy on Singapore.Choosing only soft targets, accommodating itself in practice if not in rhetoric to the power of the *Marktvolk*, drawing on nationalist passion among populations whose other political identities have become weak, it is not surprising that it is the rightist rather than the leftist response to the financial crisis that has gained the greater traction.

The only exceptions to this have been in Greece and Spain, where major new left-of-centre parties – Syriza and Unidos Podemos respectively – have been able to achieve major mobilization, restricting their criticism to national and European elites and not attacking migrants. The extreme right Golden Dawn movement in Greece has not grown as initially expected, even though Greece has experienced major waves of refugees coming from North Africa. There have been no extreme rightist movements in Spain, even though the country has experienced terrorist attacks from radical Islam. It may be relevant that Spanish conservatives never fully dissociated themselves from the Franco regime, and can still draw on its ideological support base. In both countries, the harsh terms set in the wake of the financial crisis by the coalition of the EU, the European Central Bank, the International Monetary Fund and private banks have proved more salient than any problems of immigration. The situation in Italy is more ambiguous, as the anti-elite populist movement, the Movimento Cinque Stelle, has had an uncertain profile. At times, it has joined far-right campaigns against the entry of large numbers of refugees into the country, and for a period it allied in the European Parliament with the British xenophobic party, UKIP. But it has never attacked the refugees themselves, only the Italian and European politicians it blames for not having solved the problem. The other two countries involved in the Euro debt crisis, Ireland and Portugal, have not experienced major upheaval to their party systems, though they have both seen some growth of small parties on the left.

There has also been some growth of small leftist parties in Germany, the Netherlands and the Nordic countries, and the UK Labour Party appears to be turning itself into such a party; but Syriza and Podemos are to date the only cases of major, continuing mobilizations on the left. Their future development, especially as Syriza copes with the difficult task of trying to govern Greece during prolonged austerity, needs to be studied for its more general lessons. Under what conditions does globalized capitalism take a sufficiently concrete form for mass mobilization against it to be feasible? And, more difficult, what practical policies can such mobilizations develop? (On this, see the chapters by Hilary Wainwright, and by Leo Panitch and Sam Gindin)

Different again are the movements around youthful, politically ambiguous individual leaders in France (Emmanuel Macron) and Italy (Matteo Renzi). These both came from the centre-left, but have moved to more neoliberal positions on economic issues and liberal ones on social issues. Both profess impatience with established parties, as do the new movements of both the Right and the Left. Are they merely late-arriving versions of the 1990s, Third Way phenomenon of Bill Clinton, Tony Blair and Gerhard Schroeder – in which case they are likely to repeat their errors of ignoring both the destructive tendencies of deregulated capitalism and the need for security and support of populations confronted with destabilizing change? Or are they capable of learning those lessons of their apparent predecessors?

In most countries, there is a larger concern: the new xenophobic movements are ousting moderate conservative and social democratic parties from their "share" of the fourth quarter. In some countries and at various times (Austria, Denmark, Finland, the Netherlands, Norway) conservatives have been happy to form coalitions with xenophobic parties; in others (France, Hungary, Italy, Poland, the UK, the US) right-of-centre parties have themselves moved a long way towards their positions; only in Germany has there been strong resistance to doing either. More surprisingly, liberal parties have at times done the same in Denmark and the Netherlands. Social democratic parties have so far largely stood outside this rush to the far right, though the refugee crisis has in the past produced some compromises with xenophobia in Austria, and overtures to form social coalitions against neoliberalism in Denmark. In the UK a small group called "Blue Labour" tries to develop an agenda that combines strong egalitarianism with social conservatism and respect for the traditions of local communities. This is a bid to redefine social democracy as a fourth-quarter movement.[4] Blue Labour is not at all xenophobic, and is interested in supporting Muslim communities, although most of its prominent figures campaigned for the UK to leave the EU. One

of its protagonists, David Goodhart, has recently emerged as a leading opponent of liberal attitudes towards immigration.[5]

Social democracy, nationalism and globalization

But in the face of the new xenophobic movements the quiet, implicit
nationalism of the social democracy of earlier decades is no longer
available. True, there are major historical precedents for an explicitly nationalist left. Anti-imperialist movements seeking liberation
from Austro-Hungarian, British, Dutch, French and other forms of
colonial rule frequently combined socialist with nationalist rhetoric. However, subsequent developments were not often promising. There are many examples, from the monarchical takeover of
Garibaldi's liberation movement in Italy to the disastrous dictatorship in Zimbabwe, to show that the Left does not fare well once
the goal of national independence has been achieved. Joseph Stalin,
who as a student in Vienna had studied the nationalisms that were
undermining the Austro-Hungarian Empire, made increasing use of
Russian nationalism in bolstering support for the Soviet regime. At
first the Russian revolution, which was after all based on the ideas
of two Germans (Karl Marx and Friedrich Engels), was internationalist; even the name of the new political formation, Union of Soviet
Socialist Republics, bore no national reference. After a period however came the project of building "socialism in one country". Then,
after the Second World War, during which the regime had stressed
national rather than class solidarity, Soviet socialism became
increasingly Russian in its symbolism, Jews in particular being sin-
gled out as "rootless cosmopolitans" who could not be trusted to
be true Russians. Today, as the current Russian president, Vladimir
Putin, and his associates rehabilitate elements of Stalin's legacy, not
only has the nationalist component of state ideology become overwhelming, but Putin has become an unofficial global leader of social
conservatism and homophobia. Outside the immediate Russian
sphere of influence, he is allied with extreme nationalist movements
in France, Hungary and Poland, and has won the admiration of such
right-wing leaders as Silvio Berlusconi and Donald Trump.

There are few examples of where socialist or social democratic
movements have survived compromises with nationalist social

conservatism. Today the non-aggressive de facto nationalism of the welfare state no longer meets the aspirations of those citizens who want a nationalism that excludes immigrants, turns its back on refugees, and rejects sharing sovereignty with international organizations. Globalization has stretched social democracy's capacity to sustain labour rights, redistributive taxation and a strong welfare state, but there can be no route back from globalization to the combination of free trade and national sovereignty of the first three postwar decades. That period was a temporary way station towards the ever-greater expansion of a global market economy. National economies have become far more inter-dependent, international financial flows more important, new parts of the world have joined the world market economy, enabling at least parts of their populations to climb out of poverty, making products that have reduced the cost of living in wealthy countries, and providing new markets for the products of wealthy countries.

For most of the period since the Second World War, politics was shaped around the conflict over egalitarianism, the horizontal axis in Figure 6.1. Modernizing rationalism was taken for granted, rendering the vertical axis apparently meaningless. As some observers noted more than a decade ago, the latter is today resurgent, and this is playing havoc with traditional political divisions.[6] For social democracy, there is a division between the better educated, young, mainly female professionals, especially in public services, that it attracts, who are strongly committed to modernizing rationalism, and the older, more male manual workers mainly in declining sectors, who used to form its core constituency, and who lean towards the traditionalist pole.

There are three potential ways forward from this situation, none of which would bring back the postwar compromise, and only one of which provides a viable if difficult strategy for social democracy. First, there can be a retreat into protectionism. This might seem attractive to many on the left, as it offers the possibility of restarting old manufacturing and mining industries, bringing back an industrial working class, and insulating an individual nation from neoliberal financial flows and the blackmail of international corporate investors. However, while a protectionist economy might protect a country from global capital, it creates a group of domestic insider firms who acquire strong political influence and form non-competitive cartels. Not facing international competition, they have little incentive to innovate and ensure the quality of their products. National social democracy had its greatest achievements in countries open to world trade – the Nordic lands for lengthy periods, from time to time in Germany and the UK. There have been protectionist wings to the left, as part of a general opposition to free markets and a concern for producer rather than consumer interests, but the strategy has mainly been associated with certain kinds of conservatism in France, Italy and the fascist countries, mainly concerned to protect the interests of local business elites, and is prominent today in the economic policies of Le Pen and Trump.

Working people tend not to benefit from such arrangements as they bring high prices and, eventually, poor-quality goods. Favouring producers over consumers might seem attractive to the Left, as workers are producers while the biggest consumers are wealthy individuals. But, given the automated nature of modern manufacturing, even protectionism will not bring back the large numbers of jobs of the days of pre-automation mass production. Meanwhile, all except the poorest are today consumers. A policy of restricting access to quality imports would be highly unpopular. Protectionism would be electorally sustainable under contemporary conditions only by being associated with a generalized nationalism and xenophobia, which is precisely the context in which the likes of Le Pen and Trump champion it. If citizens can be persuaded that isolation of the nation from foreign contamination is the highest priority, they might accept some loss of consumer power as a price worth paying. There is little scope here for social democracy.

A second approach to restoring economic sovereignty is that which will be followed by the UK outside Europe, seeking free-trade arrangements that are the opposite of protectionism. The dilution of sovereignty that occurs through membership of an international association of states is exchanged for increased dependence on global market competition, and what the UK government is itself willing to admit means following the "Singapore" approach to social policy and rights. This, like its opposite, protectionism, can probably only be carried through in a context of heightened xenophobia, rendering people willing to accept sacrifice.

The third strategy is to seek a more regulated global trading order. One reason for social democracy's weakness today is that its main point of strength, national democracy, is unable to access the non-democratic global level where the economy is regulated (or evades regulation). This global space is not mere anarchy. There are international agencies: the World Trade Organization, the Organization for Economic Cooperation and Development (OECD), the World Bank, the International Monetary Fund, the International Labour Organization, and regional trading blocs, of which the EU is the most advanced example. The political left is suspicious of these, as they have tended in recent decades to be neoliberal and to be far more accessible to corporate lobbying than to democratic or trade union influence. However, they are regulatory agencies and already embody important restraints on capitalism, such as the anti-corruption code of the OECD or the mass of social and cultural policies pursued by the EU.

The spread of globalization is unlikely to be reversed; in any case, if it were, the consequences would be dire, with a return to poverty in developing countries and increased risk of wars as nations began to build hostile barriers to each other's goods, services, capital and persons. The only future-oriented strategy available to social democracy is to seek a strengthening and democratization of international regulatory agencies, both global and world-regional ones. The single most effective route to their democratization is to bring discussion of their activities and parties' goals for them into national politics. Party platforms and politicians' speeches need to include declarations of what they will seek to do, *with the necessary co-operation of allied states*, to improve global regulation. This means abjuring the Quixotic temptation to wrap themselves in national flags, promising to defend the nation alone, treating other countries and international organizations as at best rivals and at worst enemies. This is what British politicians did for decades while the country was formally a member of the EU, leaving the country today facing the sober reality of an isolation that will bring heavy dependence on the unstable current administration of the US.

Objections to international social democracy

There are two different objections to this course. One is that it is doomed to fail because today's international organizations are fully tied to the neoliberal project, captive to the *Marktvolk* who can never be social democracy's allies. The second is that it means social democracy giving up all chances of sharing in the current resurgence of nationalism and general social conservatism, a phenomenon that seems to be popular among, although by no means limited to, some of its core supporters.

The first objection fails to notice the growing unease with pure neoliberalism that is affecting some international bodies. The OECD and IMF have both become concerned at the rise in income inequality, not so much because they are egalitarians at heart, but because they fear the consequences for future economic growth if the wealthy absorb too much of its proceeds, leaving middle-income households to depend on risky credit to sustain their standard of living.[7] They are also showing signs of awareness of the disillusion with globalization that is fuelling destabilizing xenophobic movements. These organizations are themselves vulnerable to the spread of these sentiments. An unfortunate exception to these recent trends in international organizations has been the growing neoliberalism of the European Union. While always mainly neoliberal, the European integration project has from the outset also included large elements of social and cultural policy, labour rights and codetermination, infrastructure and scientific research support, as well as help for declining sectors and regions. However, two major developments have made it slower to respond to the doubts about pure neoliberalism increasingly affecting the OECD or IMF. The first was the entry of new member states from the former Soviet bloc in central Europe. Although these have benefited considerably from what one might see as the social democratic agenda of the EU, their political elites are still likely, however bizarrely, to see much of that as a continuation of state socialism. They are a constant lobby for more neoliberalism. Second has been the extreme neoliberal treatment of the nations caught in the post-2008 crisis of the Eurozone.

But the EU, like the OECD, cannot remain indifferent to the destabilizing effects of what it has been doing. Neoliberals in unholy alliance with right-wing conservatives *within* nations face an alarming win-win situation: the more their policies destabilize working people's lives, the more the latter become xenophobic, and therefore the stronger becomes the conservative side of the alliance. But as an international organization this is no more available to the EU than it is to the OECD. As the chaos produced by neoliberalism intensifies, the EU has only one place to look for allies: to the weak but persistent forces of social democracy. And that gives social democracy an opportunity, provided it has strengthened its internationalist rhetoric.

The second objection to an internationalizing social democracy – the possibilities of reclaiming national social democracy's previous share in working-class social conservatism – raises dangerous temptations. As with attempts to reverse globalization, there can be no gentle road back to a period where dislike of ethnic minorities' unfamiliar cultures, general suspicion of foreigners, ostracism of unmarried mothers, men's resentment at women's entry into previously male occupations, or expressions of contempt for homosexual people could all be passed over or smiled at. The shared social democratic and liberal project of liberalization in all these and some other fields has advanced so far that revivals of social conservatism will be active, hurtful and full of hate.

The achievements of civilization can be a very thin veneer, scratched away at moments of tension and instability. Jews in mid-nineteenth-century Austro-Hungary and Germany thought that they had finally achieved an irreversible integration into their wider societies. The rise in immigration of Jews fleeing the pogroms of Tsarist Russia then legitimated talk of a "Jewish problem", which could be taken up by mainstream political leaders, like Karl Lueger, the first democratically elected mayor of Vienna, whose combination of progressive social policy and hatred of Jews made him a perfect inhabitant of the fourth quarter. Then catastrophic defeat in the First World War ripped away the final layer of the veneer, releasing the most horrifying barbarism. To take another example, it had seemed that the secular Tito government in postwar Yugoslavia had brought together a population of Orthodox, Catholic and Muslim faiths in a way that made inter-marriage and cross-confessional friendships possible. But the collapse of the Yugoslav state in 1990 ushered in an extremely violent and hate-ridden civil war of "ethnic cleansing".

The combination of economic instability resulting from rapid, inadequately regulated globalization, large-scale immigration from poorer countries to richer ones, refugees from Muslim countries, and occasional acts of Islamic terrorism, all coming at a time when social conservatism has been under general attack, is scratching at the veneer of our civilization today. In the societies of western

Europe and the United States its consequences will not be remotely similar to those in Hitler's Germany or ex-Yugoslavia, because our institutions are strongly established; but lower levels of unpleasantness can and indeed are taking place. The British and the Dutch used to be proud to be the most tolerant, multicultural nations in Europe. Now they are the sites of some of the most overt xenophobia. The Brexit vote and the election of Donald Trump were both followed by a prolonged increase in hate crimes, those in the UK not being limited to EU immigrants but extending to Muslims and Jews.

There probably are people who are irrevocably committed to strong versions of nationalism, xenophobia or other forms of aggressive social conservatism. But there are others, probably more, who, although sympathetic to such views, do not want to be associated with evil. These people are the battleground of the contemporary conflict. If established institutions and leading personalities legitimate even minor forms of xenophobia, the moral barrier moves back, and people can feel at ease with expressing and feeling a hatred of which they would in other circumstances feel ashamed. If, instead, such institutions and personalities explain what is wrong with these attitudes, they bring that barrier forward instead. This latter strategy has helped produce improvements in the place in society of immigrants, gay people and other potential victims of abuse, for example in the anti-racism campaign of the Union of European Football Associations (UEFA). Now, at least with respect to immigrants and ethnic minorities, this is being reversed. Every time a political party considers that, unless it joins the bandwagon of hostility it will be left behind, it only helps move the barrier in the direction needed by the advocates of intolerance. Once one agrees that immigration is a problem, one encourages the treatment of immigrants as strange, deviant and unwelcome. From there it is a rapid step to maltreatment, and the toleration of violence against them.

WAYS AHEAD

It might be argued that, although one should not help to legitimate hatred, it might be helpful to reduce the pressure of the forces that are causing the tension: if the numbers of immigrants could be reduced, there would be less occasion for hostility towards them.

This argument is somewhat weakened by the evidence that hostility to immigrants tends to be greater where there are fewer of them: fewer to get to know and to befriend. However, there are two social policy approaches that would enable some of the grievances of many of those who are seeing immigrants as the source of their feelings of insecurity to be met, without in any way conniving at problematizing immigrants themselves.

The first of these responds to the downward pressure on wages that at least in theory must follow any significant increase in the supply of labour, of which immigration is an example. This is best met by maintaining statutory minimum wages at a high level, and rigorously enforcing both minimum wages and labour standards in general. Immigrants are often unaware of labour rights, and in any case can usually do little to enforce them; this may be one of the motives of employers in seeking immigrant workers. Normally minimum wages are set at levels that will minimize loss of employment. If there is serious hostility towards immigrants in a particular country, it may be that this criterion should fall, minimum wages should be pushed higher, and some loss of jobs accepted. This will mainly occur where industries are viable only if immigrants can be employed at low wages. Growth will be reduced, though not per capita growth; and there will be an increase in imports. But immigration would decline. An example is the horticultural sector in eastern England, which is able to meet the tough pricing demands of supermarket chains only by employing temporary migrant workers from central Europe. This is one of the regions of the UK where hostility to the EU and to immigrants is highest. High minimum wages would probably have made the sector unviable; the British would have had to import more fruit and vegetables, probably at higher prices; but they would possibly also have felt less hostile to the EU. Similar arguments probably apply to hostility to Mexican immigrants in the US.

The second policy sphere addresses the resentment among some native white men of measures to advance the position of women, disabled people, immigrants, ethnic minorities and other historically disadvantaged groups, a resentment that seems to have been important in the votes for Trump and Brexit. These advances have been among the main achievements of a shared policy agenda of neoliberals, social democrats and moderate conservatives in recent years. However, they came as part of a compromise package in which, in deference to neoliberal prejudices, equality was defined as referring to equality of rights of categories of persons and of opportunities but not to the income inequalities of class. These latter were excluded from discussions of inequality, at a time when income inequality was rising. Lower-income native white males therefore witnessed various other categories having their disadvantages recognized, while theirs were ignored. Only the xenophobic right remained as a political force willing to define their concerns. Being of the right it necessarily attacked immigrants, the disabled and others for being "privileged" rather than criticize the truly privileged, except for attacks on the "liberal elite" for having looked after the disadvantaged categories.

In its compromise with the inequality-denying stance of neoliberal orthodoxy, Third Way social democracy lost a large part of a generation of lower-income voters to the xenophobic right. Those individuals, generally older people, can probably not be regained, but the mistake must not be repeated with the next generation. Social democracy has to stand boldly for redistribution and the interests and rights of lower-income workers as an important case among the categories that it recognizes.

The days when conservatism (or Christian democracy) and social democracy dominated political allegiances will not come back. Political forces of all kinds need to make new alliances, either within parties or across them; partly because these two great families have lost their hegemony, partly because there is a new major schism that dwarfs the divisions between them. For social democracy this means, first, seeking broader relationships with environmentalist movements, left-wing liberals and small socialist parties. But the rise of xenophobia has also broken the long-term alliance within social democracy between cosmopolitan liberals and egalitarian social conservatives. This requires action on two fronts. First, a genuine egalitarianism – and not just of "opportunity" – has to return to the forefront of social democratic policy. Second, social democrats need to become part of a broader anti-xenophobic social compromise with internationalist neoliberals and moderate conservatives, in which the latter two recognize that the globalization project can only be saved if it recognizes the repercussions of the insecurity that it brings to the lives of millions of working people. Social democracy may be weak as a political force, but its typical policies are the only means by which those repercussions can be moderated. One already sees some response to this in the changing perspectives of the OECD, the IMF and some other international organizations. There is no longer widespread enthusiasm even among neoliberal elites for the virtues of deregulated global finance and the superior capacity of the shareholder-value-maximizing firm. A coalition of forces of this kind is probably as good as things are going to get for the centre-left while the world goes through this prolonged period of global labour surplus and mobile capital.

The popular revolt that eventually took place because of neoliberal globalization is being fuelled by the extreme right, not the left. But social democracy can gain by helping shape the response to that revolt. We are back in a world of struggle between liberalizing and reactionary forces that we thought would never return after the defeat of Hitler. The liberalizing coalition needs to be very broad. Xenophobia unleashes powerful emotions and allegiances, slipping easily into violence. But only a minority of people actively want it. Humane cosmopolitanism has far less emotional power, but it probably attracts greater numbers. They are all needed now.

Elsewhere in this volume Wolfgang Streeck takes a very different approach and stresses the distance between socialism and liberalism. His position is rooted in a very pessimistic view of the values of moderately successful people in the post-industrial economy. He derives their values from what seems to be the logic of their position in the world built by neoliberalism. He therefore denies them the possibility of being able to stand back critically from that world. Thus, they can have no real concern for collective goods, and the evidence that many of them are worried about the environment is written off with the suggestion that this is merely part of their conspicuous consumption. Should the Left not instead seize on this evidence that neoliberalism has not succeeded in its attempt to destroy our awareness of collective interdependence, and build on the success that the environmentalist movement has had to extend that awareness to areas of social policy? Many of the families who are apparently coping successfully with the stresses of neoliberal employment conditions are not happy to be in that situation, and would respond positively to policies for improving the balance between work and the rest of life. They must not be written off as conspirators of contemporary capitalism just because they have to make the best of their lives within it.

Wolfgang also draws attention to immigrants and their descend-ants who seem to be more loyal to their country of origin than of destination, despite attempts of the latter to integrate them. But as well as the Turkish flag-waving Erdoğan supporters that Wolfgang perceives there are millions of other people in all classes who have succeeded in being simultaneously Turkish and German (or Muslim and French, Jewish and Dutch, West Indian and British, and so on). They demonstrate that it is entirely possible to transcend embedded-ness in a purely national sense of self to a position of multiple iden-tities – the kind of person that the world needs if human relations are to operate at the levels where the capitalist economy is already so highly active.

Both Wolfgang and I are here trading stereotypes based on casual observation. The sociological research that has been done so far on the complexities of life in societies where old conflicts between con-servatives and liberals are re-emerging to superimpose themselves on those between neoliberals and social democrats suggest a more complex picture. The research by Oesch *et al* and Kitschelt and Rehm cited above[8] suggests that the kinds of sector in which people in mid-dle- and upper-income groups work has a significant effect on where they stand in relation to the two axes of conservatism-liberalism and egalitarianism-inegalitarianism. Unsurprisingly, the research found that the higher up hierarchies in all kinds of work that people stood, the less likely they were to favour redistribution, but the more lib-eral and inclusionary they were on other dimensions. People low in the hierarchy showed the opposite characteristics, favouring redis-tribution but being more authoritarian and exclusionary. However, particularly among managerial and professional staff there were differences when work tasks were taken into account. Professionals working in inter-personal and cultural fields were the least hostile to redistribution, organizational managers the most, professionals in technical fields somewhere between. These findings seemed to hold across the 14 western European countries that Kitschelt and Rehm studied and even after controlling for income, education, gender and sector (public or private).

Research carried out in the UK and the US after the Brexit ref-erendum and Trump presidential election respectively gives further insight into current liberal and conservative values. Eric Kaufmann found that voters for Brexit and for Trump were significantly more likely than their more internationalist opponents to consider it more important that a child be "well mannered" than "considerate for others".[9] This suggests that it is quite wrong to see internationally oriented people as less able than those identifying strongly with nation to see value in caring about others.

These pieces of research are straws in the wind, but they do at least suggest that it is not misguided to seek out new coalitions of liberal and egalitarian values, and also that liberal values have not been entirely engulfed by neoliberalism. Social democracy must remain far closer to the modernizing rationalist pole than to the conservative nationalist one, sacrificing any attempt to share in the attractions of traditionalism, prioritizing *liberté, égalité,* but reducing dependence on those elements of *fraternité* that are defined in terms of nationalism and the defence of dying communities. Commitment to local community in general, and also to work communities, does not necessarily imply nationalism and interest only in decline. There is urgent work for local parties and in particular trade unions to recreate for future-oriented cities and economic sectors attachments that reinforce solidarity. Professionals and technicians, as well as the new precarious workers, in services sectors can all benefit from such a process, helping them maintain both occupational pride and resistance in the face of increasingly demanding, narrowly profit-maximizing managements.

This is not the place for a full exploration of these possibilities, but one can recall a similar situation in the early decades of industrialization. The plight of agricultural workers under the impact of modernization required the attention of the political left, but the answer was not to try to restore a doomed rural way of life. They needed to be moved on to see the possibilities of egalitarian modernization. In practice, most of them did not do so, but became the mass support base of conservatism for decades to come. The cause of egalitarian modernization was borne by industrial workers in the growing sectors and parts of the liberal middle class. Today the plight of manual workers in declining sectors will not be addressed by the nationalist conservative agendas being dangled before them, and they will probably no longer be in the vanguard of the kind of politics that can really help them. But others will be there. The precariat will never by itself be numerous or powerful enough to challenge neoliberal capitalism. But allied with progressive, liberal components of the post-industrial professional and public, cultural and personal service worker classes it stands a chance of doing so.

NOTES

1. W. Streeck, *Die Verkaufte Zeit* (Berlin: Suhrkamp, 2012).
2. D. Goodhart, *The British Dream: Successes and Failures of Post-War Immigration* (London: Atlantic, 2013); W. Streeck, "The rise of the European consolidation state", MPIfG Discussion Paper 15/1, Cologne: Max Planck Institute for the Study of Societies, 2015.
3. C. Crouch, "Globalization, nationalism and the changing axes of political identity" in W. Outhwaite (ed.), *Brexit: Sociological Responses* (London: Anthem, 2017).
4. I. Geary & A. Pabst, *Blue Labour: Forging a New Politics* (London: I. B. Tauris, 2015).
5. D. Goodhart, *The British Dream*; D. Goodhart, *The Road to Somewhere: The Populist Revolt and the Future of Politics* (London: Hurst, 2017).
6. H. Kitschelt & P. Rehm, "Occupations as a site of political preference formation", *Comparative Political Studies* 47:12 (2014), 1670–706; D. Oesch, *Redrawing the Class Map* (Basingstoke: Palgrave Macmillan, 2006); D. Oesch, "Coming to grips with a changing class structure: an analysis of employment stratification in Britain, Germany, Sweden and Switzerland", *International Sociology* 21:2 (2006), 263–88; D. Oesch & J. Rodríguez Menés, "Upgrading or polarization? Occupational change in Britain, Germany, Spain and Switzerland, 1990–2008", *Socio-Economic Review* 9:3 (2011), 503–31.
7. OECD, *Divided We Stand* (Paris: OECD, 2011); J. Ostry, P. Loungani & D. Furceri, "Neoliberalism: oversold?", *IMF Finance and Development*, June 2016, 38–41.
8. See note 6 above.
9. E. Kaufmann, "Trump and Brexit: 'Why it's again NOT the economy, stupid'", LSE blog. http://blogs.lse.ac.uk/politicsandpolicy/trump-and-brexit-why-its-again-not-the-economy-stupid/ (accessed 1 August 2017).

CHAPTER 7

WHOSE SIDE ARE WE ON? LIBERALISM AND SOCIALISM ARE NOT THE SAME

Wolfgang Streeck

Reflecting on the future of the Left we are too easily drawn into debates on what needs to be done to "solve our problems" – end exploitation, establish global peace, reverse the rise of inequality, restore the balance between nature and society. This begs the question of who wants those problems solved and is willing to do something, the right thing, to this end. Who is The Left, or can become it, apart from those of "us" who want to see it recreated and re-empowered because without it our reflections will never be more than idle chatter? Who are our constituents, our popular base waiting to be mobilized and organized, our class *an sich* whose interests, and indeed whose practicable interests, we can hope to define so as to coincide with the general interests of mankind?

VANISHING CONSTITUENCIES

Surveying the social landscape of the advanced capitalist societies from which we hail and which we know best, many of us have sympathy with and still feel somehow indebted to the *old working class*, the generation of trade union and left party members under post-war democratic, state-administered capitalism. Many of them are now retired, or about to retire. Their industries, the factories where they have toiled, have shrunk or disappeared, leaving them behind in their now depressed and decaying local communities. Their labour is no longer *die quelle allen reichtums*[1], they now depend for their livelihood on a society more-or-less willing to pay for their pensions and healthcare. In a neoliberal, turbo-capitalist society, such dependence is a stigma. Even where governments and the public treat them respectfully, the legitimacy of the social entitlements their generation has instituted is fragile, as indicated by recurring discussions on pension reform and healthcare costs. "Grandfather clauses" freezing benefits for current recipients that the next generation will not receive further de-legitimate the welfare state in its present form. They also reinforce perceptions of the old working class as an unproductive surplus population that, fortunately, will wither away with time.

When we were young, we sometimes found solace in the belief that "the revolution advances on the mortality tables". Something like this, I am sure, is today felt by the new generation of *human capital owners*, the new middle class recruited in large part from among the children of the old working class, who have moved to the cities where they live very different lives from their parents. The social marginalization their parents feel, their sense of being seen by society as an economic and social burden, is bound to breed deep resentment. The new politics of neoliberalism no longer has a place for their industrial-proletarian collectivism, not least because it required the shared experience of factory work to become politically productive. Alienated from the self-declared "knowledge society" of today and removed from their means of political production, many of them are now turning to the New Right, which has learned to cultivate their sense of undeserved inferiority. An important contributing factor seems to be that some of the new nationalist parties and movements defend the national welfare state in which the old working class has invested its political and economic capital and on which their livelihood depends. Their turn to the Right widens the gap between them and what has become the mainstream of "modern society". While the Left may pity them for their disappointment, winning them back seems difficult at best, and so would be convincing the rest of society that they are more than a demographic rustbelt from which nothing can be learned for the future.

Who remains for the Left to give support to and draw support from? To answer this strategically all-important question we may look at extant ways of life under "advanced capitalism", their different relationship to the market and to the economy, and the kinds of solidarity associated with them. One group that comes to mind has already been mentioned: the children of the old working class who have made it under post-industrial capitalism, at least so far – certified owners of expensive human capital, confident self-promoters and self-commodifiers, highly adept at marketing and networking, with a deeply engrained view of the world as a meritocratic tournament designed to detect and reward the best, according to inherited talent, acquired skills and relentless effort. They are the born, or trained, individualists *par excellence*, and therefore liberals at heart and to the bone. Nothing is left in them of the collectivism of the industrial workers of yesteryear. Individualism reigns supreme, and politics is there to protect and expand the freedom of the individual from the collectivity, whatever that collectivity may be. Democracy, then, is rights without duties, or more precisely: without authoritatively imposed and enforced duties. Rights, the model being human rights, come for free, from *a right to have rights* – and democratic progress consists in the removal of whatever obligations may in the past have been foisted on individuals as a condition of membership, detracting from the essential liberty of everyone to live the lives they deem best suited for their "self-realization".

Not that there was no place in this for compassion and indeed solidarity. Where individual rights are at stake – in particular rights to be different and not to be discriminated against in the market-place – they are almost religiously upheld. Equality comes from and is identical to the absence of discrimination on the basis of whatever ascriptive characteristic may distinguish an individual from others.[2] Democracy means above all equal access to markets and institutions. It also has a place for material solidarity and egalitarian redistribution, but ideally these should be voluntary, private not public, springing from an informally benevolent "civil society" rather than being formally obligatory. Rights of citizenship come for free, unlike in the past when they were linked, legally or morally, to military or other public service. Freedom and democracy mean the right to choose one's obligations freely. Since the draft was abolished in most western countries, no comparable civic duty has emerged anywhere to take its place. Parties or trade unions, with packages of programmatic commitments that one has to buy wholesale as a matter of organizational discipline once they have been formally adopted after "democratic" deliberation, are perceived as archaic, and so are the bureaucratic formalisms of traditional political organization. Projects, not parties, are the organizational form of choice: one can join and leave any time, as one sees fit, hang on as long as nothing more attractive appears, and not longer. Democratic centralism, as it used to be called, and party discipline of whatever kind are out.

Political parties or movements pursuing an alternative society, instead of specific, individual, and programmatically unrelated single purposes, do not thrive on this kind of motivational base. Any attempt to organize the new middle class must accommodate high fluidity of commitments, "non-ideological", fleeting enthusiasm, and a continuous building and rebuilding of individual and collective identities, as in "patchwork families", in "flexible" labour markets, and in project-group work organization. This very much corresponds to the possibilities offered by the new "social media" for individually-centred social networking, as a substitute for or, depending on one's perspective, a technological improvement over older, more stable social structures. Political engagement is voluntary in this world, funded by donations rather than dues or subscriptions, often taking the form of mass petitions on the Internet in support of specific causes. Basically, such engagement is a charitable activity. Compared to the new politics of disjointed spontaneity, the social-democratic welfare state appears like a rigid bureaucratic monster,[3] and the charitable giving of multi-billionaires like Bill Gates and Mark Zuckerberg is apt to elicit more admiration, in spite or even because of its capriciousness, than the tax-financed, routinized programmes of public social policy.

As to the political economy of the new middle class and its liberal libertarianism, we find here a strong belief in merit as the principal source of socio-economic status and in the basic fairness of educational institutions and labour markets, if properly arranged so as to offer equal opportunities to everyone. This combines with a general mood of optimism, perhaps linked to the need in the new service sector jobs to display a friendly face to everybody, customers and colleagues alike. Quasi-obligatory optimism and socially expected cheerful confidence in one's own market chances suppress concerns over social security, including in old age, and this deepens the cultural gap between the generations. That the world is a competitive meritocracy, and an open-ended rat-race is considered normal and nothing to complain about, not least since complaining may be read by others as a sign of weakness or of a disposition to underperform. With hard work in precarious employment under competitive pressure comes a demand for advanced consumption as a reward for and demonstration of personal success.[4] Conspicuous consumption often includes conspicuous attention to environmental sustainability, signaling social responsibility. Markets, for labour no less than for goods and services, are experienced as empires of freedom – whereas public provision tends to be found lacking in quality and attention to individual needs and tastes,[5] making privatization appear desirable even among progressives. As women in the new middle class are fully integrated in competitive career and consumption efforts in the money economy, families, where they still exist, have little to no time to contribute to the production and maintenance of public goods, in particular where building their human capital had required them to take up credit which they now have to service.

DIVISIVE CONFLICT: THE CASE OF IMMIGRATION

Whether the future of the Left can be in an alliance between the old working class and the new human capital owners must be doubted. Interests, worldviews and identities differ widely. An important example of political discord is immigration, an issue central to the politics and economics of contemporary societies. In the Fordist factories of the past, the political integration of immigrants, working side-by-side with their local colleagues, was promoted by trade unions, as a matter of both economic self-interest and political ideology. More recently, however, immigrants have tended to work in the small-firm service sector, which is typically not unionized. There they must be and are willing to accept any wage, outbidding their indigenous competition. Also, with precarious employment and rising unemployment, immigrants are seen as competitors for welfare state services and benefits, especially by those living on social assistance or old-age pensions, in a world of tightening public budgets where fiscal consolidation has become the order of the day. Moreover, in the larger cities where immigrants are most likely to find employment, they seek accommodation in the postwar housing developments built for and occupied by the old indigenous working class,

141

where rents are low due to public subsidies and poor maintenance. Here immigrants' ways of life jar with those of the older inhabitants, who find their accustomed societies disrupted and see their communities dissolve. In response, they look for new places to live, which they find only outside the big cities where free-market housing has become too expensive for them. As they leave, the suburbs turn into enclaves of – themselves ethnically divided – immigrant communities. Meanwhile the old working class forms its own segregated settlements in the small towns on the borders of the metropolitan areas where they live, resentfully, like a minority in their own country.[6]

Political division is reinforced by spatial segregation. In recent years, the urban–rural divide has become a main cleavage line in the politics of contemporary capitalist societies. Cities and their hinterlands have turned into political monocultures, libertarian-cosmopolitan the former and traditionalist-communitarian the latter. The result is mutually hostile, self-reinforcing political milieus that have little else in common than strong visceral contempt for one another.[7] Centre-left parties, in alliance with the libertarian wing of the political spectrum as a whole, have withdrawn into the cities and abandoned their former followers to new right-wing "populists", often insulting them for turning to the nationalist Right in search of political voice. As a result, the centre-left, locked into the cosmopolitan rhetoric of its new middle-class constituents, has in important countries lost the capacity to govern – in the United States, Britain, France, the Netherlands, Denmark and elsewhere.

While immigration is perceived as a threat by the former working class, it is not a problem for the new urban middle class. Not only can they afford to reside in the cities where they work, but they also remain undisturbed by the immigrants who live apart from them in their own quarters in the suburbs. Indeed, without continuing immigration, legal or illegal, seekers of asylum, protection, or employment, the new middle-class way of life would be unsustainable. Cheap immigrant labour is required for care and repair work of all sorts, performed on homes, children, the aged and the sick, as well as for cleaning and cooking and the delivery of goods ordered over the Internet to spare high-speed consumers from having to do their shopping in person and on site.[8] Career feminism in particular, and the family structure and family life that come with it, would be entirely impractical without poor people ready to make the long daily trips back and forth from their segregated quarters to where they perform their indispensable services.[9] If in spite of all precautions, the two urban classes come too close to one another, as in integrated schools where immigrant children threaten the proper preparation of the future elites, ways are found to stream the designated high-achievers into more private educational institutions where they get what they need for inheriting the status of their parents.

Perfectly fitting the lifeways and interests of meritocratic urban dwellers is a universalistic-cosmopolitan worldview in which free migration in and out figures as a natural human right and open borders appear as a state of political innocence with which governments must not be allowed to tamper. Communitarian insistence on older rights and local traditions easily appears racist from this perspective, and is without hesitation called so. Borders of any kind are regarded with suspicion and indeed disgust by anti-racist cosmopolitans, except where they are drawn by markets rather than by communities or states. Social integration is to be on the basis of universal values only, which makes social bonds superficial enough to allow for unlimited individual choice as well as for arms-length market relations, in all relevant spheres of life. Cosmopolitan human capital owners, with their natural affinity to market freedoms, see themselves as citizens of the world unaccountable to any national state, and the world as a duty-free market, for fine foods just as for employment and lifestyles. Their labour markets being global, or imagined to be so, they want in the name of equality and solidarity the same privilege to be extended to Philippine women desiring to care for small children in New York, Polish plumbers eager to fix toilets in Chelsea, and Moroccan marihuana dealers dying to enrich party life in Cologne. As documented by Brexit and Trump, and by Le Pen, Wilders, and many others, permissive-anarchic cosmopolitanism of this sort is unlikely to resonate positively with the old working class, let alone provide a foundation for a political alliance including it.

But what about the immigrants themselves, so cheerfully welcomed by urban cosmopolitans? For the Left, they are on the whole a political disappointment. Being happy to be where they are, they are not easy to organize. Miserable as their lives may appear to others, where they come from life was worse, or so they believe. Always scared of being expelled, especially if their legal status is less than

143

fully secure, they prefer not to stick their heads out. As their main competitive advantage is their willingness to work for less, and still less, they are unlikely to join trade unions, which in turn often see them as a new, politically hopeless *lumpen* proletariat. Moreover, they are far from a unified group, typically carrying their cultures of origin with them to form ethnically homogenous enclaves often enough at loggerheads with one another, fighting over economic turf and social status.[10] Traditional and often exploitative social relations inside immigrant communities are vigorously defended against egalitarian pressures from the surrounding society, helped by the fact that television, the new social media, and cheap airline travel enable immigrants to maintain close personal ties to their native countries.[11] Far from using host country opportunities for political participation and organization, many immigrants, and often a majority of them, not really having arrived where they now live, remain politically loyal to their home country and its parties and movements, and this seems to be so even where they are superficially well-integrated in their countries of choice.

A telling example is the large number of German Turks or Turkish Germans, often third-generation immigrants, who remain passionate Turkish nationalists. While they take sides in Turkish domestic politics, they mostly stay out of German political life, even though many now have dual citizenship (which was expressly introduced in order to advance their "integration"). The campaign in 2017 by the Turkish president, Erdoğan, for a new constitution that would greatly increase his powers involved numerous rallies in Germany and other western European countries organized by local Turkish communities, some of them accompanied by violent conflicts between supporters and opponents of Erdoğan. Members of the Turkish government addressed and were cheered by tens of thousands of flag-waving Turkish immigrants. Roughly one half of those eligible to vote did do so; of them about two thirds supported Erdoğan, to the great disappointment of the German public, left and right, who considered this a sign of insufficient "integration" (non-voters were applauded for being properly "integrated", and no-voters for having adopted democratic, i.e., German, "values" – Germans have recently developed extremely strong ideas, always nearly unanimous, as to how people in other countries should vote in their national elections: Brexit, Trump, Macron, Austria, the Netherlands…). The situation is similar with former Russian citizens who, as ethnic Germans, were admitted to Germany after 1990. In the conflicts between Germany, or "Europe", with Russia over Crimea and Ukraine they tend to take sides, as it appears almost unanimously, with the present Russian government. Also, Polish immigrants in Germany tend to support the present "nationalist" Polish government, against the freely dished-out "democratic" advice by German politicians and the German news media.

Moving on, would not the *young losers*, those who have tried but failed to join the new middle class, having in vain invested in their human capital only to be rejected by the human resource specialists and their assessment centres – would they, scared of the precarious life and not confident enough to forget their anxiety about their future, many of them supporters of Bernie Sanders and Jeremy Corbyn, not be the ideal constituency for a revived left politics? Sidelined in the rat race, overwhelmed by debt, their hopes disappointed, now eking out a marginal subsistence in jobs for which they are vastly overqualified, forever on the margins of financialized capitalist consumerism? Add to them those who may, in the not-too-far future, be made redundant by the advance of artificial intelligence – drivers of trucks, trains, tanks, and taxis, delivery men, soldiers, and meat cutters, but also lawyers, architects, journalists, and surgeons whose jobs may soon be performed by machines[12] – all of them candidates, perhaps, for a guaranteed basic income, free healthcare, and public provision of entertainment and education in the arts and humanities. Of course, we don't know how many there will be – although indications are that they will be more than just a few. Nor do we know how they will mentally manage the experience of being designated losers in a world designed for winners – low achievers disparagingly compared by others, and often enough by themselves, to the "high potentials" recognized early as such by those in charge of status assignment in contemporary capitalism. Losers tend to be demoralized; whoever wants to organize them must have a story ready that credibly reassures them that their defeat is not their fault – which is far from easy in a world so deeply individualistic and meritocratic in spirit. Ultimately, what this means is nothing less than that a new Left must somehow steer its potential constituents away from the late-capitalist lifestyle of *coping* as a test of personal worth, *hoping* as a civic duty, *doping* as a shot in the arm to either help with or substitute for individual achievement, and *shopping* as the ultimate reward in an honorable capitalist life.[13]

LIBERALISM, COLLECTIVISM, SOCIALISM

Will it be at all possible to draw the losers of digitalized capitalism, current and future, into a left political alliance with old labour, with (some of) the immigrants, even with (some of) the winners forming the new, urban middle class? Can their private frustration be transformed into public mobilization for fundamental social change, or will it continue to be culturally suppressed and politically pacified by occasional economic handouts providing them with a small share in the blessings of consumerism? One question is about the channels by which the Left would be able to communicate with them – a question that is in different ways also relevant in relation to the immigrants: how to lure the losers away from their Facebook and Instagram studies of Justin Bieber's and Selena Gomez's latest exploits – from their captivated entanglement in the unsocial diversion networks provided for them by Silicon Valley tycoons with certificates from Harvard College? More important, however, is what an alliance that includes them, assuming that their numbers will rise, is to offer them as a programme to act upon.

My claim here is that, today, a left politics that is not from the beginning doomed to let down its constituents must be more than liberal politics, while in important respects it must also be less than liberal. What Americans mean by liberalism is by and large what Europeans call social democracy: a progressive politics of individual freedom from traditional social constraints combined with corrective egalitarian intervention in free markets under capitalist relations of production. American-style liberalism emerged when classical liberalism, a doctrine for which individual freedom depended on a state-free market economy and a government devoted to economic laissez-faire, co-opted under the pressure of circumstances "programmes" like the New Deal and the Great Society, the War on Poverty, No Child Left Behind, and the like.[14] In Europe, by comparison, liberalism did not turn social-democratic since the political space of social democracy was occupied early on by the political parties of the labour movement. Liberal parties, unless they temporarily become social-liberal to govern together with social democrats, usu-ally side with the centre-right. Culturally, they may be either con-servative or progressive, mostly somewhere in between. Their core constituency being business, small and large, they continue to repre-sent strong preferences for free markets, balanced budgets, and low state spending, which they ideologically link to their central theme, the freedom of the individual citizen as a *bourgeois*.

Both European social democracy and American New Deal lib-eralism disintegrated under the pressures of the successive crises of capitalism after the 1970s.[15] The postwar combination of liberal-ism with welfare state interventionism, (also known as democratic capitalism) had never been more than tenuous; now, with "globali-zation", labour as a class, acting as a counter-party to capitalism on behalf of society, lost any capacity to strike mutually beneficial deals with capital and its management, except heavily lopsided ones due to dramatically changed power relations.[16] In response, American-style liberalism – and in Europe, social democracy – transformed into neoliberalism. In the United States this involved a re-definition of the "social question" addressed by the New Deal into the "social issues" of current "culture wars" over almost anything sexual, from abortion to transgender restrooms. In Europe, liberal parties turned life-style libertarian, dissociating themselves from more traditionally bourgeois values, and social democrats basically followed suit, often to the unease of their core membership. Politics, with class issues suspended under the dictates of "Third Way" globalization, turned liberal-pluralist, as ever new "cultural" concerns were paraded before the public by ever new groups claiming attention for their particular demands for free choice and social recognition.

This, I argue, is where *socialism* must come in. A renewed left politics cannot be a revamped version of American liberalism or European social democracy: global capital is not a class with which national societies can negotiate a productive class compromise. And it cannot be neoliberal-libertarian either, neoliberalism as an eco-nomic doctrine having collapsed in 2008,[17] and libertarianism being taken care of by neoliberalism's remaining liberal-pluralist politics of individual liberty, self-realization and choice, with its critique of pre-established social identities and moral obligations. The left counter-programme to libertarian consumerism can only be social-ist. However it may in detail be defined, socialism comes with the idea of society as a moral community, both imperfect and capable of being improved by its members, a collective order of human interdependence that precedes its individual members, or a collective good that needs to be protected from falling into the hands of individualistic predators who would privatize and thereby destroy it.

Socialist politics is stewardship for a social community that human beings need as much as their natural environment. It is collectivistic, both respectful and critical of tradition, as well as constructivist; and it recognizes individuals' existential dependence on a community, which in turn depends on and is entitled to the support of its more fortunate members in particular. As much as socialism wants individuals to be happy, it knows and lets it be known that a hedonistic life is not a responsible life; that people owe something to their weaker neighbours; and that a good life is impossible without responsible collective maintenance, not just of natural but also of social resources. Socialists also know that societies and communities that can effectively demand and attract moral commitment – that can, in other words, create and enforce social obligations – are and must be smaller and "thicker" than the imagined global society of contemporary neoliberalism-cum-libertarianism; citizenship, with the rights and duties that flow from it, just like the government by which it is constituted, is always particular and never universal.[18] Socialist politics requires and is possible only in collectivities that have a capacity to make effective demands on their members. In the modern world, such collectivities are organized as states that draw their moral authority from being democratic. While socialists must be, and are, willing to find a place in society for organizations other than states, socialism has been and continues to be intricately bound up with statehood – democratic and in need of democratization – and with its territorially delimited monopolistic control over legitimate violence.

In its move toward universal liberalism, the Left has largely abandoned collectivism – which can exist only as particularism, today predominantly invested in nation-states and national politics – to the radical Right, allowing it to pose as defender of last resort of the national arena of collective interest articulation and binding government. In the 1990s, with left-liberal and increasingly neoliberal individualism riding on the coat-tails of market expansion, the Left began to define itself as anti-nationalist – ergo anti-racist, ergo anti-fascist, in effect allowing collectivism to become associated with nationalism, racism and fascism. As a result, nationalists, racists and fascists could present themselves as the only remaining allies of those seeking national protection from international markets and corporations. On the Third Way, what had once been *left anti-capitalism* turned into *liberal-libertarian pro-capitalism*, if not intentionally then by default, by dissociating itself from the politically most effective collectivism, that of the nation-state. As a consequence, collectivism came to be captured by the Right, and in fighting the Right the Left allied itself with neoliberalism – with free trade, free markets and state-free globalization. Economic prosperity and social protection were to come, no longer from collective action, but from the beneficial effects of free trade made possible by neoliberal national reforms in response to international market conditions and constraints. In the new left-universalist-cosmopolitan frame of mind, borders became anathema, as did localized solidarity – discounting national-state government in favour of liberal-voluntaristic governance by experts, epistemic communities, well-meaning NGOs and problem-solving, knowledge-processing international conferences.

Having declared national politics and the nation-state obsolete, and having placed its hopes on global cosmopolitanism as the social solidarity of the future, centre-leftism has become indistinguishable from libertarian liberalism, most of all in the United States. The radical Left, for its part, seems to lack the ideological imagination to recognize phenomena like the one-nation Toryism of the post-Brexit British Prime Minister as an invasion of political territory that is by tradition theirs. Instead many on the Left feel a sense of sympathy with what one can call Silicon Valley progressivism: with its universalistic pro-immigration language confusing solidarity with charity, with its billionaire philanthropy, and with its utopian social policy projects such as a guaranteed minimum income for everybody, presumably worldwide. Redefining international relations to make them a vehicle of high-tech globalization while rebuilding social structures into networks of global consumerism, Silicon Valley progressivism needs politics to provide for effective demand in its borderless markets, so that electronic gadgets can be sold to "users" and advertisement space to corporations seeking customers able to pay for their products. There is no underestimating the attraction for much of the former Left, now (neo-)liberal Left, of the Silicon Valley utopia of a borderless global society based on universal civil rights – essentially the right not to be discriminated in free trade on ascriptive criteria – and governed by a stateless *lex mercatoria* in conjunction with circles of elite experts disposed to protect global universalism from the temptations of particularistic, national, state-organized solidarity.

Of course, socialism is more than just community-building and good government. Ultimately the reason why socialism must be at the heart of left politics is *capitalism*. Speaking of a Left that wants to be more than just liberal, or what has remained of liberalism, simply makes no sense without speaking of capitalism. It is capitalism, not democracy, that constitutes the unity of modern society, and it is from this unity that a left politics must derive its – socialist – programmatic and practical coherence. Capitalism with its peculiar "laws of motion" is the inevitable vantage point for any socialist project concerned, as it must be, with society as a whole. It is the fight against capitalism, and it alone, which makes left politics socialist – that is, makes it more than a collection of unrelated worthy causes advancing individual liberty and well-being. This does not preclude sympathy with, and indeed support for, such causes as equal civil rights for gays, lesbians, transgenders and others, although they can be served just as well and perhaps even better in a single-purpose, liberal-pluralist organizational format. To be closer to the core of a socialist agenda, causes must be related to the overall confrontation between capitalism, as a socially destructive political-economic order, and society as organized by left-socialist politics. Socialist feminism, for example, demands that men and women not allow themselves to be pitted against one another in the labour market; it has nothing in common with the exploitative "leaning-in" feminism proclaimed by American corporate business, or for that matter with centre-left ideas to make it obligatory for large companies to have a specific percentage of women on their boards of directors. Characters like Marissa Mayer and Sheryl Sandberg are capitalist icons created to elicit treacherous hopes and misguided identifications in real-life women struggling from day to day to make ends meet – propaganda tools just like other celebrities making money by way of the glorification of capitalist consumption and production.

FIGHTING CAPITALISM TODAY

This raises the question of what capitalism is, a question that I obviously can no more than touch on. I define capitalism for present purposes as a social regime dependent for its survival on the continuous expansion of the range and nature of monetized social relations, producing "economic growth" (as measured by the total volume of monetized transactions) by eating into its surrounding social context. "Growth" under capitalism results in, and serves the purpose of, continuous accumulation of monetized capital available to be invested in further accumulation – a process that is fundamentally inegalitarian as capitalist capital is privately owned and new capital accrues mostly to those possessing or commanding old capital. Capitalist capital accumulation is conditional on the social values that govern non-monetized social relations being replaced with market prices, making it possible to extract profit from them. Capital is invested – that is, combined with human labour – for profit maximization only, subordinating all substantive purposes of economic activity to the single, formal purpose of increasing the sum total of (privately owned) monetized capital. In particular, capitalism's need for endless growth requires that subsistence economies be transformed into profit-maximization economies, a transformation that requires complex means of social control, especially in societies where the level of material satisfaction is high enough to allow in principle for a less "capitalistically rational" life. Moreover, capitalism's dependence on endless growth, breeding with the help of ever more absurd motivational technologies an unnatural psychology of greed as the centrepiece of modern culture, diverts attention from the finiteness of the natural and social world, and from the wastefulness of production for its own sake. It also hides the senselessness of ever-intensifying competitive effort in a world of obscenely increasing inequality amidst unprecedented abundance, as well as from the increasing risks of collapse inherent in a growth model that is beginning to reach its limits.

Since the 1990s at the latest, capitalism has been a global system. But the social structures with which it interacts – from which it draws support while at the same time commodifying and thereby consuming them – differ by locality as repositories of territorially situated histories and cultures. As a result, the intersection between

151

capitalism and society where the conflictual relationship between the two is institutionally and politically regulated is not universally the same, and neither are the problems that pose themselves in it. That capitalism is now global does not mean that the battles between capitalism and society, even though they result from the same general tension, are the same everywhere. Political interventions to minimize economic risks and maximize social protection, slow down resource consumption, correct asymmetries and inequalities, defend substantive against formal rationality, and in general manage the contradictions entailed in a capitalist production process must take different forms in different places. In fact, they may have to protect local particularisms against the universalism of capitalist monetized profit-making: not everything has a sales price that can be compared to its production cost, and nobody can impose on us non-commercial obligations other than the particular social system to which we owe who we are.

The need to act locally to gain control over what is now a global system is one of the many problems facing a socialist politics today. How to coordinate across political jurisdictions, cultural divisions, linguistic barriers and economic interests if we cannot and do not want to speak the universal language of the general equivalent, treating social conditions and human needs as though they were convertible like convertible monies? What would a comprehensive and coherent socialist project for a global capitalist society have to be like to take into account the diversity and particularity of the human condition? Even if we limit ourselves to the "developed" societies of "the West", the task of inventing a "future of the Left", and indeed for a socialist Left, appears nothing short of awesome. In the past socialists could rely on collective action for economic self-interest as a preschool for socialist politics, although demanding "more" was as such never socialist, even if done collectively. Now we face a situation where an entire culture, that of "the West", has been made to believe in an open-ended happiness scale, corresponding to an open-ended needs scale motivating and necessitating the open-ended work and consumption effort required for the unending accumulation of capital under conditions of material abundance – the capitalist rationalization and monetization of the last remaining non-commercialized social relations. What we are dealing with here is a cultural problem, not one of inefficient production, and only partly one of unequal distribution. Our most formidable task may well be to talk people out of the myth that they will be happier in proportion to how much more they consume, proportionate in turn to how much more "money they make" – a myth spread and pressed into people's minds and souls every day, every hour by the most gigantic, most sophisticated, most expensive propaganda machinery mankind has ever seen.

Dispelling that myth and breaking its hold over our fellow citizens, and in particular those of them who have to struggle hard to keep up with evermore-demanding consumption standards, requires nothing less than a cultural revolution: a deep re-definition of progress and modernity. Remember how Soviet communism by the 1960s at the latest turned into goulash communism, promising its citizens to catch up with and overtake capitalism in private consumption. Not kept, that promise contributed to communism's demise and fuelled the consumerist greed that has, since the transition to capitalism in the 1990s, beset the countries of the former Soviet empire. What socialists must explain if capitalism is to be put back in the cage is that progress is not in having more of the same, but in replacing it with something else, not in a *plus* but in an *aliud* – since in today's capitalism, continued capitalist plus-making[19] depends vitally on non-capitalist plus-wanting, plus-working, and plus-consuming.

Ending *the era of plus* is not just a matter of whether one finds a less materialist life ethically superior – which most socialists probably do. If anything is certain, then that the capitalist-consumerist lifestyle of "the West" is not generalizable to humankind as a whole; here Malthus finally wins his case. Any left project must take this to heart. Ultimately it will have to answer the question how it will convincingly communicate the need for a global modernity that learns to conserve resources, physical and social, rather than continuing to use them up; to switch from creative destruction to creative protection, including protection from excessive free trade (not leaving this to the Trumps of this world); to appreciate the economics of subsistence as opposed to expansion; to slow down rather than speed up; and to start a *perestroyka* that does not amount to *uskoreniye*, meaning acceleration, which was the late-communist reform project of Gorbachev, but to controlled deceleration, de-capitalization, more local development, more collectivism and solidarity – in short, a project as utopian as it can possibly be. In the real world, perhaps, such a turn from, essentially, private to public and purchasable to non-purchasable means of satisfaction may be started by saturation or, on the contrary, frustration, or simply by exhaustion from the daily struggle for the latest-model SUV, running shoes, or mobile phone. Left to itself, however, it is likely to be nipped in the bud by social pressures, fear of the future, seductive design, sexualized advertisement and the like. To turn political, it needs to be supported by an ideology of, well, abstention – a social equivalent of veganism that is amenable to being politicized, meaning organized into something like a political movement.[20]

Is this asking too much – at a time when people are working so hard to turn their creative powers into "human capital"? If the revolution that is required to replace capitalism with something better is indeed a cultural revolution, then what might be needed for it is a modern, perhaps postmodern, variety of religion, both critical of the world and self-critical – a post-protestant spirit, as it were. There is little in the established religions of "the West" that could be of use here. Contemporary Protestantism has lost all distance to modern consumerism, having firmly settled in the *juste milieu* of the new middle class, perhaps with a guilty conscience once in a while that is, however, easily appeased if the eggs one has for breakfast are from organically fed, free-range chickens. Catholicism, as it always has, reserves asceticism to its various cadres of religious virtuosi (Weber) – and is even there under pressure to become less strict or else die out. Veganism is still a basically private obsession, limited to a very few urban dwellers; in fact, it has already been accommodated within the consumer goods industry's ever more individualized product range. Private abstention is not a problem in a liberal society; resistance sets in, however, if it is to be politicized. In Germany during the 2013 election campaign, the Greens suggested that Germans should commit to one "veggie day" a week, and employers should on that day offer vegetarian meals in their cafeterias. This was scandalized by the media as an attack on freedom of choice and contributed to the party's disastrous election result. The incident was reminiscent of earlier episodes when the same party called for the price for a litre of gasoline to be doubled, to the equivalent of €2.50, or for people to fly by air into their holidays only every other year. Both times voters abandoned the party in droves.

The only significant religious holdout against western consumerism today happens to be Muslim fundamentalism – which, however, can attack the consumerist lifestyle only from the outside by violence rather than from the inside by moral argument. Muslim fundamentalism may be seen as a "sour grapes" response to the end of hopes on the capitalist periphery for a kind of "development" that would ultimately give those living there equal access to North American and Western European prosperity. Thus a generational disappointment, in combination with Islam's historical culture of both strict sobriety and warlike militancy, is transformed into an activist ideology. Parallels between the Taliban and early Calvinists or Puritans are many: black dress, no music, no dancing, no alcohol, no fun, and a harshly restricted sexual life – a collective asceticism rigorously enforced in tightly knit and densely controlled social communities. Muslim fundamentalism must appear terrorist in Western societies, not just because it finds itself at war with the sinful consumerist West, but also because the atavistic social organization it prescribes for its adherents makes it entirely unsuitable for an anti-capitalist politics in western societies. In fact Islamist terrorism is today drawn upon to reinforce and legitimize the consumerist lifestyle claimed to embody "Western values", as after the massacre in Paris in November 2015 when European leaders called upon citizens not to allow the terrorists to disrupt their libertarian way of life and continue to go out, dance, drink, and listen to rock music, as their heroic contribution to the war on terror.

A left agenda worth its name must be a socialist agenda, conceived to heal society from the disease of plus-making: more money, more work for money, more consumption with money, more transformation of nature into garbage. But while there can be no new socialist Left without a politicized culture of de-commodification, no such culture is anywhere in sight. Perhaps the historical moment for it has passed, at the latest when Socialist Man was allowed, or had to be allowed, or allowed himself, to be as greedy as Capitalist Man? How will another attempt at socialism assemble a constituency willing and able to fight for it? Others writing in this volume seem to be more confident than I am that such a constituency, one for a Left that is more than just liberal while also in important respects less, will somehow be cobbled together as the need for it becomes even more obvious than it is already now. I am not so sure that the human species will in any foreseeable future rediscover society and in the process rid itself of its late-capitalist addiction to privatized, competitive, socially and physically destructive consumerism. Maybe capitalism as a political economy will expire because of systemic disintegration while capitalism as a culture and way of life will carry on, in helpless and hopeless libertarian confusion and disorganization, and more destructively than ever exposed to the vagaries of – increasingly unstable – global markets?

NOTES

1. In English, "the source of all wealth", as in the SPD's *Gothaer Programm* of 1875 and Marx's "Critique" of it. The labour theory of value (which goes back to Adam Smith) was a central tenet of early socialism.
2. For example, Tufts University's "non-discrimination statement" lists "race, color, national or ethnic origin, ancestry, age, religion or religious creed, disability or handicap, sex or gender (including pregnancy, sexual harassment and other sexual misconduct including acts of sexual violence such as rape, sexual assault, sexual exploitation and coercion), gender identity and/or expression (including a transgender identity), sexual orientation, military or veteran status, genetic information, or any other characteristic protected under applicable federal, state or local law".
3. Remember Jürgen Habermas, who in the mid-1980s, after his conversion from "critical theory" to liberalism, found the "lifeworld" under attack from two sides, the market and the welfare state, which he considered equally socially destructive.
4. And as a precondition of ever-increasing work effort. As Durkheim already observed in his *Division du travail*, we are in modern capitalist societies not working as hard as we do because we want to consume more, but we must consume more in order to be able to work harder.
5. On this, see W. Streeck, "Citizens as customers: considerations on the new politics of consumption", *New Left Review* 76, July/August 2012, 27–47.
6. C. Guilluy, *Le Crépuscule de la France d'en haut* (Paris: Flammarion, 2016).
7. K. J. Cramer, *The Politics of Resentment: Rural Consciousness in Wisconsin and the Rise of Scott Walker* (Chicago, IL: University of Chicago Press, 2016); D. Eribon, *Rückkehr nach Reims. Aus dem Französischen von Tobias Haberkorn* 10 Auflage (Berlin: Suhrkamp, 2016); and A. R.

Hochschild, *Strangers in Their Own Land: Anger and Mourning on the American Right. A Journey to the Heart of Our Political Divide* (New York: New Press, 2016).

8. Not to mention the regular supply by immigrant family businesses of the illegal drugs required for increasing the performance and enhancing the leisure activities of the creative classes. Immigrants also bring in and prepare at affordable prices the exotic foods needed for advanced cosmopolitan consumerism. For an impressive ethnographic account see B. Judah, *This is London: Life and Death in the World City* (London: Picador, 2016).

9. N. Fraser, "Contradictions of capital and care", *New Left Review* 100 (2016), 99–117.

10. B. Judah, *This is London.*

11. This makes them unlikely political allies for the urban middle class with its liberal causes, in spite of their symbiotic relationship with it. That relationship is in fact one of master and servant, and sometimes one of charity.

12. R. Collins, "The end of middle-class work: no more escapes" in I. Wallerstein *et al.* (eds), *Does Capitalism Have a Future?* 37–69 (Oxford: Oxford University Press, 2013).

13. W. Streeck, *How Will Capitalism End? Essays on a Failing System* (London: Verso, 2016).

14. It helped that in American English, the semantic spectrum of "liberal" overlaps with that of "generous" – and that "free" can mean free of charge, as in "free lunch".

15. Streeck, *How Will Capitalism End?*

16. This was different under "Fordism". See J. Rogers & W. Streeck, "Productive solidarities: economic strategy and left politics" in D. Miliband (ed.), *Reinventing the Left*, 128–45 (Oxford: Polity, 1994).

17. J. Ostry, P. Loungani & D. Furceri, "Neoliberalism: oversold?", *Finance & Development* 53:2 (2016), 38–41.

18. As the British Prime Minister, Theresa May, pointed out in October 2016 at the Conservative Party conference, where she promised to stand by the result of the Brexit referendum. In his 2017 Reith Lecture, the philosopher Kwame Anthony Appiah let it be known that this made her a hopeless western chauvinist. For a brilliant comment that says everything that needs to be said on this, see D. Rodrik, "Global citizens, national shirkers", *Social Europe*, 22 February 2017.

19. *Plusmacherei*, as Marx calls it in *Capital I*, with the sarcastic undertone that is characteristic of his writing. The English translation, "appropriation of surplus-value", has nothing of the caustic flavour of the original.

20. One should not forget that in the first half of the twentieth century, the Left produced a good number of radical-socialist movements and parties devoted not just to a planned economy but also, as for example the SAP in Germany, to what was then called *Lebensreform* (life reform). In the last years of the Weimar Republic, the young Willy Brandt was a member of the SAP. So was Otto Brenner, a man of enormous political importance for the democratic development of postwar Germany, where he was until his death in 1972 president of the country's leading trade union, IG Metall. Today the puritanism of the socialist life reformers, if it is at all remembered, tends to be considered a strange aberration and is easily ridiculed. Still, we might venture the thought that their commitment to a simpler, more modest life may today be more relevant for socialism than their belief in state-led economic planning with nationalized means of production.

CHAPTER 8

CLASS, PARTY AND THE CHALLENGE OF STATE TRANSFORMATION

Leo Panitch and Sam Gindin

In 1917, not only those parties engaged in insurrectionary revolution but even those committed to gradual reform still spoke of eventually transcending capitalism. Half a century later social democrats had explicitly come to define their political goals as compatible with a welfare-state variety of capitalism; and well before the end of the century they would be joined in this by many who had formerly embraced the legacy of 1917. Yet this occurred, just as the universalization of neoliberalism rendered threadbare any notion of distinct varieties of capitalism. The realism without imagination of the so-called "Third Way" was shown to lack realism as well as imagination.

However reactionary the era of neoliberal globalization has been, it has seemed to confirm the continuing revolutionary nature of the bourgeoisie, at least in terms of creating "a world after its own image". Nevertheless, the financialized form of capitalism that greased the wheels not only of global investment and trade, but also of globally integrated production and consumption, was clearly crisis prone. The first global capitalist crisis of the twenty-first century was rooted in the contradictions attending the new credit-dependent forms through which, amidst stagnant wages in the neoliberal era, mass consumption was sustained. Yet as the crisis has unfolded over the past decade, in sharp contrast to the two great capitalist crises of the twentieth century, it did not lead to a replacement of the regime of accumulation that gave rise to it. Unlike the break with the gold standard regime in the 1930s and the Bretton Woods regime in the 1970s, neoliberalism persisted. This could be seen in the rescue and reproduction of financial capital, the reassertion of austerity in fiscal policy, the dependence on monetary policy for stimulus, and the further aggravation of income and wealth inequality – all of which was made possible by the continuing economic and political weaknesses of global working classes through this period.

We are now in a new conjuncture; one very different from that which had led to the perception, at the height of its embrace by Third Way social democracy, that neoliberalism was "the most successful ideology in world history".[1] While neoliberal economic practices have been reproduced – as has the American empire's centrality in global capitalism – neoliberalism's legitimacy has been undermined. As the aftershocks of the US financial crash reverberated across the Eurozone and the BRICS, this deepened the multiple economic, ecological, and migratory crises which characterize this new conjuncture. At the same time, neoliberalism's ideological de-legitimation has enveloped many political institutions which sustained its practices, from the European Union to political parties at the national level. What makes the current conjuncture so dangerous is the space this has opened for the far right, with its ultra-nationalist, racist, sexist and homophobic overtones, to capture popular frustrations with liberal democratic politics in the neoliberal era.

The de-legitimation of neoliberalism has at the same time restored some credibility to the radical socialist case for transcending capitalism as necessary to realize the collective, democratic, egalitarian and ecological aspirations of humanity. It spawned a growing sense that capitalism could no longer continue to be bracketed when protesting the multiple oppressions and ecological threats of our time. And as austerity took top billing over free trade, the spirit of anti-neoliberal protest also shifted. Whereas capitalist globalization had defined the primary focus of oppositional forces in the first decade of the new millennium, the second decade opened with Occupy and the Indignados dramatically highlighting capitalism's gross class inequalities. Yet with this, the insurrectionary flavour of protest without revolutionary effect quickly revealed the limits of forever standing outside the state.

A marked turn on the Left from protest to politics has also come to define the new conjuncture, as opposition to capitalist globalization shifted from the streets to the state theatres of neoliberal practice. This is in good part what the election of Syriza in Greece and the sudden emergence of Podemos in Spain signified. Corbyn's election as leader of the British Labour Party attracted hundreds of thousands of new members with the promise to sustain activism rather than undermine it. And even in the heartland of the global capitalist empire, the short bridge that spanned Occupy and Sanders' left populist promise for a political revolution "to create a government which represents all Americans and not just the 1%", was reflected in polls indicating that half of all millennials did not support capitalism and held a positive view of socialism.

This transition from protest to politics has been remarkably class oriented in terms of addressing inequality in income and wealth distribution, as well as in economic and political power relations. Yet as Andrew Murray has so incisively noted, "this new politics is generally more class-focused than class-rooted. While it places issues of social inequality and global economic power front and center, it neither emerges from the organic institutions of the class-in-itself nor advances the socialist perspective of the class-for-itself".[2] The strategic questions raised by this pertain not only to all the old difficulties of left parties maintaining a class focus once elected; they also pertain to how a class-rooted politics – in the old sense of the connection between working class formation and political organization – could become revolutionary today. Given the manifold changes in class composition and identity, as well as the limits and failures of the old working-class parties and unions in light of these changes, what could this mean in terms of new organizational forms and practices? And what would a class-focused *and* class-rooted transformation of the capitalist state actually entail?

While leaders like Tsipras, Iglesias, Corbyn and Sanders all have pointed beyond Third Way social democracy, their capacity to actually move beyond it is another matter. This partly has to do with their personal limitations but much more with the specific limitations in each of their political parties, including even the strongest left currents within them not preparing adequately for transforming state apparatuses. The experience of the Syriza government in Greece highlights this, as well as how difficult it is for governments to extricate their state apparatuses from transnational ones.

161

All this compels a fundamental rethink of the relationship between class, party and state transformation. If Bolshevik revolutionary discourse seems so archaic a hundred years after 1917, it is not just because the legacy of its historic demonstration that revolution was possible has faded. It is also because Gramsci's reframing, so soon after 1917, of the key issues of revolutionary strategy – especially regarding the impossibility of an insurrectionary path to power in states deeply embedded in capitalist societies – rings ever more true. What this means for socialists, however, as we face up to a long war of position in the twenty-first century, is not only the recognition of the limitations of twentieth-century Leninism. It above all requires discovering how to avoid the social democratization even of those committed to transcending capitalism. This is the central challenge for socialists today.

CLASS STRUGGLE BEFORE CLASS: THEN AND NOW

The *Communist Manifesto* of 1848 introduced a new theory of revolution. Against the conspiracies of the few and the experiments of the dreamers, an emerging proletariat was heralded with the potential to usher in a new world. The argument was not that these dispossessed labourers carried revolution in their genes; rather it pointed to their potential for organization, which was facilitated by modern means of communication as well as by the way capitalists collectivized labour. Even though their organization would be "disrupted time and again by competition amongst the workers themselves", it indeed proved to be the case that "the ever expanding union of the workers" would lead to "the organization of workers into a class, and consequently into a political party".[3]

It was this sense of class formation as process that led E. P. Thompson to argue so powerfully that class was not a static social category but a changing social relationship, which historically took shape in the form of class struggle *before* class. Out of the struggles of the dispossessed labourers against the new capitalist order in England in the last half of the eighteenth century and the first half of the nineteenth came the growing collective identity and community of the working class as a social force.[4] Moreover, as Hobsbawm subsequently emphasized, it was really only in the years from 1870 to

1914 – as proletarianization reached a critical mass, and as workers' organizational presence developed on a national and international scale through mass socialist parties and unions – that the revolutionary potential in the working class that Marx had identified looked set to be realized.[5] However arcane the very term "workers' state" now may seem, it made sense to people in 1917 – and not least to nervous bourgeoisies.

Yet there was much that made this problematic even then. The fact that so many new trade unions and workers' parties had emerged that did not aim to create socialism reflected how far even the newly organized industrial proletariat stood from revolutionary ambitions. And where there was a commitment to socialist purposes, as was ostensibly the case with the social democratic parties of the Second International, this was compromised in serious ways. The winning of workers' full franchise rights had the contradictory effect of integrating them into the nation state, while the growing separation of leaders from led inside workers' organizations undermined not only accountability, but also the capacity to develop workers' revolutionary potentials. This was of course contested in these organizations even before Robert Michels' famous book outlined their oligarchic tendencies.[6] But these two factors – a class-inclusive nationalism and a non-revolutionary relationship between leaders and led in class organizations – combined to determine why the catastrophic outcome of inter-imperial rivalry announced with the guns of August 1914, far from bringing about the international proletarian revolution, rather ambushed European social democracy into joining the great patriotic war and making truce in the domestic class struggle.

What made proletarian revolution ushering in a workers' state still credible after this (perhaps all the more credible) was the Russian Revolution. But what Rosa Luxemburg discerned within its first year – that a revolutionary process which in breaking with liberal democracy quickly narrowed rather than broadened the scope of public participation could end as a "clique affair" – would definitively mark the outcome. Lenin, she noted, saw the capitalist state as "an instrument of oppression of the working class; the socialist state, of the bourgeoisie", but this "misses the most essential thing: bourgeois class rule has no need of the political training and education of the entire mass of the people, at least not beyond certain narrow limits". The great danger was that:

Without general elections, without unrestricted freedom of press and assembly, without a free struggle of opinion, life dies out in every public institution, becomes a mere semblance of life, in which only the bureaucracy remains as the active element. Public life gradually falls asleep, a few dozen party leaders of inexhaustible energy and boundless experience direct and rule. Among them, in reality only a dozen outstanding heads do the leading and an elite of the working class is invited from time to time to meetings where they are to applaud the speeches of the leaders, and to approve proposed resolutions unanimously – at bottom then, a clique affair.[7]

Isaac Deutscher, looking back some three decades later, succinctly captured the dilemma which had led to the Bolsheviks bringing about a dictatorship that would "at best represent the idea of the class, not the class itself". He insisted that in consolidating the new regime the Bolsheviks had not "clung to power for its own sake" but reflected a deeper quandary. Even though anarcho-syndicalists seemed "far more popular among the working class", the fact that they "possessed no positive political programme, no serious organization, national or even local", only reinforced the Bolsheviks identification of the new republic's fate with their own, as "the only force capable of safeguarding the revolution".

Lenin's party refused to allow the famished and emotionally unhinged country to vote their party out of power and itself into a bloody chaos. For this strange sequel to their victory the Bolsheviks were mentally quite unprepared. They had always tacitly assumed that the majority of the working class, having backed them in the revolution, would go on to support them unswervingly until they had carried out the full programme of socialism. Naive as the assumption was, it sprang from the notion that socialism was the proletarian idea par excellence and that the proletariat, having once adhered to it, would not abandon it ... It had never occurred to Marxists to reflect whether it was possible or admissible to try to establish socialism regardless of the will of the working class.[8]

The long term effects of what Luxemburg had so quickly under-stood would contribute to reproducing a dictatorial regime regard-less of the will of the working class – and relatedly, also to the gaps in the "political training and education of the entire mass of the people" – was chillingly captured by what a leader of the local trade union committee at the Volga Automobile plant said to us in an interview in 1990 just before the regime established in 1917 collapsed: "Insofar as workers were backward and underdeveloped, this is because there has in fact been no real political education since 1924. The workers were made fools of by the party".[9] The words here need to be taken literally: the workers were not merely fooled, but *made* into fools; their revolutionary understanding and capacity was undermined.

The fillip that 1917 had given to fueling workers' revolutionary ambitions worldwide was more than offset by the failure of the rev-olution in Germany and the Stalinist response to an isolated and beleaguered Soviet Union after Lenin's death, with all the adverse consequences this entailed. Though the spectre of Bolshevism hardly faded, it was the spectre of fascism that dominated radical change in the interwar years. Nevertheless, there was also widespread recog-nition of the potential of the working class as the social force most capable of transforming state and society. This perception was not least based on worker organization and class formation in the US during the Great Depression. As the US already was the new world centre of capitalism, even before the Second World War, this con-tributed to the sense on the part of leading American capitalists and state officials that among the barriers to the remaking of a liberal capitalist international order, "the uprising of [the] international pro-letariat ... [was] the most significant fact of the last twenty years".[10]

The strength of the organized working class as it had formed up to the 1950s was registered in the institutionalization of collec-tive bargaining and welfare reforms. The effects of this were highly contradictory. The material gains in terms of individual and fam-ily consumption, which workers secured directly or indirectly from collective bargaining for rising wages as well as from a social wage largely designed to secure and supplement that consumption, were purchased at the cost of union and party practices that attenuated working-class identity and community – especially in light of the restructuring of employment, residency and education that accom-panied these developments. To be sure, the continuing salience of working-class organization was palpable. This was increasingly so in the public sector, but it was also measurable in class struggles in the private sector which resisted workplace restructuring, as well as in the wage-led inflation that contributed to the capitalist profitability crisis of the 1970s. Yet the failure to renew and extend working-class identity and community through these struggles opened the way to the neoliberal resolution of the crises of the 1970s through the defeat of trade unionism, the assault on the welfare state and the interpellation of workers themselves as "taxpayers".

By the beginning of the twenty-first century, aided by the realization of a fully global capitalism and the networked structures of production, finance and consumption that constitute it, there were more workers on the face of the earth than ever before. New technologies certainly restricted job growth in certain sectors, but this also introduced entirely new sectors in both manufacturing and especially high tech services. Though this weakened the leverage of class struggles in important ways, it also introduced new points of strategic potential: strikes at component plants or interruptions of supplier chains at warehouses and ports could force shutdowns throughout a globally integrated production network; and whistle-blowing could expose vast stores of information hidden by corporations and states.

The precarious conditions workers increasingly face today, even when they belong to unions, speaks not to a new class division between precariat and proletariat. Precariousness rather reflects how previous processes of working-class formation and organization have become undone. Precariousness is not something new in capitalism: employers have always tried to gain access to labour when they want, dispose of it as they want and, in between, use it with as little restrictions as possible. There is in this context limited value in drawing new sociological nets of who is or is not in the working class. Rather than categorizing into different strata nurses or baristas, teachers or software developers, farmhands or truckers, sales people or banktellers, what needs to preoccupy our imaginations and inform our strategic calculations is how to visualize and how to develop the potential of new forms of working-class organization and formation in the twenty-first century.

There are indeed multitudes of workers' struggles taking place today in the face of an increasingly exploitative and chaotic capitalism. Yet there is no denying that prospects for working-class revolutionary agency seem dim. It was factors internal to working-class institutions, their contradictions and weaknesses, which allowed, in the developing as well as the developed countries, for the passage of free trade, the liberalization of finance, the persistence of austerity, the further commodification of labour power, the restructuring of all dimensions of economic and social life in todays' global capitalism. The inability of the working class to renew itself and discover new organizational forms in light of the dynamism of capital and capacities of the state to contain worker resistance has allowed the far right today to articulate and contextualize a set of common sentiments linked to the crisis – frustrations with insecurity and inequality and anger with parties that once claimed to represent workers' interests. Escaping this crisis of the working class is not primarily a matter of better policies or better tactics. It is primarily an *organizational* challenge to facilitate new processes of class formation rooted in the multiple dimensions of workers' lives that encompass so many identities and communities.

This organizational challenge will have to include developing socialist parties of a new kind. As can be seen from the two examples to which we now turn, the recent shift from protest to politics has already shown the popular resonance which a renewed socialist appeal can have today, even if it has only begun to probe what a consistent socialist politics would actually entail, and the barriers that will be encountered.

POLITICAL REVOLUTION TODAY? FROM SANDERS TO SYRIZA

"Election days come and go. But political and social revolutions that attempt to transform our society never end." The speech with which Bernie Sanders closed his Democratic primary election campaign began with these sentences; it ended by pointing to future historians who would trace the success of the long effort to transform American society from oligarchy to social justice as beginning with the "the political revolution of 2016".[11] It is tempting to treat as ersatz the rhetoric of revolution deployed here, taking the meaning of the word from the sublime to the ridiculous, or from tragedy to farce. The last time an American politician vying for the presidency issued a call for a political revolution it came from Ronald Reagan. But for all the limits of Sanders' populist campaign, the national attention and massive support garnered by a self-styled democratic socialist who positively associated the term revolution with the struggle against class inequality in fact represented a major discursive departure in American political life, which can be a resource for further socialist organizing.

Of course, the specific policy measures advanced by Sanders were, as he constantly insisted, reforms which had at some point been introduced in other capitalist societies. But when the call for public medicare for all, or free college tuition, or infrastructure renewal through direct public employment, is explicitly attached to a critique of a ruling class which wields corporate and financial power through the direct control of parties, elections and the media, this goes beyond the bounds of what can properly be dismissed as mere reformism, even if the demands hardly evoke what the call for bread, land and peace did in 1917. And it is no less a significant departure, especially in the US, to make class inequality the central theme of a political campaign in a manner designed to span and penetrate race and gender divisions to explicitly pose the question of who stands to benefit more from high quality public healthcare and education and well compensated work opportunities than African Americans and Latinos, while pointing to the need to move beyond the ghettoes of identity towards building a more coherent class force.

The key question is whether Sanders' campaign really could lay the grounds for an ongoing political movement capable of effecting this "political revolution". Sanders' argument during the campaign that he could be sustained in the White House amidst a hostile Congress and imperial state apparatus by a "mass movement" marching on Washington DC was not very convincing. Much more serious was his call after he lost the primary campaign for a shift from protest to politics at every level, including "school boards, city councils, county commissions, state legislatures and governorships". But even if this happened, such engagement would also have to be directed at the institutions in which workers have heretofore been organized.

The very fact that the Sanders campaign was class-focused rather than class-rooted may be an advantage here. It opens space for a new politics which can become "rooted" in the sense of being grounded in working-class struggles but committed to the radical transformation of the generally exhausted institutions of the labour movement. This ranges across turning union branches into centres of working-class life, leading the fight for collective public services, breaking down the oligarchic relationship between leaders and led, contributing to building the broadest member capacities, empha-sizing the importance of expressing a clearer class sensibility, and even becoming ambitious enough to introduce socialist ideas. This also applies to Workers Action Centers, which have spread across the US but which are so often overwhelmed by having to reproduce themselves financially in order to continue providing vital services to Black, Latino, immigrant and women workers. Becoming more class-rooted and effective would require building the institutional capacities to creatively organize workers in different sectors into new city-wide organizations, as well as develop a coordinating national infrastructure.

Similar challenges would need to be put to consumer and credit cooperatives, which are broadly identified with the Left, but whose primarily narrow economic activities need to be politicized, above all in the sense of opening their spaces to radical education about the capitalist context in which they operate, actively participating in radical left campaigns, and contributing a portion of their revenue to funding organizers to carry out such tasks. And to get beyond the frustrations so often voiced in the environmental movement with workers' defensive prioritization of their jobs, turning this into a pos-itive rather than negative class focus by speaking in terms of "just transitions" to a clean energy economy would also mean raising the necessity for economic planning to address both environmental and social crises, with the corollary of challenging the prerogatives of private property and capitalist power structures.

A new class politics cannot emerge *ex nihilo*, however. The Sand-ers campaign, initiated by an outsider in the Democratic Party, con-firmed that if you are not heard in the media you are not broadly heard. But whatever the advantages of initially mobilizing from with-in established institutions in this respect, the impossibility of a polit-ical revolution taking place under the auspices of the Democratic Party needs to be directly faced (it is hard enough to imagine that what Corbyn represents in the Labour Party could be sustained with-out a major institutional recalibration). After it had become clear he would not clinch the nomination, Sanders and the loose "movement" that had begun to take shape around him appeared at risk of falling

169

into a myopic strategy of internally transforming and democratizing the Democratic Party. In part, this is one of the contradictions in Sanders' choice to run as a Democrat. While the Sanders campaign showed that Democratic Party institutions offer certain bases from which to advance a left politics – lending his campaign a certain legitimacy and credibility within mainstream discourse – in the long run, an alternative political pole will have to be constructed around which social struggles can condense.

It was far from surprising that the thousands of Sanders supporters who gathered at the People's Summit in Chicago after the primary campaign ended did not come to found a new party. What happened there, as Dan La Botz described it, "was about vision, not organization or strategy", so that one could at best only hear "the sound made by the *Zeitgeist* passing through the meeting rooms and the halls, brushing up against us, making its way, sometimes gracefully, sometimes clumsily, to the future".[12] One key test will be whether, as it "makes its way", lessons are learned from the US labour party project of the 1990s, and links are made with attempts already underway to spawn new socialist political formations, escaping the traces of either Bolshevik sectarianism or Third World romanticism while nevertheless also abandoning the naïve admiration for Canadian and European social democracy that has long characterized so much of the US Left.[13]

This takes us from Sanders to Syriza, the only party to the left of traditional social democracy in Europe that has actually succeeded in winning a national election since the current economic crisis began. Syriza's roots go back to the formation of Synaspismos, first as an electoral alliance in the 1980s, and then as an independent, although factionalized, new party in the early 1990s. This was part of the broader institutional reconfiguration inaugurated by the Eurocommunist strategic orientation, searching for a way forward in the face of communist and social democratic parties having lost their historic roles and capacities as agencies of working-class political representation and social transformation. This search went all the way back to the 1960s and accelerated after the collapse of the Soviet bloc and social democracy's embrace of the "Third Way". In Greece especially, the Eurocommunist orientation was characterized by continuing to embrace the tradition of political revolution as experienced in the Civil War after 1945, even while distancing itself from the Soviet regime; and it would increasingly be characterized by the inspiration it took from, and a willingness to work with, new social movements.

Although Synaspismos through the 1990s offered enthusiastic support of European integration, as the neoliberal form of Economic and Monetary Union buried the promises of a European Social Charter, the grounds were laid in Greece, as elsewhere on the European radical left, for a more "Eurosceptical" orientation.[14] This new critical posture towards the European variety of capitalism was a crucial element in Synaspismos explicitly defining by the turn of the millennium its strategic goal as "the socialist transformation of Greek society" while increasingly encouraging "dialogue and common actions" not only with the alter-globalization movement, but with radical ecologists and political groups of a Trotskyist or Maoist lineage. The goal of the Coalition of the Radical Left, with the acronym Syriza, which emerged out of this as an electoral alliance was, as Michalis Spourdalakis put it, "not so much to unify but rather to connect in a flexible fashion the diverse actions, initiatives and movements ... and to concern itself with developing popular political capacities as much as with changing state policy". But actually turning Synaspismos, and through it Syriza, into such a party was, as Spourdalakis immediately adds, "more wishful thinking than realistic prospect".[15]

As the Eurocrisis broke, however, with Greece at the epicentre of the attempt to save the euro through the application of severe austerity at its weakest point, all the elements of Syriza threw themselves into the 2011 wave of protests, occupations and strikes, while supporting the 400 or so community solidarity networks around the country to help the worst affected cope. This prepared the ground for Syriza's electoral breakthrough of 2012. Syriza's active insertion into the massive outbursts of social protest from below across Greece the year before was a source of radical democratic energy that went far beyond what can be generated during an election campaign, however successful. What this meant was eloquently articulated at Syriza's Congress in 2013 when it finally turned itself from an electoral alliance into a single party political organization, in the conclusion to its founding political resolution. It called for "something more" than the programmatic framework that resolution set out. Since "for a Government of the Left, a parliamentary majority – whatever its size

— is not enough", the something more it called for was "the creation and expression of the widest possible, militant and catalytic political movement of multidimensional subversion".

> Only such a movement can lead to a Government of the Left and only such a movement can safeguard the course of such a government ... [which] carries out radical reforms, takes on development initiatives and other initiatives of a clear environmental and class orientation, opens up new potentials and opportunities for popular intervention, helps the creation of new forms of popular expression and claims ... Syriza has shouldered the responsibility to contribute decisively to the shaping of this great movement of democratic subversion that will lead the country to a new popular, democratic, and radical changeover.[16]

This sort of language, articulating this sort of understanding, was rare on the European radical left, let alone anywhere else. Yet as the Syriza leadership contemplated the dilemmas it faced as it stood on the doorstep of government, its concern to appear as a viable government in the media's eyes led them to concentrate, as was evident in the Thessalonika Manifesto proclaimed just a year later, on refining and scaling down the policy proposals in the 2013 party programme. This was done with little internal party consultation, with the leadership mainly primarily concerned with there not being enough experienced and efficient personnel in the party to be brought into the state to change the notoriously clientelistic and corrupt state apparatus. Little attention was paid to who would be left in the party to act as an organizing cadre in society. The increase in party membership was not at all proportionate to the extent of the electoral breakthrough. Even when new radical activists did join, the leadership generally did very little to support those in the party apparatus who wanted to develop these activists' capacities to turn party branches into centres of working-class life and strategically engage with them, preferably in conjunction with the Solidarity Networks, in planning for alternative forms of production and consumption. All this spoke to how far Syriza still was from having discovered how to escape the limits of social democracy.

SYRIZA AND THE PROBLEM OF STATE TRANSFORMATION

[This] is not a "betrayal". It's not about the well-known sce-
nario "they have sold out". We have seen that there was real
confrontation. We have seen the amount of pressure, the
blackmailing by the European Central Bank. We have seen
that they want to bring the Syriza government to its knees.
And they need to do that because it represents a real threat,
not some kind of illusion of a reformist type. So the reality
is that the representatives of the Greek government did the
best they could. But they did it within the wrong framework
and with the wrong strategy and, in this sense, the outcome
couldn't have been different ... The people who think that
"the reformists will fail" and that somehow in the wings
stands the revolutionary vanguard who is waiting to take
over somehow and lead the masses to a victory are I think
completely outside of reality.[17]

All this was said within a month of Syriza's election at the end
of January 2015 by Stathis Kouvelakis, whose interpretation of the
dramatic unfolding of events in his country garnered widespread
attention on the international left. Himself a member of the party's
Central Committee as a partisan of the Left Platform, he was speaking at a meeting in London and addressing the disappointments
already felt when the new government agreed to new negotiations
with the EU and IMF. Less than five months later, as these negotiations infamously came to a climax, he would, along with many
others, leave Syriza in response to what he now called the government's "capitulation", which indeed became the most common epi-
thet used by the international left. Yet the need to ask whether the
outcome could really have been different was now greater than ever.
And while the answer did indeed hinge on the adequacy of Syriza's
strategy in relation to Europe, that in turn related to deeper issues of
party organization, capacity building and state transformation – as
well as the adequacy of strategies on the wider European left, at least
in terms of shifting the overall balance of forces.

The common criticism of Syriza, strongly advanced by the Left
Platform, was that it had not developed a "Plan B" for leaving the
Eurozone and adopting an alternate currency as the key condition

for rejecting neoliberal austerity and cancelling debt obligations. What this criticism recoiled from admitting was that the capital and import controls this also would require would lead to Greece being forced out of the EU as a whole. After 35 years of integration, the institutional carapace for capitalism in Greece was provided by the manifold ways the state apparatus became entangled with the EU. Breaking out of this would have required Syriza as a party and government to have been prepared for an immediate systemic rupture. It could certainly be said that Syriza was naïve to believe that it could stop the European economic torture while remaining in the Eurozone, let alone the EU. At the very least, this simultaneously posed two great challenges: could such a state as Greece be fundamentally changed while remaining within the EU, and could the EU itself be fundamentally changed from within at the initiative of that state?

For a small country without significant oil resources, a break with the EU would have entailed economic isolation (along the lines of that endured by the Cuban revolution, yet without the prospect of anything like its geostrategic and economic support from the former USSR). The Syriza government faced the intractable contradiction that to fulfil its promise to stop the EU's economic torture, it would have to leave the EU – which would, given the global as well as European balance of forces and the lack of alternative production and consumption capabilities in place, lead to further economic suffering for an unforeseeable period. Despite the massive popular mobilization the government unleashed by calling the referendum in July to support its position against that of the EU-IMF, the intractable dilemma was the same as it had been when it first entered the state. That the government managed to win reelection in the autumn while succumbing to and implementing the diktats of the "Institutions" indicated that Kouvelakis's observation when it entered into the negotiations back in February still held: "People support the government because the perception they have is that they couldn't act otherwise in that very specific situation. They really see that the balance of forces was extremely uneven".

Costas Douzinas, another prominent London-based Greek intellectual newly elected as a Syriza MP in the Fall of 2015, hopes the story may not be over. He outlines the "three different temporalities" through which the radical left must "simultaneously live" once it enters the state.[18] There is "the time of the present": the dense and difficult time when the Syriza government, "held hostage" to the creditors as a "quasi-protectorate" of the EU and IMF required "to implement what they fought against", and thus "to legislate and apply the recessional and socially unjust measures it ideologically rejects". This raises "grave existential issues and problems of conscience" which cannot go away, but can be "soothed through the activation of two other temporalities that exist as traces of futurity in the present time". This begins with "the medium term of three to five years" when time for the government appears "slower and longer" as it probes for the space it needs to implement its "parallel programme" so as not only to "mitigate the effects of the memorandum" but also to advance "policies with a clear left direction ... in close contact with the party and the social movements". This is the bridge to the third and longest temporality, "the time of the radical left vision", which will be reached "only by continuously and simultaneously implementing and undermining the agreement policies". As this third temporality starts unfolding, freed from the neoliberal lambast, "the full programme of the left of the 21st century" will emerge. "It is a case of escaping into the future, acting now from the perspective of a future perfect, of what will have been. In this sense, the future becomes an active factor of our present".

It is indeed significant that the Syriza government's continuing ideological rejection of neoliberal logic – even as it implements the measures forced upon it – is precisely what distinguishes Syriza from social democratic governments in the neoliberal era. The crucial condition for the three temporalities to coexist, however, is precisely the "close contact with the party and the social movements", which Douzinas only mentions in passing. Even in terms of its relations to the party, let alone the social movements, the Syriza government has failed to escape from familiar social democratic patterns, as it distanced itself from party pressures, and seemed incapable of appreciating the need for activating party cadre to develop social capacities to lay the grounds for temporality two and eventually three. The neglect of the party turned to offhand dismissal when the government called the second election of 2015. As so many of its leading cadre left the party in the face of this – including even the General Secretary rather than asserting the party's independence – the promise that Syriza might escape the fate of social democracy in neoliberal capitalism was left in tatters. There are still those in Syriza, inside and outside the government who, operating with something very like the three temporalities in mind, are trying to revive the party outside government as the key agent of transformation. But whether they can manage to create the conditions for "Syriza to be Syriza again" is now moot indeed.[19]

Yet the problem goes far broader and deeper than with those who still have hopes for Syriza. It was ironically those who advanced the ostensibly more radical plan B who seemed to treat state power most instrumentally. Little or no attention was paid by them to how to disentangle a very broad range of state apparatuses from budgetary dependence on EU funding, let alone to the transformations the Greek state apparatuses would have to undergo merely to administer the controls and rationing required to manage the black and grey markets that would have expanded inside and outside the state as Greece exited the Eurozone. This was especially problematic given the notorious clientelistic and corrupt state practices which Syriza as a party had been vociferously committed to end, but once in government did not have the time to change, even where the inclination to do so was still there. When confronted with a question on how to deal with this, one Syriza MP who was a leading advocate of Plan B responded privately that in such a moment of rupture it is necessary to shoot people. But this only raised the bigger question of whom the notoriously reactionary coercive apparatuses of the Greek state, as unchanged as they were, would be most likely to listen to, and most likely to shoot.

Perhaps most tellingly, advocates of Plan B showed no more, and often rather less, interest in democratizing state apparatuses by linking them with social movements. This stood in contrast with the Minister of Social Services, who had herself been the key founder of the federation of solidarity networks, Solidairty4All, and openly spoke to her frustrations that Syriza MPs, even while paying over a sizeable portion of their salaries to the networks, insisted that they alone should be the conduits for contact with solidarity activists in their communities. The Minister of Education visited one school a week and told teachers, parents and students that if they wanted to use the school as a base for changing social relations in their communities they would have his support. However, the Ministry of Education itself did not become actively engaged in promoting the use of schools as community hubs, neither providing spaces for activists organizing around food and health services, nor the technical education appropriate to this, nor other special programmes to prepare students to spend periods of time in communities, contributing to adult education and working on community projects.

Yet it must be said that the social movements themselves were largely passive and immobilized in this respect, as if waiting for the government to deliver. Activists from the networks of food solidarity were rightly frustrated they could not even get from the new Minister of Agriculture the information they asked for on the locations of specific crops so they might approach a broader range of farmers. But they did not see it as their responsibility to develop and advance proposals on how the state apparatuses should be changed, even minimally, so as to cope with the economic crisis. For instance, how the agriculture ministry could have been engaged in identifying idle land to be given over to community food production cooperatives, and in coordinating this across sub-regions; or how the defence ministry might have been engaged in directing military trucks (at least those sitting idle between demonstrations) to be used to facilitate the distribution of food through the solidarity networks.

The point is this. Insofar as the Syriza government has failed the most crucial democratic, let alone revolutionary test, of linking the administration up with popular forces – not just for meeting basic needs but also for planning and implementing the restructuring of economic and social life – there were all too few on the radical left outside the state who really saw this as a priority either.

SIGNPOSTS TOWARDS DEMOCRATIC SOCIALISM

Whatever the final outcome in Greece, it is useful to look back at Nicos Poulantzas's "Towards a Democratic Socialism", especially given its formative influence on those who founded Synaspismos in the 1980s (Syriza's research institute bears his name to this day).[20] Written in 1978 as the epilogue to his last book, what Poulantzas articulated was reflective of a much broader orientation on the European left, already represented by Gorz, Magri, Benn, Miliband, Wainwright and others, towards trying to discover new strategic directions beyond both the Leninist and social democratic "models"

177

which, despite taking different routes, nevertheless evinced in their practices a common distrust of popular capacities to democratize state structures.[21] As Poulantzas put it: "There is no longer a question of building 'models' of any kind whatsoever. All that is involved is a set of signposts which, drawing lessons of the past, point out the traps to anyone wishing to avoid certain well-known destinations". For Poulantzas, the "techno-bureaucratic statism of the experts" was the outcome not only of the instrumentalist strategic conception of social democratic parliamentarism, but also of the "Leninist dual-power type of strategy which envisages straightforward replacement of the state apparatus with an apparatus of councils...":

> Transformation of the state apparatus does not really enter into the matter: first of all the existing state power is taken and then another is put in its place. This view of things can no longer be accepted. If taking power denotes a shift in the relationship of forces within the state, and if it is recognized that this will involve a long process of change, then the seizure of state power will entail concomitant transformations of its apparatuses ... In abandoning the dual-power strategy, we do not throw overboard, but pose in a different fashion, the question of the state's materiality as a specific apparatus.[22]

Notably, Poulantzas went back to Luxemburg's critique of Lenin in 1918 to stress the importance of socialists building on liberal democracy, even while transcending it, in order to provide the space for mass struggles to unfold which could "modify the relationship of forces within the state apparatuses, themselves the strategic site of political struggle". The very notion *to take* state power "clearly lacks the strategic vision of a process of transition to socialism – that is of a long stage during which the masses will act to conquer power and transform state apparatuses". For the working class to displace the old ruling class, in other words, it must develop capacities to democratize the state, which must always rest on "increased intervention of the popular masses in the state ... certainly through their trade union and political forms of representation, but also through their own initiatives within the state itself". To expect that institutions of direct democracy outside the state can simply displace the old state in a single revolutionary rupture in fact avoided all the difficult questions of political representation and opens the way for a new authoritarian statism.[23]

Indeed, as Andre Gorz had already insisted in his pathbreaking essay on "Reform and Revolution" a decade earlier, taking off from liberal democracy on "the peaceful road to socialism" was not a matter of adopting "an *a priori* option for gradualism; nor of an *a priori* refusal of violent revolution or armed insurrection. It is a consequence of the latter's actual impossibility in the European context".[24] The advancement of what Gorz called a "socialist strategy of progressive reforms" did not mean the "installation of islands of socialism in a capitalist ocean", but rather as involving the types of "structural reforms or non-reformist reforms" which could not be institutionalized so as to close off class antagonism but which allowed for further challenges to the balance of power and logic of capitalism and thereby introduce a dynamic that allowed the process to go further. In calling for the creation of new "centres of social control and direct democracy" outside the state, Gorz was far sighted in terms of what this could contribute to a broad process of new class formation with revolutionary potential, not least by extending to "the labour of ideological research" and more generally to the transformative capacities of "cultural labour aiming at the overthrow of norms and schemata of social consciousness". This would be essential for ensuring that "the revolutionary movements' capacity for action and hegemony is enriched and confirmed by its capacity to inspire ... the autonomous activity of town planners, architects, doctors, teachers and psychologists".[25]

What this left aside, however, were the crucial changes in state structures that would need to attend this process. Poulantzas went to the heart of the matter, a decade later, stressing that on "the democratic road to socialism, the long process of taking power essentially consists in the spreading, development, coordination and direction of those diffuse centres of resistance which the masses always possess within the state networks, in such a way that they become real centres of power on the strategic terrain of the state". Even Gramsci, as Poulantzas pointed out "was unable to pose the problem in all its amplitude", since his "war of position" was "conceived as the application of Lenin's model/strategy to the 'different concrete conditions of the West' without actually addressing how to change state

179

apparatuses".[26] Yet it must also be said that Poulantzas, even while highlighting the need for taking up the challenge of state transformation, did not himself get very far in detailing what actually changing the materiality of state apparatuses would entail in specific instances. Lurking here was the theoretical problem Miliband had identified of not differentiating state power from class power and therefore not specifying sufficiently how the modalities and capacities involved in exercising capitalist state power would be changed into different modalities with structurally transformative capacities.[27] And as Goran Therborn pointed out, in envisaging an important role for unions of state employees in the process of transforming state apparatuses, it was necessary to address the problem that "state bureaucrats and managers will not thereby disappear, and problems of popular control will remain", thereby continuing to pose "serious and complicated questions" for the state transformation through socialist democracy.[28]

Far too little attention has since been paid by socialists to the challenges this poses.[29] While the recognition that neither insurrectionary politics to "smash the state" nor the social democratic illusion of using the extant state to introduce progressive policies became more and more common, this was accompanied with a penchant for developing "market socialist" models in the late 1980s which has subsequently been succeeded by a spate of radical left literature which – almost in a mirror image of neoliberalism while entirely avoiding coming to grips with the transformation of the state – weakly point to examples of cooperatives and self-managed enterprises as directly bearing socialist potential.[30] Replicated here is exactly what Poulantzas identified in the conception of those for whom "the only way to avoid statism is to place oneself outside the state. The way forward would then be, without going as far as dual power simply to block the path of the state from the outside". Yet by concentrating exclusively on "breaking power up and scattering it among an infinity of micro-powers", the result is that the "movement is prevented from intervening in actual transformations of the state, and the two processes are simply kept running along parallel lines".[31]

CONCLUSIONS

Political hopes are inseparable from notions of what is possible. And possibility is itself intimately related to class formation, the role of parties in this and developing confidence in class institutions, and especially the question of potentials to transform the state. The alliances that socialist parties would have to enter into, not least in face of the growing threat from the far right of the political spectrum, should not just be amongst elites but be directed at new working-class formation of the broadest possible kind; and given the uneven capacities of the class, also be directed at developing its actual potential to become the transformative agent in a transition to socialism. New socialist parties cannot, however, see themselves as a kind of omnipotent *deus ex machina* in society. Precisely in order not to draw back from the "prodigious scope of their own aims", as Marx brilliantly wrote in *The Eighteenth Brumaire*, they must "engage in perpetual self-criticism" and deride "the inadequacies, weak points and pitiful aspects of their first attempts".[32] Developing commitments to socialism – getting socialism seriously on the agenda – consequently requires not only addressing the question of political agency, but overcoming a prevailing sense that even sympathetic governments will either be stymied by state apparatuses hostile to the socialist project, and/or that in a globalized world the problem in any case lies beyond the nation state.

To stress the importance of a democratic socialist strategy for entering the state through elections to the end of transforming the state is today less than ever – amidst the deep political and social as well as economic contradictions of the neoliberal era – a matter of discovering a smooth gradual road to socialism. Ruptures, or extended series of ruptures, are inescapable. This is so because of the contradictions inherent in reaching beyond capitalism while still being of it, and the virtual inevitability of conditions being premature as the project is attempted in "circumstances not of our own choosing". The contradictions for any radical government that would be engaged in this process will include responsibilities for managing a capitalist economy that is likely in crisis while simultaneously trying to satisfy popular expectations for the promised relief, and yet also embarking on the longer-term commitment to transform the state, i.e., not pushing the latter off to an indefinite future. It is this tension among the various new state responsibilities that makes the role of new socialist parties which will bring such governments to office so fundamental.

Given the legitimacy and resources that inevitably will accrue to those party leaders who form the government, the autonomy of the party is crucial in order to counter the pull of those leaders towards social democratization. The party must more than ever keep its feet in the movements and, far from trying to direct them, remain the central site for democratic strategic debate in light of their diverse activities. This is why strategic preparations undertaken well before entering the state on how to avoid replicating the experience with social democracy are so very important. But even with this, the process of transforming the state cannot help but be complex, uncertain, crisis-ridden, with repeated interruptions and possibly even reversals. Beginning with election to local or regional levels of the state would allow for developing capacities of state transformation before coming to national power. Developing alternative means of producing and distributing food, healthcare and other necessities depends on autonomous movements moving in these directions through takeovers of land, idle buildings, threatened factories and transportation networks. All this in turn would have to be supported and furthered through more radical changes in the state that would range over time from codifying new collective property rights to developing and coordinating agencies of democratic planning. At some points in this process more or less dramatic initiatives of nationalization and socialization of industry and finance would have to take place.

For state apparatuses to be transformed so as to play these roles, their institutional modalities would need to undergo fundamental transformations, given how they are now structured so as to reproduce capitalist social relations. State employees would need to become explicit agents of transformation, aided and sustained in this respect by their unions and the broader labour movement. Rather than expressing defensive particularism, unions would need to be changed fundamentally themselves so as to actively be engaged in developing state workers' transformational capacities, including by establishing councils that link them to the recipients of state services.

Of course, the possibility of such state transformations will not be determined by what happens in one country alone. During the era of neoliberalism state apparatuses have become deeply intertwined with transnational institutions, treaties and regulations to manage and reproduce global capitalism. This has nothing at all to do with capital bypassing the nation state and coming to rely on a transnational state. Both the nature of the current crisis and the response to it have proved once again how much states still matter. Even in the most elaborate transnational institutional formation, the European Union, the centre of political gravity lies not in the supranational state apparatus headquartered in Brussels. It is, rather, the asymmetric economic and political power relations among the states of Europe which really determines what the EU is and does. Any project for democratization at an international scale, such as those being advanced by many of the Left for the EU in the wake of the Syriza experience, still depends on the balance of class forces and the particular structures within each nation state. Changes in international institutions are therefore contingent on transformations at the level of nation states. And the changes in international state apparatuses that should be pursued by socialists are those that would allow more room for manoeuvre within each state. What socialist internationalism must mean today is an orientation to shifting the balances of forces in other countries and in international bodies so as to create more space for transformative forces in every country. This was one of the key lessons of 1917, and it is all the more true a century later.

NOTES

1. P. Anderson, "Renewals", *New Left Review* 1 (Jan–Feb 2000), 7, 13; "Whatever limitations persist to its practice, neo-liberalism as a set of principles rules undivided across the globe: the most successful ideology in world history".

2. A. Murray, "Jeremy Corbyn and the battle for socialism", *Jacobin*, 7 February 2016, www.jacobinmag.com/2016/02/corbyn-socialism-labour-left-tony-benn-miliband/ (accessed 6 August 2017).

3. Marx, *Later Political Writings*, (Cambridge: Cambridge University Press, 1996), 9–10.

4. See E. P. Thompson, *The Making of the English Working Class* (New York: Pantheon, 1964), 9–11; and "Eighteenth-century English society: class struggle without class", *Social History* 3:2 (1978), 133–65.

5. E. H. Hobsbawm, "The making of the working class, 1870–1914", chapter 5 of *Uncommon People: Resistance, Rebellion and Jazz* (New York: New Press, 1999), 58–9. See especially, G. Eley, *Forging Democracy: The History of the Left in Europe, 1850–2000* (New York: Oxford University Press, 2002).

6. R. Michels, *Political Parties: A Sociological Study of the Oligarchical Tendencies of Modern Democracy* [1911] (New York: Free Press, 1962).

7. "The Russian Revolution" in P. Hudis & K. Anderson (eds), *The Rosa Luxemburg Reader* (New York: Monthly Review Press, 2004), 304–6.

8. I. Deutscher, *The Prophet Armed* (Oxford: Oxford University Press, 1954), 505–6.

9. Quoted in L. Panitch & S. Gindin, "Moscow, Togliatti, Yaroslavl: Perspectives on Perestroika" in D. Benedict *et al.* (eds), *Canadians Look at Soviet Auto Workers' Unions* (Toronto: CAW, 1992), 19.

10. "An American proposal", *Fortune*, May 1942. See L. Panitch & S. Gindin, *The Making of Global Capitalism: The Political Economy of American Empire* (London: Verso, 2012), 67–8.

11. Bernie Sanders, "Prepared remarks: the political revolution continues", 16 June 2016, https://berniesanders.com/political-revolution-continues/ (accessed 6 August 2017).

12. D. La Botz, "Life after Bernie: people's summit searches for the movement's political future", *New Politics*, 21 June 2016, http://newpol.org/content/life-after-bernie-people%E2%80%99s-summit-searches-movement%E2%80%99s-political-future (accessed 6 August 2017).

13. See S. Williams & R. Awatramani, "New working-class organizations and the social movement left" and M. Dudzic & A. Reed, Jr., "The crisis of labour and the left in the United States", *Socialist Register 2015*.

14. See C. Eleftheriou, "The uneasy 'symbiosis': factionalism and radical politics in Synaspismos", paper prepared for Fourth Hellenic Observatory PhD Symposium, n.d..

15. M. Spourdalakis, "Left strategy in the Greek cauldron: explaining Syriza's success", *Socialist Register 2013*, 102.

16. https://left.gr/news/political-resolution-1st-congress-syriza (accessed 6 August 2017).

17. "Syriza and socialist strategy", *International Socialism* 146 (April 2015), transcript of a debate between Alec Callinicos and Stathis Kouvelakis, London, 25 February 2015.

18. C. Douzinas, "The Left in power? Notes on Syriza's rise, fall and (possible) second rise", http://nearfuturesonline.org/the-left-in-power-notes-on-syrizas-rise-fall-and-possible-second-rise/ (accessed 27 May 2016).

19. M. Spourdalakis, "Becoming Syriza again," *Jacobin*, 31 January 2016 https://www.jacobinmag.com/2016/01/syriza-memorandum-troika-left-platform-tsipras-austerity-government/ (accessed 6 August 2017).

20. N. Poulantzas, "Towards a democratic socialism", *State, Power, Socialism* (London: New Left Books, 1978).

21. A. Gorz, "Reform and revolution", *Socialist Register 1968*; L. Magri, "Problems of the Marxist theory of the revolutionary party", *New Left Review* I:60 (Mar/Apr 1970); T. Benn, *The New Politics: A Socialist Reconnaissance*, Fabian Tract 402 (1970); R. Miliband, "Moving on", *Socialist Register 1976*, and *Marxism and Politics* (Oxford: Oxford University Press, 1977).

22. N. Poulantzas, "Towards a democratic socialism", 257–8, 260–1.

23. *Ibid.*, 256, 258, 261.

24. A. Gorz, "Reform and revolution", 112.

25. *Ibid.*, 132–3. Lucio Magri similarly called for new workers councils "right across society (factories, offices, schools), with their own structures as mediating organizations between party, union, and state institutions, for which all of the latter needed to act as elements of stimulus and synthesis". And even though he presented this in terms of the "need for a creative revival of the theme of *soviets* [as] essential to resolve the theoretical and strategic problems of the Western Revolution", this was directed at offsetting the total dominance of the party, and emphatically did not mean re-endorsing a dual power strategy for smashing the state ("Problems of the Marxist theory of the revolutionary party", 128.)

26. Poulantzas, *State, Power, Socialism*, 256, 258.

27. R. Miliband, *Class Power and State Power* (London: Verso, 1983), esp. chapters 2–4.

28. G. Therborn, *What Does the Ruling Class do When it Rules? State Apparatuses and State Power under Feudalism, Capitalism, and Socialism* (London: New Left Books, 1978), 279–80.

29. See, however, G. Albo, D. Langille & L. Panitch (eds), *A Different Kind of State: Popular Power and Democratic Administration* (Toronto: Oxford University Press, 1993).

30. See the critique of recent books in this vein by Alperowitz, Wolfe and Wright in S. Gindin, "Chasing Utopia", *Jacobin*, 10 March 2016. https://www.jacobinmag.com/2016/03/workers-control-coops-wright-wolff-alperovitz/ (accessed 6 August 2017).

31. Poulantzas, *State, Power, Socialism*, 262.

32. Marx, *Later Political Writings*, 35.

CHAPTER 9

CLOSING THOUGHTS

Matthew Watson

This volume makes for inspirational reading. The analysis is never anything less than penetrating, the conclusions profound. Read individually, we begin to see the current political predicaments of both the parliamentary and the extra-parliamentary left through the eyes of leading thinkers of their generation, every one of whom has gained a well-deserved reputation for the clarity of their writing on the never-ending drama of left politics in a largely hostile world. I am merely one member of a following generation who was schooled in the issues of left-political reinvigoration through familiarising myself with their work when I was a student. Read collectively, their contributions remind me once again today of lessons that a younger me learnt from their earlier insights. The world moves on, the issues of the day change, the targets for our opposition come in different forms, our aspirations for the future likewise, but one thing remains steadfastly the same. Together the individual essays collected here show that there is no magic bullet that will suddenly make everything right, no better world that will miraculously drop from the skies and be embraced by political friend and foe alike. There is still much work to be done, much ink to be spilt, many meetings to attend, many demonstrations to go on, many disagreements to be had, as different versions of a shared progressive future are suggested, discussed and argued over. All of that requires clarity of analysis as the first step to outlining the pathologies of the current condition, and it would be hard to imagine a single volume making a better start to such a task than this one does.

Of course, exactly *where* one starts is a function of historical experience, historical memory and historical imagination. Inevitably when setting off to reflect on the issues that the contributors were asked to write about, the question of whether we have been here before asserts itself as a significant background presence. Echoes of past debates and past struggles will naturally be called to mind. As the preceding chapters amply demonstrate, though, it is equally natural that they will do so in different ways. The "here" from the past to which different authors' analysis refers when asking "have we been here before?" thus spreads backwards across many diverse timeframes. The volume is all the more enticing for that as the complex relationship between past and present is brought to the fore.

It would have been impossible to have created a collection of essays such as this and to have expected everyone to have come to the same conclusions. Indeed, it is more remarkable that eight distinguished scholars on the left have produced pieces that have so much in common. Each has chosen their own point of departure, their own emphasis, and their own sense of priorities. This is exactly as it should have been, because they each come to debate the future of the left from their own political subject position from within that broad alliance, their own view of the world, and their own sense of where the most important lessons from the past are to be located. Despite this, it is clear that, when taking a step back from the deeply personal accounts that provide the spark for seven separate analyses of where the left might go from here, everyone is talking about the same basic thing. Some are more optimistic than others about how far the capacities already exist for creating a world cast in a progressive image, but nobody disputes that talking about what such a world might look like is as important today as it has ever been. The continued necessity of left politics rings throughout the volume in the face of its many recent obituaries. The task that I have set myself in preparing these brief concluding thoughts is how to read the individual chapters as a whole, in an attempt to keep that necessity at the forefront of further discussions regarding future progressive political agency.

CELEBRATING DIVERSITY OF OPINION

The different political timeframes invoked by the individual chapters are mirrored in the different political subjects that the contributors place under their analytical gaze. "Who is The Left?", asks Wolfgang Streeck (p. 137) in the most explicit recognition that all is not necessarily straightforward when it comes to identifying the most likely standard bearers of future progressive politics. The double capitalisation of "The" and "Left" is notable for its presence in this instance because of either its partial absence or its complete absence elsewhere in the volume. The equivocation over the "who" also leads to similarly differentiated understandings of "what" to study when reflecting on the future of the left. Even the opening paragraph of David Coates's (p. 2) introductory chapter provides four different glimpses of what the contributors could have chosen to focus on: it might have been "left-wing prospects" broadly defined and borne by whoever chooses to position themselves to carry the flame; it might have been "the Left" as a more or less monolithic bloc of like-minded political agents; or it might have been either "the centre-left" or "the revolutionary left" as two potential organizational forms around which these people could find themselves being mobilised.

The open-ended nature of the engagement that follows is very definitely a strength of the volume. If there are any doubts about that, think briefly of what the alternative would have looked like. A united position could have been imposed in advance and the contributors could have been instructed to have followed it to the letter. However, the reputation for creative thinking for which all of them have been so well known for so long has been earned for something substantially different to devotion to a pre-imposed line. The political left may well be known historically for its party lines, but the scholarly left much less so. The contributors brought together here would almost certainly have declined any invitation to have taken part on the basis of fleshing out someone else's framework for analysis, but why would such an invitation have been issued in the first place? The whole objective of the book is to provoke a discussion about how progressive forces might transcend the current impasse in which the parliamentary left appears to find itself, and the current distance that is placed between the extra-parliamentary left and the scope for genuine societal transformation. This involves trying to define exactly

189

where successful progressive agency might currently be located, how it might be further harnessed, and with what ultimate destination in mind. The particular political subject position of the authors will necessarily impact on the way in which they answer these questions. So too will their degree of optimism in the possibility of moving beyond what so many people, both politically and economically, now take for granted as normal conditions of existence.

One observation in David Coates's (p. 90) chapter really jumped off the page at me in this regard. It was his remark that "the Left has lots of experience of losing". If I look back at the political frustrations of the teenage me in the late 1980s, I can now nod in defiant appreciation of how frequently we have subsequently been proved to have been on the right side of history back then. We demanded that people beyond the advanced industrialised countries be given a voice in their own destiny, rather than being told that they should be the grateful and forever passive recipients of western developmental programmes. We joined the stand against apartheid when, in my case at least, my government was telling me that the struggle was being led by a proscribed terrorist organization. We asked for a debate – this time, one that we are still waiting for – about what a proper structure of reparations would look like for our countries' colonial pasts. We wanted all barriers to social equality to be torn down, at a time at which fully protected characteristics under equalities legislation was still a pipedream. Without the benefit of hindsight that I now possess, however, all the teenage me was aware of at the time was one setback after another. Every election that really mattered was lost; every policy that began the process of changing the way we lived, worked and subsisted was therefore enacted by a politically hostile government.

I wonder whether one of the differences that underpins the individual chapters is the degree to which these electoral and legislative reversals were felt personally. There is an obvious discrepancy when the volume is read as a whole, between those contributors who see the route to a successfully institutionalised progressive politics passing through parliaments reconfigured with suitable numbers of centre-left legislators, and those who believe that the same end can only be achieved through a broad-based extra-parliamentary social realignment. What takes place through the policy process in the former vision must occur through transformative social movements in the latter. The elaboration of policies that embed progressive ideals, and show how progressive political language can become the new language of political common sense, therefore takes on two different roles in different places in the book. It is either what needs to be done now as a matter of urgency, or it is a potential diversion that might take attention away from the much more profound changes that are necessary. Nobody has said that the future of the left can be reduced solely to the question of the best possible policy platform on which to fight upcoming elections, but there are diverse positions within the volume on how much emphasis should be placed on electoral processes more generally. Perhaps if you have taken the mounting electoral losses suffered by parties with progressive aspirations very much to heart, then the immediate priority is likely to be to want to stop this from happening again. Focusing on how best to reset the policy programme through which self-identifying centre-left politicians seek to connect to the electorate seems from this perspective to be an eminently sensible first-up objective. However, if you have always been convinced that the parliamentary road to socialism is blocked from the outset because of the very nature of the capitalist state, then you cannot be blamed for thinking that there must be something more to strategising for a progressive future than worrying about the detail of short-term policy reform.

Something very interesting thus emerges as a dominant theme of the book when read as a whole. The prognosis is the same wherever we look. The status quo of centre-left parliamentary politics, all of the contributors agree, has become a dead end for the political parties that have been entrusted in the recent past with the nurturing of progressive ideals. Moreover, their continuing electoral weaknesses threaten to bring down the wider progressive project, and to cause perhaps insuperable damage to the left's dream of a society forged on the principles of fairness, justice and equality. Yet for all the similarity in prognosis there is no common ground on the diagnosis of exactly what sort of a crisis it is that the left is currently experiencing. Indeed, it could be said that the contributors often reveal themselves to be looking at different patients. The eclectic terminology being used to describe the subject under investigation might have been a difficulty had this been a single-authored book, but in the context of what the volume has set out to achieve it performs the invaluable function of indicating just how much needs to be discussed if a clearer view of the way ahead is ever to be achieved. "Who is The Left/the Left/ the left?" indeed. This is a question that we should not be afraid of continuing to ask, because the most straightforward answers are not necessarily the most illuminating.

THE TEMPORALITY OF CHANGE

Of course, there is a possibility that I am reading somewhat too much into these differences. Could it be instead that the contributors are looking not at different patients so much as the same patient but over different points in its recovery to rude health? After all, there is no simple political portal that can take a currently fragmented collective of social movements to the promised land of successful left government in a single step. The image of the final destination is clearly not going to take shape in the mind in exactly the same form as the image of the embarkation point. What needs to be done over an unspecified time horizon to meet all the demands of progressive politics is equally clearly not going to be the same as what needs to be done tomorrow so that we can convince ourselves that the journey has begun. Nobody can tell us before the fact about how many tomorrows it will take to turn what Dean Baker (p. 40) calls "a slice and dice incrementalist agenda" into the "extended series of ruptures" that Leo Panitch and Sam Gindin (p. 181) describe as the hallmark of a genuine socialist transformation. Nor can they say for sure at what point on that journey, in Fred Block's (p. 62) words, it will become "possible to build a durable bridge that connects those engaged in the 'politics of everyday life' with electoral politics". However, there is no disputing the fact that these tomorrows will have to be lived sequentially, one at a time, if the future of progressive politics is to amount to something more than the occasional electoral victory to interrupt the normality of defeat.

It is chastening to recall what has recently been treated as an admirable electoral performance on the left. Neither "they did better than expected" nor "think how much worse it could have been" equate to stopping the legislative onslaught of neoliberalism. Yet the achievement of avoiding the worst possible of all predicted scenarios has recently given cause not only for cheer but for outright celebration amongst the liberally-minded commentariat. That in itself tells us something important about the rather depressing level at which expectations have recently been set.

Yes, there are reasons to be extremely heartened by the way in which Jeremy Corbyn managed to connect with voters in the June 2017 UK general election through ripping up the Third Way playbook of promising to be a more competent manager of an increasingly toxic neoliberal legacy. Yet during the post-election Queen's Speech debate Theresa May was still able to use her position at the government despatch box to congratulate him sarcastically for having come "a good second".[1] As David Coates (p. 83) observes, Corbyn still has an uphill struggle to convince even some of his ever-sceptical MPs that it could ever amount to more than this. The problems of the Labour Party's "Parliamentarism", as Hilary Wainwright (p. 96) documents, remain unresolved and, perhaps, are fundamentally unresolvable. Yes, Emmanuel Macron's victory in the May 2017 French presidential election provoked a wholly necessary sigh of relief that the Front National candidate Marine Le Pen had not fared better in the final run-off. Yet his victory came on a heavily pro-business platform that will roll back workplace protections and sacrifice hard-earned labour rights that any genuine progressive would surely want to defend.[2] Macron's not being Le Pen does not make it all right that his policies will further rig markets in the direction of "upward redistribution" as described by Dean Baker (p. 24). And yes, Bernie Sanders kept the race for the Democratic nomination for the US presidency alive for much longer than anyone initially expected in the face of the Clinton millions. Yet whilst there may well be useful lessons to learn from the manner in which he ran his campaign, then this still counts at most as a near miss. Moreover, it was a near miss whose policy content might have looked unusual for a US presidential candidate but, as even he himself has pointed out, was only too familiar from the perspective of a contemporary European social democracy that so many of the contributors depict as being part of the broader problem.

This hopefully highlights just what a parlous electoral position meaningful progressive strategies must begin from. Throughout the last forty years, whenever the question of the future of the parliamentary left has been raised it has been within the context of a collective intake of breath at the difficulties posed by the political centre being dragged significantly to the right. If Stuart Hall and his colleagues at *Marxism Today* were able to write about "the great moving right show" as early as the late 1970s, it is very hard to think of what the equivalent terminology would be today.[3] When parties that profess their progressive heritage now try to engage their electorate with programmes that not even the most hardened neoliberal ideologues of the 1970s would have considered sellable, perhaps it is little wonder when suitable descriptive words fail to come to mind. Two things, the contributors agree, must now happen as a matter of priority. The first is that these parties must cease the pretence that accommodating neoliberalism provides them with an appropriate basis for asking their public to trust them to govern. The second is to realise that governing is itself only partly about finding that you have ostensible control of the legislative agenda.

As some of the contributors hint at and others say explicitly, it is at least possible that the structure of the modern capitalist state is simply not amenable to the successful long-term progressive transformation of society. It reflects a balance of social forces that is inimical to even the most basic principles of a progressive society. Leo Panitch and Sam Gindin (p. 161) are most vocal in taking such a stance. They presume that little is to be gained if the outer limits of ambition are simply to capture state power for existing centre-left parties and their new cadres of career politicians. The transition to something beyond a merely different version of the status quo, they argue, requires a radical shift to a whole new state form if the left is to pursue, in Hilary Wainwright's (p. 100) terms, "power-as-transformative-capacity". It hardly needs saying that the tomorrows being envisioned in this instance are likely to be further in the future than the tomorrows that are implied by the chapters that are more policy focused. There are simply more intermediate stages through which it is necessary to pass if the goal is nothing less than total state and societal transformation than if it is devising the policies that will win the next election on a clearly progressive ticket.

THE RECENT PAST

Viable tomorrows are obviously linked to the lived experiences of recent yesterdays. As all of the contributors highlight, the parliamentary left has hardly covered itself in glory in this regard. This is not just, or even not primarily, about its distinctly patchy record when it comes to fighting national-level elections. It is much more about how centre-left parties have chosen to fight those elections: what they have told their watching publics they now believe in and are now prepared to stand up for, as well as who they are seeking to represent. Even though some degree of change over time is to be expected, because the context in which questions about the future of the left are asked never remains as it previously was, still both the extent and the direction of the parliamentary left's recent travels is quite extraordinary. Colin Crouch (p. 120) describes the way in which "all major social democratic movements had shared in the neoliberal consensus, no longer able to appear as its antagonists".

Indeed, the talk throughout the chapters is of the parliamentary left's poor recent record as the guardian of progressive ideals. Centre-left parties are called out time and time again for having been complicit in further institutionalising the neoliberal settlement whose introduction they had earlier failed to stop. It has also been repeatedly pointed out that their deal with the devil has not worked even in its own terms. The Third Way social democrats of the 1990s and 2000s seemingly understood their mission to be a passive response to the assumption that the medium voter had moved away from the progressive end of the political spectrum in the preceding decades.[4] However, this left them merely to reproduce the worst excesses of an economic model that demands that most people have to commit more of their waking hours to work tasks, whilst simultaneously becoming aware that livelihood struggles are becoming ever more precarious and increasingly reliant on short-term debt fixes.[5] If these Third Way social democrats have often been left to carry the can for the spectacular implosion of this economic model during the global financial crisis, they have a point when they say that it is not *all* their fault. Yet they are sufficiently responsible that the effect might be much the same anyway, even if blame were to be apportioned strictly proportionately. Certainly, this sense of blameworthiness seems to be the perception that has developed across large parts of the electorate, who have withheld their support whenever, in Fred Block's (p. 45) words, centre-left parties have chosen not to "reinvent themselves".

It is worth remembering that whilst Macron was heading towards what ultimately proved to be a comfortable 2017 French presidential election victory, Benoît Hamon, the candidate of the Parti Socialiste, the party of the sitting president, François Hollande, who Macron had served as Minister of Finance between August 2014 and August 2016, polled at just 6 per cent. Jean-Luc Mélenchon of La France Insoumise, campaigning well to Hamon's left, gained over three times as many votes. Equally tellingly, Blairite candidates in the metropolitan mayoral elections held in England just five weeks before the 2017 UK general election fared much worse when campaigning independently of the party's national leadership than when the latter campaign was spearheaded across the country by Corbyn's personal brand of anti-austerity and anti-establishment politics. In the constituency in which I live, for instance, a 63-vote Labour majority in May 2017 turned into a more than 15,000-vote Labour majority in June 2017 in the context of a 15 percentage point increase in the Labour vote compared with the 2015 general election.

Voters therefore seem to have a long memory when it comes to punishing Third Way social democrats. Some even retain loyalty to earlier and more radical visions of a progressive society. Even new voters can easily discern the difference in what sort of parliamentary left stands before them appealing for their support. They are enthused by parties that are willing to speak in an unambiguously progressive voice, but remain apathetic when being told that the left has to strike a pragmatic rapprochement with the political forces now lined up against it. Colin Crouch (p. 113) captures the essence of those forces perfectly when describing their extreme economic neoliberalism ("representing the extraordinary power of business wealth") and their extreme social conservatism ("representing the power of mass fear and hatred"). If we did not already know it before, we certainly should be under no illusions following recent elections: promising a more humane version of all those things that the right currently cherishes is a road to nowhere.

However, this realisation presents some problems of its own. There are many career politicians amongst the ranks of the parliamentary left who owe their careers to being the face of the argument that it is possible to accept much of the right's programme for government, but to want to lessen its excesses, soften its edges, and introduce it with a human face. It is surely too late to expect them to display a total change of mind now. More importantly, the very fact that the accommodation to neoliberalism has for so long been the only thing on offer economically has had a significant effect on the way in which many people have attempted to future-proof their lives. Those who have had enough money not to worry unduly about how they are going to live from day to day have typically branched out beyond passive savings. They have sought instead to accumulate assets, having become convinced that the state pension will not be sufficiently generous to cater for their consumption needs in later life.[6] This has created an important new division within society that any successful left strategy will need to find a way of navigating around.

There have always been the asset-rich and the asset-poor, but the source of that distinction in the past served to engender a relatively straightforward class politics. The asset-rich in general owed their wealth to the good fortune of birthright, and their inherited wealth placed them in a consumption bracket that was beyond the wildest dreams of all blue-collar and the vast majority of white-collar workers. The difference was between those who could consume beyond the level of the income they earned from paid work and those for whom that income represented a non-negotiable upper limit on their consumption. There are still those for whom inherited wealth gives them a head start throughout the whole of their lives, but the asset-rich now extend significantly beyond these people. This is one of the legacies of Third Way social democrats' time in government that now provides a very real obstacle for the progressive politics of the future.

It is very unusual for anyone whose job still pays reasonably well not to have used a proportion of their forgone current consumption to have created some sort of asset-based nest egg.[7] They have been able to accumulate assets out of unspent income at the same time that other workers have had to make good the consumption gap produced by stagnant wages by taking on personal debt.[8] The same recycling of funds through financial markets that keeps asset values high for the former group simultaneously sets up debt traps for the latter. There is no simple distinction to be drawn here between rentiers and workers. As Dean Baker (p. 25) argues, the most important upward redistribution of the last twenty years has been from workers in the bottom five income deciles to workers in the top five income percentiles. When we take the upward redistribution from asset ownership into account as well, the bottom five income deciles look as if they have been increasingly cut adrift. Throughout western

Europe and North America, social democrats were in government for a good proportion of the time in which this divisive trend was being embedded.

THE LANGUAGE OF "THE ECONOMY"

As David Coates (p. 75) rightly insists, the parliamentary left has historically proved least able to safeguard progressive values when it dances most conspicuously to the beat of somebody else's drum. The contributors all agree that, perhaps in particular, it needs to become the economic agenda-setter if it is to avoid becoming captive of distinctly non-progressive interests. As is abundantly clear from the preceding chapters, there is no dearth of ideas about how the economy might be run through a series of near-term tomorrows in a way that will make life materially better for countless numbers of people. There is also ample evidence of how longer-term tomorrows might be built around a mode of organization that today is only really found in various social movements. What might still be visible only in tentative outline – what might be missing, even – is a language of "the economy" that can speak to broad progressive aspirations, but that can also narrate a choice of life that those who are most in need of progressive policies will be willing to embrace.

By such a language, I mean something rather different to whether the parliamentary left in government can boost headline growth rates every bit as much as those of parties of government from across the aisle. This is another road to nowhere that has already been all-too-extensively explored by Third Way social democrats of the recent past. Almost anyone can preside over relatively unbroken periods of economic growth if they do not care whether they are destroying the environment, and if they are unabashed by the fact that the rewards to paid work have been squeezed horrendously for the bottom half of the income distribution. What I mean is finding a suitable political vocabulary that can act upon our basic intuitions concerning what it is, at heart, that we want out of the economy: the instincts it will embody, the cultures of entitlement it will override, the self-awareness it will promote. This is about laying waste to what Wolfgang Streeck (p. 155) so memorably describes as "the disease of plus-making", but doing so not through legislative decree but by establishing the vision of a world within which people really want to live.

This, of course, is much easier said than done. Difficult as the task would be likely to prove at any time, it is made trickier in contemporary circumstances by what the very phrase "the economy" has come to mean to so many people. The introduction of permanent austerity has taken its toll in this regard. This is not to say that there are not some very important experiments currently taking place in debt-free living and resistance to debt that have begun to create spaces of economic interaction beyond the logics of austerity.[9] However, these movements are by no means mainstream as yet, and it will take another level of experimentation altogether before anyone can be sure if they can be successfully scaled up to anything beyond the niche level. Until then, for most people austerity will continue to be experienced as something that simply bears down on them. Politicians who remain wedded to the fools' gold of fiscal retrenchment through slashing public expenditures will always preside over economic systems in which the majority of people are required to up their efforts for increasingly paltry rewards.

"The economy" has therefore taken on a far from unproblematic image in the popular consciousness.[10] When politicians speak about "the economy" today, they tend to do so in one of two ways. On the one hand, they like to put forward any evidence that they can muster, genuinely meaningful or otherwise, that "the economy" is doing well and that indicators of ostensible success are pointing in the right direction. This is often no more than a way of saying "hasn't my party done well to preside over a period of enhanced prosperity?", in the hope that this will lead to opinion polls also pointing in the right direction. Such assertions, however, fly in the face of lived experience for so many people, whereby the positive economic performance that people are being asked to celebrate is not felt personally, especially amongst the asset-poor. The feeling that actually materialises is usually one of slipping still further behind. On the other hand, recent experiences of one financial crisis after another have also positioned "the economy" in politicians' discourse as something that needs to be saved. Collective national sacrifice has hence been promoted as a means of putting "the economy" back on an even keel, of correcting prior mistakes and of providing us with the security we all crave. Yet no serious thinking person believes that this has resulted in anything other than the asset-rich being able to widen the gap they already enjoyed with the everyday subsistence struggles of the asset-poor. The financial system that was the site of the original crisis continues to be used to lock the asset-rich into an ever more parasitic relationship with the asset-poor, all in the name of doing what is best for "the economy".

It is hardly surprising, then, if there is increasingly widespread scepticism when politicians start talking about the requirement for the public to defer to the needs of "the economy". As both Leo Panitch and Sam Gindin (p. 171) and Hilary Wainwright (p. 102) document, there are distinctly cautionary tales to be gleaned from the recent experience of progressives with a mandate for government that entailed them trying to do significantly more than Third Way social democrats were ever inclined to do. They have been faced with powerful institutions of governance for whom the needs of "the economy" will always equate to the reproduction of the social divisions that have helped to propel popular trust in political processes to new lows. This, then, is the scale of the task that the left has in front of it: to perfect a new economic language that provides more people with more belief in the power of politics to make their lives better, knowing all the time that this will be challenged by those who have the institutional affiliation to speak up for the interests that do well out of the current structure of "the economy".

There are resources from progressive pasts that might well prove useful to this end. The left has always had its instinct towards egalitarianism to help frame the way in which it assesses what is, and what is not, an economic priority. Yet as Colin Crouch (p. 116) points out, it now faces political opponents who think that there are votes to plunder by demarcating the national "in group" and arguing that it alone is worthy of preferential treatment relative to anyone else who might be socially othered on the grounds of race, ethnicity, religion or place of birth. The left can also rely on ongoing movement-based experiments in radical democracy to invert today's dominant language of "the economy". The question then becomes not what people must do to serve the needs of "the economy", but what new forms of everyday economic life might be created to serve the needs that people have to live in flourishing communities, a flourishing society and a flourishing environment. Yet it has to be expected that this will also be met with resistance by those who continue to benefit from the organization of what Wolfgang Streeck (p. 155) calls a plus-based society that stands at odds with Fred Block's (p. 52) notion of a "habitation society".

FINAL WORDS

It is not the job of the person who is invited to write the final chapter of a book of this nature to adjudicate between the individual chapters. It is also not up to them to try to drag the discussion onto radically new territory. I have attempted instead to harness the spirit of dialogue in which the volume has been put together so as to provide some sort of guide as to how the chapters might be read as a whole. They were written to reflect the way in which each of the contributors personally views the world around them, but they are indisputably all part of a broader collective endeavour to think through the future that the left might be able to make for itself and, more importantly, for those people who need it the most.

If my experience is in any way representative of that of other readers, then the journey that has been undertaken to reach this point in the book will have been an exhilarating one. It is also likely to have proved to be something of a rollercoaster ride. The preceding pages are packed full of reasons to be optimistic. The volume makes it crystal clear that there are still plenty of thinkers on the extra-parliamentary left for whom the progressive values that first brought them into politics burn as brightly as ever. This might not always seem to be as true for all members of the parliamentary left, which is why, whatever the future of the left holds, it must be pursued within society through extra-parliamentary means every bit as much as through winning elections. However, the analysis contained in this book is never written through misleadingly rose-tinted spectacles. There is always a recognition that being able to say what needs to be done is not the same as actually being able to do it. There are obstacles to be overcome in terms of how society is currently constructed, how so many within that society currently conceive of their relationships to other people, including their future selves, and how deeply lots of people have been socialised into aspiring for things that are antithetical to genuinely progressive values. It is one of the strengths of the volume that these issues of contemporary life are not simply wished away, but are confronted head-on.

There are self-inflicted problems for the parliamentary left resulting from memories of its recent failures to assert a governing strategy that differed noticeably from a simple accommodation to neoliberalism. There are also problems for the left more broadly of always having to fight a better resourced foe that enjoys direct access to propaganda arms of the media. The starting point for the struggle to win hearts and minds for a genuinely progressive alternative to what we now have is therefore far from auspicious. It is not one that anybody on the left would willingly have chosen for themselves. But as the book has shown beyond all doubt, it is a challenge that so many people are still prepared to take up. The knowledge that there will always be strength in numbers is comforting in itself. It makes the thought of the journey considerably less daunting than it might otherwise be. That journey will necessarily remain a test of stamina, but the volume's overriding lesson as a whole is that it is eminently worthwhile persevering. The future of the left depends on nothing less, as does the future of all those people around the world whose lives a re-energised left can make qualitatively better.

NOTES

1. http://www.bbc.co.uk/news/live/uk-politics-40347339 (accessed 3 August 2017).
2. https://www.bloomberg.com/news/articles/2017-04-24/macron-wins-french-executives-backing-in-contest-versus-le-pen (accessed 3 August 2017).
3. S. Hall, "The great moving right show" in his *Selected Political Writings* (London: Lawrence & Wishart, 2017).
4. C. Hay, *The Political Economy of New Labour: Labouring Under False Pretences?* (Manchester: Manchester University Press, 1999).
5. G. Standing, *The Precariat: The New Dangerous Class* (London: Bloomsbury, 2011).
6. R. Martin, *Financialization of Daily Life* (Philadelphia, PA: Temple University Press, 2002).
7. P. Langley, *The Everyday Life of Global Finance: Saving and Borrowing in Anglo-America* (Oxford: Oxford University Press, 2008).
8. J. Montgomerie & D. Tepe-Belfrage, "A feminist moral-political economy of uneven reform in austerity Britain: fostering financial and parental literacy", *Globalizations* 13:6, 890–905.

9. L. Tooker, "Ordinary Democracy: Reading Resistances to Debt after the Global Financial Crisis with Stanley Cavell's Ordinary Language Philosophy", unpublished PhD thesis, Department of Politics and International Studies, University of Warwick, 2017.

10. I have explained the lack of traction of the official Remain campaign during the 2016 EU referendum in the UK through this lens: M. Watson, "Brexit, the left behind and the let down: the political abstraction of "the economy" and the UK's EU referendum", *British Politics*, forthcoming.

INDEX

Note: **bold** page numbers indicate figures; numbers in brackets preceded by *n* are chapter endnote numbers.

absentee state 83
activism/activists 13, 14, 15–16
    transition to politics from 161
agency 15, 38, 181, 190
agriculture 104, 131, 135, 177
American Left 13, 170
anarcho-syndicalists 164
apartheid 190
apprenticeships 80
Árnason, Árni 3
asset-rich 197, 199–200
Attlee, Clement 74
austerity 8, 77, 86, 90, 98–9, 107, 160, 167, 199
    and Greece 103–4, 123, 171, 174
Austria 123
Austro-Hungarian Empire 124, 129
auto industry 46–7, 50

Bailey, David 6
Baker, Dean 12, 82
Balls, Ed 81
banks 61–2, 92(*n*11), 120, 122
    collapse of 28
    see also financial crisis (2008); financial sector
basic income 81, 145
Benn, Tony 98, 175
Berlusconi, Silvio 124
Berman, Sheri 3

Blair, Tony 7, 21(*n*17), 51, 72, 75, 79, 110, 123
Blue Labour 123–4
Bolshevism 164, 165
bourgeoisie 115, 159, 163
Brexit referendum (2017) 3, 4–5, 45, 68, 121–2, 123, 131
    and inequality 58
    and Labour Party 8, 69
    and liberal/conservative values 134–5
    and xenophobia 130
Britain (UK)
    Coalition Government 7
    Conservative Government 121–2, 126
    Conservative Party *see* Conservative Party
    economics–politics separation in 105–6
    "economy" of 198–200
    general election, 1997 3
    general election, 2010 68, 73
    general election, 2015 81, 84, 196
    general election, 2017 *see* general election, 2017
    Labour Party *see* Labour Party
    postwar consensus in 74, 120
    social settlements in 71–3
    xenophobia in 130
Bullman, U. 89
Bush, George W. 7, 77

California (US) 30, 31, 32, 33, 34, 40
Calvino, Italo 95
Cameron, David 7
Canada 34
capacity-building 62, 63, 101, 104, 106, 169, 182
capital 5, 119
    global movement of 119, 125
    and labour 9, 14, 25, 70, 72, 89
    and social settlements 72, 73
capitalism 12, 19, 119, 159, 160, 166
    and political mobilization 121–3
    precariousness of 166
    progressive 15, 69, 70, 78, 160–1
    restraints on 127
    and social settlements 71, 72
care crisis 59
Center for American Progress 81
centre-left parties 2, 68–9
    accommodation of neoliberalism by 75–6, 79, 160, 194, 195, 196–7, 202
    crisis/electoral weakness of 4, 5–8, 67–9, 191
    emergence of 46
    and EU 3, 8–9
    parliamentary 189, 193–5, 196, 198, 201, 202
centre-left parties, reinvention/renewal of 14, 45, 70, 70–91
    and agency 85–9
    and austerity 77
    and contemporary situation 70–3, 189–90
    and economic growth models 76–7
    and electoral cycle 75–6
    four stages of 70
    moderate/radical policies for 81–4
    and politics of transition 72, 73–6
    and progressive policy proposals 79–85
    and supply/demand 77–8
    and think-tanks 82, 83–4
    and transformational policies 89–90
centre-left reinvention in US 45–64
    and changes in economy/consumption patterns 50–1
    and federal/state government focus 47–9
    and habitation society see habitation society
    and local level 47–8, 49–50
    organizational challenge of 46–50
    programmatic challenge of 45, 50–2
centre-right parties 16

childcare 80, 83, 84, 92(n10)
China 53, 54
cities 52, 53, 54, 58, 107–8, 109, 135
    and rural space 60
civil rights 68, 69, 72
civil society policy 79, 80–1
class 16, 72, 89, 120, 161, 183
    formation 162, 165, 166, 167, 181
    inequality 132, 160
    and transformation of capitalism 161–2
    see also working class
class struggle 162–7
    and collective bargaining/welfare reforms 165–6
    and elites/cliques 163–4
    new forms of 166–7
Clause 4 108
climate change 84, 106–7
Clinton, Bill 48, 50, 75, 79, 123
Clinton, Hillary 3, 47–8, 69, 81, 193
coalition politics 9
Coates, D. 88
Cold War 71
    end of 5, 72, 170
collective bargaining 165
colonialism/neocolonialism 71, 72, 124, 190
Communist Manifesto (Marx/Engels) 162
communities 59, 66(n16), 117, 135, 175–6
    and Blue Labour 123
    and democratization 61, 62–3, 101
    and habitation society 51–2
    and markets 54
competition 27, 141, 162
    global 5, 13, 17, 27, 28, 125–6
conservatism 113–4, 115, **116**, 119, 131–2, 135
    and nationalism 117–8
Conservative Party 3, 72
    and 2017 general election 2, 5
consumer/credit cooperatives 169
consumption 62, 73, 126, 133, 159, 165, 166
    and asset-rich 197
cooperatives 62, 169, 177, 180
copyright 34–5
    see also patent/copyright protection
Corbyn, Jeremy 1, 3, 8, 67, 89
    campaigns of 47
    progressive policies of 83–5
    and young people 86, 98
Corbyn-led Labour 3, 8, 11, 16, 68, 86–7, 89, 95–110, 161, 169, 193

and Corbyn's leadership style 97, 108–9
and economics–politics separation
105–6
and Labour's old politics 96–7
manifesto of 108–9
and new politics 95–6, 97, 99
and parliamentarism 96, 97, 99, 110
and participatory ethos 98, 99, 108–9
and PLP 97–8, 109–10
and power/knowledge 95–96, 99–103,
106
and social transformation 106–7
and strategic/entrepreneurial state
83, 84
and Syriza, compared 95, 96, 97, 103–5,
110
and young/first-time voters 69–70, 86,
110
corporations 50, 56, 60, 119, 125, 127
CEOs' pay see executives' pay
corrupt governance structure of 26–7
tax avoidance by 80, 81
corruption 26–7
cosmopolitanism 133
Cox, Joe 84
credit 120, 159
cooperatives 169
Crouch, Colin 17
Cruddas, Jon 1, 10
Cuba 174

Danish People's Party 114
decentralization 61, 62, 63–4, 65(n9)
deindustrialization 76
Delaware (US) 36
democracy/democratization 61, 64,
103–4, 109, 114, 126–7, 178–9, 182
and conservatism 115, 117
of Democratic Party 170
of international agencies 127
and knowledge/power 101–2, 103
and "the economy" 200–1
Democratic Party 9, 41, 69, 72, 81
and activism 14
central government focus of 48–9
decline of 47–8, 74, 85–6, 87
and identity/class politics 88
lessons from Republicans for 14, 23–4,
87
need for progressive policies in 87–9
and Sanders 169–70
democratic socialism 177–80
Denmark 7, 21(n14), 123

deregulation 6, 16, 72–3, 76, 119, 120
Detroit (US) 46–7
Deutscher, Isaac 164
developing countries 127, 167
Diamond, Patrick 8–10, 11
DiEM25 104
disabled people 81, 131, 132
Douzinas, Costas 174–5

economic growth 55, 76–7, 85, 198
austerity route to see austerity
in contrast to lived experience 199
inhibited by inequality 84
progressive policies for 78–9
and social settlements 71–3
Economic and Monetary Union 171
economic policy 1
economic recession 5–6
economic transformation 50–2, 57
economics profession 28–9, 43(n4)
economics–politics separation 105–6
education 52, 53, 55, 57, 59, 81, 84, 113,
168
and empowerment 107, 108
radical 169
reform of tuition fees 80, 83, 168
and revolution 163–4, 165
and solidarity networks 176–7
egalitarianism 14, 15, 60, 105, 123, 125,
134, 135, 200
and liberalism 116
Einstein, Albert 19
elections/electoral politics 75–6, 87, 90,
97, 99, 110, 182, 190, 191, 192–4,
195–6
and local level organization 47–8
and social struggles 105–10, 181
elites 46, 63, 99, 104, 105, 117–8, 121,
128
liberal 132
local business 126
neoliberal 133
employment 120
entrepreneurial state 84
entrepreneurs 57
environmental issues 10, 55, 59–60, 79,
98, 109, 132, 169, 198
see also climate change; green economy
equality 38, 48, 52, 80, 131–2, 190, 191
Erdoğan, Recep 134
ethnic cleansing 129
Euro debt crisis 103–4, 122, 128, 171
Eurocommunism 170–1

European Central Bank 122, 173
European Social Charter 171
European Union (EU) 2, 3, 4, 12, 114
   and Greece *see* Greece
   and immigration/refugee crisis 8
   and neoliberalism 7, 127, 128–9, 160
   power relations in 183
   and social democracy 128–9
Eurozone 104, 160, 173, 173–4, 176
executives' pay 13, 25, 27–8, 29, 39
   progressive policy for 35–6

Facebook 50
families 15, 30, 59, 79, 119, 133, 141,
   142–3
far right 45, 121, 122, 133, 160, 167, 181
   in US 3, 4, 16
Farage, Nigel 6, 74
fascism 118, 121, 126, 165
financial crisis (2008) 5–7, 26, 55, 62, 73,
   75, 200
   and economics profession 28–9
   no major changes following 23, 120
   rescue of capital following 160
   see also housing bubble
financial markets 120
financial policy 79
financial sector 13, 26, 29, 41, 61–2
   progressive policies for 32–3, 62, 80, 82,
     83, 85, 92(*nn*10, 11)
financial transactions taxes 32, 33
First World War 129, 163
food cooperatives/solidarity networks
   62, 177
Ford, Robert 5
Fordism 71, 72, 76
France 4, 45, 50, 114–5, 123, 126
   Front National/Le Pen 114, 126, 193
   National Assembly election, June 2017
     1–2
   nationalism in 114, 124
   Parti Socialiste 195–6
   presidential election, May 2017 193,
     195–6
Frank, Barney 82
fraternité 114, 115, 117
free market/trade 13, 28, 126, 167
   and Blairites 110
   and monopolies 29, 33, 34
free-trade agreements 17, 26, 126
French Revolution 114, 115
French Socialist Party 1–2
full employment 41, 42, 74

Gates, Bill 28
gay rights 13, 48, 66(*n*18), 130
   see also transgender people
gender 49, 78, 121, 125, 129, 134
   inequalities 57, 60, 79, 88
   see also women
general election, 2017 1–2, 3, 5, 8, 11,
   67–8, 90, 192–3, 196
   Labour manifesto in 83
   young/first-time voters in 69–70
Germany 8, 30, 31, 45, 122, 126, 129, 165
   lessons from 81, 84
   Nazi period 118, 130
gerrymandering 49, 58
Gilbert, Jeremy 10
Gindin, Sam 19
globalization 10, 16, 17, 27, 63, 81, 113,
   119–20, 125, 129
   and bourgeoisie 159
   and Brexit referendum 121–2
   and employment 120
   of labour market 13
   regulated 89, 126–7
Golden Dawn 122
Goodhart, David 117, 124
Google 50
Gorz, Andre 177, 179
Gramsci, Antonio 74, 91, 162, 179
Great Depression 72, 165
Great Recession 25, 28
Greece 4, 8, 19, 50, 95, 96, 97, 103–5, 110,
   122–3
   corruption in 176
   solidarity movement in 104–5
   Synaspismos in 170–1, 177
   see also Syriza
green economy 51, 79, 82, 89
Green Party 9

habitation society 13, 45, 51–64, 65(*n*8),
   201
   and budget constraints 56, 58, 59, 60
   and care crisis 59
   China model 53, 54
   and communities 51–2, 54, 61, 62–3
   and decentralization 61, 62, 63–4,
     65(*n*9)
   and definitions of socialism 60–1
   and democratization 61, 64
   and environmental crisis 59–60
   and finance sector reform 62
   four challenges for 54–60
   and industrial era structures 52–3, 54

and inequality/social exclusion 57–8
and innovation *see* innovation
and lost economic dynamism 55–6
and market flaws 53–4
Hacker, Jacob 82
Hall, Stuart 11, 193–4
Hamon, Benoît 195–6
healthcare 39, 48, 52, 55, 113, 168
    and care crisis 59
    and doctors' pay 27, 28, 37–38
    in Greece 104–5
hedge-fund managers 25, 26
Hobsbawm, Eric 11–12, 15, 162–3
Hollande, François 196
homophobia 88, 124, 129, 160
housing bubble 23, 25, 28–9, 33, 42–3(*n*2)
human rights 79
Hungary 123, 124
Hutton, Will 84

Iceland 20–1(*n*6)
identity
    multiple 134
    politics 88
    social 120–1
    working-class 165, 166
Illinois (US) 32, 40
IMF (International Monetary Fund) 104,
    122, 127, 128, 173
immigration 1, 7, 8, 17, 18, 114, 125, 129,
    130–1, 132
    and left 124
*Inclusive Prosperity, Report of the
    Commission on* (2015) 81–2
income 24, 25, 27
Indignados 102, 160
industrial decline 46–7, 63
industrial policy 79, 80
inequality 5, 27–9, 73, 80
    class 132, 160, 168
    and Corbyn's leadership election 98
    and economic growth 84
    and habitation society 57–8
    as issue in political campaigns 88
    and markets 13
    metropolitan–rural 58
    and neoliberalism 77, 89, 119–20, 132
    see also upward redistribution
inflation 13, 25
infrastructure 51–52, 53, 55, 56, 58, 113
    progressive policies for 80, 82, 83, 84,
    92(*n*10), 168, 169
inherited wealth 197

innovation 52, 55–6, 57, 65(*n*9), 77
    constraints on 56, 126
    regional 81
    social 107
intellectual property *see* patent/copyright
    protection
international institutions 125, 127, 183
International Labour Organization 127
International Monetary Fund (IMF) 104,
    122, 127, 128, 173
internationalism 10, 17, 117, 124, 129,
    183
Internet 38, 49, 50, 107
investment 81, 83
    corporate 125
Ireland 8, 122
Italy 8, 118, 122, 123, 126

Jews 124, 129, 130
job security 80, 89

Karitzis, Andreas 103–4, 105
Kaufmann, Eric 134–5
Keynesian economics 11, 50, 71, 72, 74,
    76, 78, 119
Kitschelt, H. 134
knowledge 95–6, 101–2
    and democracy 101–2
Kouvelakis, Stathis 173, 174
Krugman, Paul 82
Kuttner, Robert 82

La Botz, Dan 170
La France Insoumise 196
labour/labour market 7, 25, 78, 131
    changes in 50
    and dismissal/severance pay 31–2
    EU 8
    and full employment policy 41, 42, 74
    globalized 13, 28
    and healthcare insurance/pensions 31
    low-wage service employment 76
    and paid vacations 30, 40
    progressive policies for 30–2, 40, 80,
    83, 84–5
    women in 78, 79, 81, 92(*n*10)
    and work-sharing 30–1
    and working hours 30, 80, 84
    see also executives' pay; wage
    distribution
labour movement 23, 71, 76, 116, 168–9
    emergence of 162–3
    and globalization 119

Labour Party 83–5, 117, 122
  in 2015 general election 81, 84
  in 2017 general election *see* general
    election, June 2017
  Corbyn's leadership of *see* Corbyn-led
    Labour
  and EU Referendum 8
  and Left 9–10, 11
  loss of support for 7–8, 74, 85, 86
  and movements/locally-based groups
    86
  and neoliberalism 7
  "old politics" of 96
  parliamentarism of 96, 99, 110, 193
  reconnection with electorate by 86–7
  reconstruction of alliance in 9–11
labour productivity 71
labour rights *see* workers' rights
Lawson, Neal 1, 8, 9, 10
Le Pen, Marine 114, 126, 193
Left
  and activism 13, 14
  alliances in 9–11, 14, 17–18
  and creation of new social settlement
    15
  crisis in/weakness of 2, 3–4, 113
  and democracy 103–4
  and Enlightenment 114–5
  future of, four questions for 12, 189
  lessons from Right for 14, 23–4, 87
  and nationalism 123–4
  parliamentary 97–8
  and protectionism 125–6
  and socialism 18
  and Thatcherism/neoliberalism 11–12
  three strategies for 11
  in US *see* American Left
left populism 99
Lenin, Vladimir 163, 165, 178, 179
Leslie, Chris 69
Leuger, Karl 129
LGBT rights 39
Liberal Democrats 9
liberalism 114–5, 116, **116**, 119, 123, 134
  and socialism 133, 178–80
liberté, fraternité, égalité 114, 115–6
Libya 8
local government 32, 34–5, 98, 168
low-income workers 17
Luxemburg, Rosa 163–4, 165, 178

McDonnell, John 98–9
Macron, Emmanuel 110, 123, 193, 195–6

Magri, Lucio 177, 185(*n*25)
manufacturing sector 50–1, 52, 72, 125,
  126, 166
  decline of 73, 76, 119
  progressive policies for 80, 82
market restructuring 24, 29, 38–40, 60–1
  successes in 39
markets 17, 114, 125
  and habitation society 53–4
  and inequality 13, 24, 27
  labour *see* labour/labour market
Marktvolk 114, 119, 120, 121, 122, 127–8
Marx, Karl 54, 124, 162, 163, 181
Marxism Today 11, 194
maternity/paternity leave 80, 83, 84
May, Theresa 16–17, 69, 96, 114, 121–2
mayoral elections, 2017 196
Mazzucato, Mariana 84
media 90, 110, 169, 172
Medicaid/Medicare 34, 38, 41, 168
Mélenchon, Jean-Luc 196
Meyerson, Harold 82
Michels, Robert 101, 163
Michigan (US) 47, 48
Middle East 7, 121
Miliband, Ed 84
Miliband, Ralph 15, 19, 96, 110, 175, 180
military spending 79, 82
millennialism 23
minimum wage 17, 30, 43(*n*7), 80, 82, 84,
  92(*n*11), 131
Mitterand, François 50
mobilizing capacity 16, 113, 115, 119, 161
modernization 4, 31, 32, 82, 92(*nn*10, 11),
  118
  egalitarian 135
modernizing rationalism 114, 125, 135
money supply 106
monopolies 29, 107
Montana (US) 31
Movimonto Cinque Stelle 122
Münchau, Wolfgang 67
Murray, Andrew 161
Muslims 7, 123, 129, 130

Napoleon 115
national debt 81, 92(*n*10)
National Health Service (NHS) 83, 84
national socialism 118
  see also fascism
National Union of Teachers (NUT) 109
nationalism 4–5, 16, 117–8, 124–7, 128,
  160

left 123–4
and protectionism 126
see also xenophobia
nationalization/renationalization 80, 83, 182
neoliberalism 5, 6, 7, 10, 11, 15, 16, 89, 113, 115, 127–8, 159
and austerity *see* austerity
centre-left's accommodation of 75–6, 79, 160, 194, 195, 196–7, 202
de-legitimation of 128, 133, 160
and economic growth 71, 77–8
emergence of 119
and equal rights 131–2
and inequality 77, 89, 119–20, 132
and nationalism/xenophobia 121, 123
and protectionism 125–6
and social democracy 120–1, 124–8
Netherlands 4, 30, 122, 123, 124
xenophobia in 130
networks 101–2, 104–5, 166
Nevada (US) 48
New Deal 74, 85, 88, 90
New Democrats 73
New Labour 3, 68, 73, 75–7, 86
New left 18, 50, 64
New York (US) 30, 31
NHS (National Health Service) 83, 84
Nordic countries 117, 122, 126
Nunns, Alex 98

Obama, Barack 3, 7, 47, 48, 51, 66(*n*18), 73, 121
Occupy 23, 62, 102, 121, 160, 161
OECD (Organization for Economic Cooperation and Development) 127, 128
Oesch, D. 134
oil crisis (1973) 75
Old Labour 11, 72, 76
Osborne, George 77
Ossoff, Jon 42
outsourcing 72–3, 76

Panitch, Leo 19
parliamentarism 96, 97, 99, 110
parliamentary left 189, 193–5, 196, 198, 201, 202
Parti Socialiste 195–6
patent/copyright protection 13, 26, 29
progressive policy for 33–5, 40
pension funds 32, 40, 62
pensions 29, 31, 33, 39, 82, 89, 113

personal debt 73, 76, 195, 197
PIIGS economies 8
Piketty, Thomas 57
Pisani-Ferry, Jean 6
Podemos 50, 96, 122, 161
Polanyi, Karl 60–1, 65(*n*8)
political participation 120–30
and globalization/nationalism 121–3, 124–7
and social identity 120–1
political revolution 162, 167–72, 178–9
political space 115–8, **116**, 125, 127, 134
class-focused 168–9
Pollin, Robert 82–3
Portugal 8, 118, 122
Post Office, renationalization of 83
postindustrialism 50–2
see also habitation society
postwar period 9, 50, 71, 74, 99, 124, 125
Poulantzas, Nicos 177–9
poverty 57, 88, 92(*n*11), 127
power-as-transformative-capacity 15–16, 100–3, 106, 107, 194
power/power relations 15–16, 89, 95–6, 99–103
devolution of 108
as domination 100, 102–3, 107
and EU 183
and globalization/neoliberalism 113
state/class 180
pre-distribution policies 84–5
prescription drugs *see* patent/copyright protection
private-equity partners 25, 26, 40
productivity
and austerity 77–8
and automation 71, 72
and wages 73, 76
progressive alliances 9, 10, 20, 38–40, 89, 135, 171, 181
political strategy of 40
and social media 38–9
successes of 39
progressive capitalism 15, 69, 70, 78–9
proletariat 144, 162, 163, 164, 165
property/property relations 36, 60, 114, 115
protectionism 125–6
and nationalism/xenophobia 126
protest movements/rebellions 23, 62, 100–101
public procurement policies 82
public sector 77, 166

public services 98, 101, 102, 120, 125, 139, 169
  collective 169
public–private collaborations 55–6, 81
Putin, Vladimir 124

quality of life 30, 55, 56, 77
quantitative easing 78

racism 7, 16, 17, 88, 160
  anti- 130
railways, renationalization of 83, 98
Rasmussen, P. N. 89
Reagan, Ronald 7, 90, 167
  social settlement of 71, 72–3, 75–6, 77
refugee crisis 8, 121, 122, 123, 125, 129
Rehm, P. 134
Reich, Robert 82
religion 120–1
rent taking 13, 26, 40
Renzi, Matteo 123
Republican Party 3, 14, 29–30, 41, 72, 73, 87, 89
  gerrymandering by 49, 58
  and inequality 57
  and low taxation 58
  state government focus of 49
retail sector 76
retirement savings plans 32–33, 39, 43–4(n9), 62
revolution
  and education 163–4, 165
  political see political revolution
revolutionary gradualism 107
right-wing alliance 113, 115
right-wing populism 4, 63
Romney, Mitt 48
rural communities 58, 65(n8)
Russia 124
  see also Soviet Union
Russian Revolution 159, 162, 163–5, 168

Sanders, Bernie 7, 19, 38–9, 82, 87–8, 89, 161, 165, 193
  class-focused campaign of 168–9
  and Democratic Party 169–70
  and political revolution 167–70
Saville, John 19
Schäuble, Wolfgang 103, 104
Schmidt, Ingo 1
Schroeder, Gerhard 123
Schumpeterian democracy 46
Schweiger, Christian 1

Second International 163
service sector 73, 120, 135
sexism 129, 160
"Singapore" approach 122, 126
social conservatism 10, 117, 121, 123, 128, 129, 196
  and xenophobia 123–4, 130
social democracy 16, 83, 85, 89, 96, 113–36, 159
  and American Left 170, 193
  and EU 128–9
  future of 130–6
  and global economy 126–7
  international, objections to 127–30
  and neoliberalism/globalization 120–1, 124–7, 160, 195
  persistence of 113–4
  and political participation see political participation
  and political power 113, 114
  and political space 115–8
  regeneration of 17, 19
  retreat of 8–9
  and right-wing alliance 113
  Third Way see Third Way
  and upward redistribution 197–8
  see also centre-left parties
social housing 81, 83
social justice 68, 69, 85, 167
social media 38–9
social movements 13, 15–16, 19, 95, 100, 110, 190–1, 192, 198, 200
  in Greece 171, 175, 176, 177
social relations 107, 144, 162, 176, 182
  monetized 151, 152–3
social settlements 71–3
  collapse of 72, 73, 74
  progressive 75, 79
  Thatcher/Reagan 71, 72–3, 75–6, 77
social structures of accumulation (SSAs) 71, 72, 73–4, 76
socialism 60–1, 115–16, **116**, 162–7, 181–3
  emergence of see class struggle
  and liberal democracy 133, 178–80
  revolutionary strategy of see political revolution
  Soviet 124
Socialist Campaign Group 98
Socialist Register 19
solidarity organizations/networks 104–5, 176–7
sovereignty 125, 126

Soviet Union 124, 165, 171
    collapse of 5, 72, 170
    see also Russian Revolution
Spain 4, 8, 118, 122, 161
Spourdalakis, Michalis 171
SSAs (social structures of accumulation) 71, 72, 73–4, 76
Staatsvolk 114, 119, 120
stagflation 72, 75
Stalin, Joseph 124, 165
statism 178, 179, 180
Stiglitz, Joseph 82
strategic state 83
Streeck, Wolfgang 114, 117
strikes 166, 171
student debt 80, 83
Summers, Larry 81
Sweden 50, 117
Synaspismos 170–1, 177
Syria 8
Syriza 19, 50, 95, 96, 97, 103–5, 122–3, 161, 183
    capitulation/scaling down by 172, 173
    and Eurozone 104, 173–4, 176
    and plan B 173–4, 176
    and political revolution 170–7
    and social democracy 172, 175–6
    and social movements 175, 176–7
    and solidarity networks 171, 172
    and state transformation 173–7
    and Synaspismos 170–1
    and three temporalities 174–6

Tawney, R. H. 67
tax avoidance 80, 81
tax/transfer policy 24, 28
taxation 36, 43(*n*4), 44(*n*9), 58, 77, 113
    financial transactions taxes 32, 33
    progressive 81, 82, 83, 84, 92(*n*10), 125
Tea Party 85, 87
technology 27, 47, 50, 51, 52, 55–6, 57, 78, 81, 166
terrorism 121, 122, 129, 190
Thatcher, Margaret 3, 7, 11, 71, 90
    social settlement of 71, 72–3, 75, 77
Thatcherism 86
Therborn, Goran 180
think-tanks 82, 83–4
Third Way 7, 16, 50, 123, 132, 159, 160, 161, 170, 193, 195, 196
    and inherited wealth 197
Thompson, E. P. 162
trade 79, 106, 126–7

trade agreements 27
trade unions 12, 14, 38, 72, 80, 84–5, 89, 92(*n*11), 117, 165
    and Corbyn 98, 99
    decline/defeat of 47, 166
    emergence of 162, 163
    and Labour's "old politics" 96, 97
    rollback of rights of 49
    transformative capacity of 178, 180, 182
traditionalist egalitarianism 116–7, **116**
training 80, 81, 84
transformational policies 89–90, 106, 109, 110
transformative capacity 15–6, 106, 107, 179, 181–3
    power as 15–6, 100–103, 106, 107, 194
    and trade unions 178, 180
transgender people 49, 147, 150, 156(*n*2)
trickle-down economics 77
Trump, Donald J. 16, 29, 45, 58, 88, 121, 126, 127
    election of 3, 4, 6, 68, 69, 74, 124, 131
    and liberal/conservative values 134–5
    mobilization against 39, 41, 86
    and xenophobia 130
Turkey 134
Twitter 56

UKIP 4–5, 6, 74, 122
unemployment 25–6, 43(*n*3), 58, 73, 77
    and inflation 13, 25
    and work-sharing 30–1
United States (US) 2, 12, 13–14, 23–42, 45–64
    Affordable Care Act 41, 48, 66(*n*18)
    balanced budget policy in 42
    black/immigrant/ethnic minorities in 25, 42, 48, 72, 88, 168, 169
    centre-left in 69
    centre-left in, reinvention of *see* centre-left reinvention in US
    CEOs' pay in *see* executives' pay
    Congress/Senate 29–30, 41, 43(*n*8), 87
    Democratic Party *see* Democratic Party
    doctors'/professionals' pay in 27, 28, 37–8, 44(*n*13)
    economic transformation in 50–2
    emergence of socialist parties in 46
    financial sector in 26, 29, 61–2
    grass-roots/labour movement action in 13, 19
    Great Depression 72, 165
    as habitation society 13, 45, 51–3

industrial decline in 46–7, 63
infrastructure spending in 82
labour party in 170
Left in 13, 170
market restructuring in *see* market
    restructuring
and Mexican immigrants 131
and Middle East 7
political culture of 85–6
poverty in 57
presidential election 2012 68
presidential election 2016 *see* US
    presidential election 2016
progressive finance policy in 32–3
progressive labour market policy in
    30–2
progressive patent/copyright policy in
    33–5
racism/exclusion of minorities in 25,
    72, 88
Republican Party *see* Republican Party
rural–urban divide in 58
social settlements in 71–3
tax/transfer policy in 24, 28
Trump administration *see* Trump,
    Donald J.
unemployment in 25–6, 43(*n*3)
upward redistribution in 24–7, 28
see also specific states/cities
universalism 115, 117
upward redistribution 24–7, 28, 193,
    197–8
and patent/copyright protection 26, 29
reversal of 41
urban areas 53, 54, 58, 60
US presidential election 2016 3, 4, 6, 68,
    69, 74, 87, 124, 131
see also Sanders, Bernie
utility companies 83

Varoufakis, Yanis 103, 104
Vietnam War 72

wage distribution 25–6
wages 79, 80, 81, 159, 165, 166
and immigration 131
minimum 17, 30, 43(*n*7), 80, 82, 84,
    92(*n*11), 131
and productivity 73, 76, 79
stagnant 76, 159, 197
Wahl, Asbj¢rn 4, 7
welfare policy 1, 74, 81
welfare reforms 165–6
welfare state 117, 125, 166
Wisconsin (US) 4, 48
women 78, 79, 81, 92(*n*10), 101, 131,
    169
work-sharing 30–1
Workers Action Centers 169
workers' councils 182, 185(*n*25)
workers' rights 84, 85, 89, 101, 125
see also trade unions
workers' state 163
working class 11, 76, 116, 160
emergence as movement *see* labour
    movement
formation 162–3, 165, 166, 167, 181
industrial, decline of 46–7, 120
and nationalism 117–8
organizational challenge with 167
political realignment of 4, 5–6, 7, 68,
    85, 88
in political space 116–7
struggle of *see* class struggle
working hours 30, 80, 84
work–life balance 30, 78, 89, 133,
    195
World Bank 127
World Trade Organization 127

xenophobia 16, 17, 113, 114, 121, 123,
    124, 129, 132, 133
and protectionism 126

Yugoslavia, former 129, 130